THE STRUCTURE
OF PORTUGUESE
SOCIETY

THE STRUCTURE
OF PORTUGUESE
SOCIETY

The Failure of Fascism

DIAMANTINO P. MACHADO

New York
Westport, Connecticut
London

Library of Congress Cataloging-in-Publication Data

Machado, Diamantino P.
    The structure of Portuguese society : the failure of fascism /
Diamantino P. Machado.
        p.   cm.
    Includes bibliographical references and index.
    ISBN 0-275-93784-4
    1. Portugal—Politics and government—1910–1974. 2. Portugal—
Social conditions—20th century. 3. Portugal—History—Revolution,
1974. 4. Fascism—Portugal—History—20th century. 5. Portugal—
Economic conditions—1918–1974.   I. Title.
DP680.M233   1991
946.904′2—dc20   91-9646

British Library Cataloguing in Publication Data is available.

Library of Congress Catalog Card Number: 91-9646
ISBN: 0-275-93784-4

First published in 1991

Praeger Publishers, One Madison Avenue, New York, NY 10010
An imprint of Greenwood Publishing Group, Inc.

Printed in the United States of America

∞™

The paper used in this book complies with the
Permanent Paper Standard issued by the National
Information Standards Organization (Z39.48-1984).

10 9 8 7 6 5 4 3 2 1

Copyright Acknowledgments

To the memory of Maria Ilda, my mother,
and
to Virginia, my wife, who made it all possible.

Contents

Tables

Abbreviations

ACAP	Associação Central de Agricultura Portuguesa (Central Association of Portuguese Farmers)
ACL	Associação Comercial de Lisboa (Commercial Association of Lisbon)
ACP	Associação Comercial do Pôrto (Commercial Association of Pôrto)
AD	Aliança Democrática (Democratic Alliance)
AIP	Associação Industrial Portuguesa (Portuguese Industrial Association)
AIp	Associação Industrial Portuense (Industrial Association of Pôrto)
CGT-IN	Confederação Geral dos Trabalhadores-Intersindical (General Confederation of Workers-Interunion)
CGTP	Confederação Geral dos Trabalhadores Portugueses (General Confederation of Portuguese Workers)
COPCON	Comando Operacional do Continente (Continental Operations Command)
CR	Conselho da Revolução (Council of the Revolution)
CUF	Companhia União Fabril (United Fabric Company)
EEC	European Economic Community
EFTA	European Free Trade Association
FUR	Frente Unida Revolucionária (United Revolutionary Front)
GDP	Gross Domestic Product
GNP	Gross National Product

GNR	Guarda Nacional Republicana (Republican National Guard)
MFA	Movimento das Forças Armadas (Armed Forces Movement)
PAIGC	Partido Africano para a Independência da Guiné e de Cabo Verde (African Party for the Independence of Guinea and Cape Verde)
PCP	Partido Comunista Português (Portuguese Communist Party)
PIDE/DGS	Polícia Internacional de Defesa do Estado/Direção Geral de Segurança (International Police for the Defense of the State/General Security Directorate—secret police)
PRP	Partido Republicano Português (Portuguese Republican Party)
PSP	Partido Socialista Português (Portuguese Socialist Party)
PSP	Polícia de Segurança Pública (Public Security Police)
SEDES	Sociedade de Estudos de Desenvolvimento Económico e Social (Society for the Study of Economic and Social Development)
UIE	União de Interesses Econômicos (Union of Economic Interests)
UN/ANP	União Nacional/Acção Nacional Popular (National Union/Popular National Action)

Preface

The purpose of this book is twofold. First, it is to probe the nature of Portuguese society and the role played by the state during the period 1926–1974. Second, it is to probe the causes and the nature of the 1974 revolution, and its consequences up to 1976.

My investigation will unravel the Portuguese paradox. Portugal is one of the oldest Western European states. It has existed as a sovereign political entity since 1140, many years before the emergence of the United Kingdom, Spain, Italy, and Germany as coherent political entities. Only France can equal the state of Portugal in terms of longevity. Moreover, Portugal possessed, for more than 500 years (until 1975), a vast and immensely rich colonial empire.

At the same time, however, during the period under investigation Portugal was the most backward country in Europe with the lowest per capita income. As late as 1971, Portugal's infant mortality rate was among the highest in Europe (41.4 per 1,000 live births); slightly over one-third of its population was illiterate, and 76 percent of the people had less than four years of schooling. Furthermore, "Forty-eight years of supposedly efficient fascist dictatorship, from the mid-1920's to the mid-1970's, also did little or nothing to make Portugal into a modern European state" (Keefe et al. 1977, 1).

Since I reject the pluralistic view of the state as a neutral coordinator or agent of society as a whole, in this work the state will be viewed in its concrete forms, disrobed of ideological mystification. As Miliband notes:

The state is an essential means of class domination. It is not a neutral referee arbitrating between competing interests: it is inevitably a deeply engaged partisan. It is not "above" class struggles but right in them. Its intervention in the affairs of society is crucial, constant and pervasive; and that intervention is closely conditioned by the most fundamental of the state's characteristics, namely that it is a means of class domination. (1977, 66–67)

And Henri Lefebvre reminds us that

critical analysis of the state in any Marxian sense must be based on specific studies of every known mode of production, every historical phase, every country. And this in terms of both the structural aspect (classes) and the conjunctural aspect (conquests, domination, characteristics of the conquerors and their armies, etc.). Governments reveal the particularities of the society they administer and set themselves above: they sum up, as we have seen, its struggles and conflicts. Conversely, specific sociological and historical studies help us understand governments by taking into account the multiple conditions under which one or another state was formed. (1969, 159)

My argument is, therefore, that the form the state takes is conditioned by the prevailing mode of production and its peculiarities in each country and conjuncture (here, a *colonial*, yet *dependent*, society). The theoretical perspective guiding my investigation is broadly based on social class and class conflict.

It will be obvious to the reader that any of the chapters which follow can be expanded into a lengthy thesis. This assertion can even apply to some of the subjects treated in each chapter. Surely one could write a book on the secret police, PIDE (discussed in Chapter 3). In this study, however, I have attempted to obtain and give an overall picture of Portuguese society and explain the role played in it by the state, up to the time of the revolution of 1974. I felt that a study of a narrow subject would not make possible a proper, macrosociological account of almost fifty years of Portuguese history and society. Naturally, in doing so, I hope to present a relatively complete account of the Portuguese paradox.

On the other hand, not even a wide approach such as I have undertaken can encompass all pertinent aspects of structure or of the ubiquitous social transformations. Some, such as the position and function of the Roman Catholic Church during the period being studied, are not properly treated in this work. Others, such as the foreign policy of Salazar and Caetano, have not been included in this analysis.

In order to keep my work within a manageable form, I limited the field of investigation to those topics and activities which I considered to be most relevant to the task, especially (1) the transition from latifundial agriculture to industrial oligopolies; (2) the role played by the state in the reactionary coalition's regime (1926–1974); (3) the African wars; (4) the changing structure of the Portuguese military officer corps; (5) the revolution of 1974 and its aftermath. With these purposes in mind, I have organized this book as follows.

Chapter 1 concerns the agrarian nature of Portuguese society in the earlier 1920s and identifies the core of the reactionary coalition. Then the political economy of the reactionary coalition is explained, and its reproduction, transformation, and fall are demonstrated. In this chapter I also explain the transition from latifundial agriculture to industrial oligopolies, and demonstrate how indispensable emigrants' remittances and tourism were to the international balance of payments of the reactionary coalition, and why the African wars expedited the fall of the Estado Novo.

Chapter 2 is first a historical description of the fall of the First Republic and of the seizure of power by the military. Second, it is an analysis of the contrast between the political rhetoric and the empirical reality of the Estado Novo. It is also an explanation of Salazar not as dictator but as the "organic intellectual" of the coalition, and of the National Union, the coalition's party. In this chapter I also argue that the coalition's political regime can, and must, be classified as a type of bureaucratic–authoritarian state, and that the peculiarity of the Portuguese case, a *colonial* yet *dependent* society must be considered.

Chapter 3 deals with the imposition of the Estado Novo from above, and with the role of the state in Portuguese society. The repressive state apparatuses, the role of the military and paramilitary forces, and other instruments of class domination, such as censorship and ideology, are analyzed and demonstrated. I also show how the secret police, PIDE/DGS, operated on behalf of the reactionary coalition.

Chapter 4 introduces the physical characteristics of the vast and immensely rich Portuguese empire. Then the "metaphysical" nature of Portuguese colonialism and its beneficiaries is analyzed. The paradoxical contradiction of the Portuguese case, a colonial imperial power and, at the same time, the poorest country in Western Europe, is analyzed in terms of the nature of the coalition's colonial exploitation.

Chapter 5 concerns the nature of the opposition in Portugal until the late 1960s. I pay particular attention to the "freed" time regarding presidential elections. I also argue that the unsatisfactory presidential election of 1958 demonstrates that political pluralism, even "limited pluralism"—interelite opposition—was absent in Portugal during the rule of the reactionary coalition.

Chapter 6 discusses the "guardianship" role of the armed forces until 1974, and demonstrates that the African wars, in addition to causing transformations in the political economy of the reactionary coalition, caused concomitant changes in the patterns of recruitment and in the ensuing composition of the military officer corps. Since armed forces do not exist in a vacuum, but operate in a class society that inevitably influences their behavior, the Armed Forces Movement (MFA) and the coup of April 25, 1974, are analyzed in terms of a multiplicity of causal factors and not of either military or economic reductionisms. Besides the social background of the military conspirators, other variables determined the appearance of the MFA and the coup of 1974.

Chapter 7 presents the Portuguese conjuncture from April 1974 to 1976, after the fall of the Estado Novo. I demonstrate that the MFA was a broad coalition of bourgeois and petit bourgeois officers, and that the revolution was not a real social revolution but a bloodless democratization from above. The popular power and spontaneous activities from below, while very active and influential on the MFA during the postcoup period of ambivalence and uncertainty, ultimately were not sufficiently organized or strong, enough to play a key role in the future of Portugal.

Acknowledgments

I would like to thank Philip Evanson of the Department of History and Magali Sarfati-Larsen, Sherri Grasmuck, and Kyriakos Kontopoulos of the Department of Sociology at Temple University for their assistance and suggestions. Special thanks must be given to the members of the Inter-library Loan Department of Temple University for their gracious assistance. I want to thank my wife, Virginia, and my children, Camilla and João, and the new member of our family, son-in-law Eugene Okamoto, for their patience and support during many long months of research and writing. Among the people who helped me with this manuscript, I wish to thank especially Sharon Gehm and Mike Krippendorf, whose assistance was invaluable, and Virginia for her assistance in editing the manuscript. I also wish to thank the people at Praeger, especially Mary Glenn and Talvi Laev, who made this book possible.

The Rise and Fall of the Political Economy of the Reactionary Coalition

STATISTICAL INTRODUCTION

In 1926, when the reactionary coalition seized power through the military, Portugal was an agricultural country with a population of 8.5 million inhabitants. Located at the westernmost corner of Europe, continental Portugal had an area of 34,377 square miles. The agricultural character of the Portuguese economy and society is easily discernible when we look at the composition of the labor force, the level of literacy, and the urban/rural population distribution.

With more than 50 percent of its active population engaged in the agricultural (primary) sector of economic production in 1930, Portugal could not be anything but agrarian (see Table 1.1). The level of industrialization was extremely low, and heavy industry was nonexistent. Portugal had to import most of its machinery, heavy equipment, and fuel. Its exports consisted of wine, cork, canned fish, and textiles.

The nonindustrialized character of Portugal is also illustrated in the rates of illiteracy. In 1920, 1930, and 1940, the rates were 66.2, 61.5, and 48.8 percent respectively. However, since the levels of illiteracy were not evenly distributed, it is necessary to look at the rates in each of the eighteen districts of continental Portugal.

The data in Table 1.2 enable us to see how serious the illiteracy problem was in Portugal. Twelve districts had a rate over 70 percent in 1920, between 60 and 70 percent in 1930, and between 50 and 60 percent in 1940. In 1930, only one district had a rate of between 40 and 50 percent.

In terms of population distribution, at the time the reactionary coalition seized state power, Portugal was an essentially rural country (see Table 1.3).

Table 1.1
Active Population, by Economic Sector, 1930 and 1940 (percent)

SECTOR	1930	1940
Primary	56.0	50.0
Secondary	17.0	20.0
Tertiary	27.0	30.0

Sources: For 1930, Joel Serrão, ed., *Dictionário de história de Portugal*, vol. V (Lisbon: Iniciativas Editoriais, 1975), 160; for 1940, *Analise social* 3(1965), quoted in Carlos Almeida and Antonio Barreto, *Capitalismo e emigração em Portugal* (Lisbon: Prelo, 1976), 254.

It was to remain so for many years. Data for 1960 (see Table 1.4), thirty-four years after the seizure of power, show that between 1930 and 1960 Portugal's rural and urban populations had changed very little. In 1930 only 19.4 percent of the population lived in urban centers. In 1960 the figure had increased to 23 percent.

The agricultural character of Portugal is also discernible in the prevailing ideological worldviews. Anselmo de Andrade, one of the last ministers of the monarchy, wrote in 1912:

Portugal is neither a commercial nor an industrial country. . . . Much damage is done to the country in any attempt to transform into industrial, activities that truly can only be agrarian, and in so doing we create future industrial crises that will be more difficult to solve than agrarian crises.[1]

This defense of rural Portugal is also found in a popular book written in 1923:

Disorders caused by industrialism were manifested recently in the demands of the workers, in the spirit of dissipation evident in the large masses of working people and in the lack of interest in maintaining things as they are and in conserving the present working conditions.[2]

The agrarian, traditional, and, in some areas of the country, feudal nature of Portuguese society, in terms of interpersonal relationships and social distance between employers and employees or owners and nonowners, was defended by Integralismo Lusitano (Lusitanian Integralism) and by some individuals who held positions of power, such as João Pereira da Rosa and Alfredo da Silva. The Integralismo was a traditional, conservative, monarchist, and antiliberal movement formed shortly before World War I under the influence of Charles Maurras's Action Française. It gave the reactionary coalition the theoretical basis for considering the political economy of republican liberalism as illegitimate. Its goal was the total destruction of the liberal system of Republican Portugal.

João Pereira da Rosa was the owner of the Lisbon daily newspaper *O Século*

Table 1.2
Rate of Illiteracy, by District, 1920–1940 (percent of population older than 7)

District	1920	1930	1940
Aveiro	64.2	60.4	47.5
Beja	77.7	75.1	64.0
Braga	69.4	65.6	54.2
Braganca	75.0	70.6	55.6
Castelo Branco	79.4	76.4	61.7
Coimbra	70.2	64.7	61.7
Evora	73.5	68.3	55.0
Faro	74.0	69.1	52.4
Guarda	71.2	68.2	50.6
Leiria	76.1	71.5	54.2
Lisboa	45.6	40.4	31.2
Portalegre	74.7	68.3	56.0
Porto	56.4	52.0	42.1
Santarem	72.6	65.6	54.2
Setubal	70.7	63.5	51.6
Viana do Castelo	67.9	65.1	52.2
Vila Real	66.5	65.1	53.3
Viseu	71.8	68.0	54.7

Source: Compiled from Banco Nacional Ultramarino (Lisbon), *Boletim* no. 75/76 (1968): 25.

Table 1.3
Rural and Urban Population, 1920–1940 (percent of population)

Year	Rural	Urban
1920	82.3	17.7
1930	80.2	19.4
1940	80.2	19.4

Source: Compiled from Banco Nacional Ultramarino (Lisbon), *Boletim* no. 75/76 (1968): 25.

and a former member of the União de Interesses Economicos (UIE; Union of Economic Interests). A founding member of the latter, he was also a member of the reactionary coalition that seized control in 1926. He was a strong anti-industrialist and took much pleasure in attacking the Associação Industrial Portuguesa (AIP; Portuguese Industrial Association) in the early 1920s, when the AIP asked the state to extend financial assistance to industrial enterprises (Medeiros 1978, 115).

Alfredo da Silva was the Portuguese Henry Ford. He was a ruthless entrepreneur, interested in capital accumulation without much risk, without class struggle and demands from below. He had funded the right-wing UIE, was a main financial backer of the seizure of state power, and was minister for corporations from 1930 to 1933. Da Silva and his successors were perhaps the

Table 1.4
Urban and Rural Population, 1960

District	Total (000)	Urban (000)	%	Rural (000)	%	Urban Share By Dist. %
TOTAL	8,293	1,931	23	6,362	77	100
Aveiro	525	41	8	483	92	2.2
Beja	277	16	6	261	94	0.8
Braga	597	65	11	533	89	3.3
Braganca	233	8	4	225	97	0.4
C. Branco	317	38	12	279	88	2.0
Coimbra	434	57	13	377	87	3.0
Evora	220	24	11	196	89	1.2
Faro	315	47	15	268	85	2.4
Guarda	283	9	3	274	97	0.5
Leiria	406	30	7	375	93	1.5
Lisboa	1,383	908	65	482	35	47.0
Portalegre	189	23	12	166	88	1.2
Porto	1,193	450	38	743	62	23.3
Santarem	462	16	4	445	96	0.8
Setubal	377	152	40	226	60	7.9
V. Castelo	278	14	5	263	95	0.7
Vila Real	325	24	7	302	93	1.2
Viseu	482	17	3	465	97	0.9

Note: In 1930 only district capitals and areas officially designated as cities were considered urban centers. In 1940 urban centers were those areas with more than 2,000 inhabitants. In 1960 the Portuguese National Intitute of Statistics classified as urban centers those areas, demarcated by local municipalities, with 10,000 or more inhabitants.

Source: A. Sedas Nunes, *Sociologia e ideologia do desenvolvimento* (Lisbon: Morais Editora, 1969), 198.

greatest beneficiaries of the reactionary coalition's political economy. The company he built in the late nineteenth century was to become the biggest, best-known, and most diversified Portuguese enterprise. The seemingly contradictory positions of Pereira da Rosa and da Silva will be explained in Chapter 2.

When the reactionary coalition seized power in 1926, the center of hegemonic control was held by the latifundists, owners of extensive parcels of land. Table 1.5 shows how the ownership of land was distributed in the period 1930–1931.

The pattern of landholding in Portugal has been, historically, minifundia in the northern region and latifundia in the central and southern regions. The former consist of small holdings and unproductive plots. The latter consist of great estates cultivated by hired labor or sharecroppers. Southern Portugal was the country of the landed aristocracy, the nonmodern power-holding sector, the unenlightened Portuguese Junkers. The extremes in the sizes of farms are obvious. The data in Table 1.5 indicate the predominance of the latifundia in four districts: Évora, Beja, Setúbal, and Portalegre. In Évora, for example, during

Table 1.5
Distribution of Land Ownership, by District, 1930–1931

District	Hectares	Parcels (No.)	Proprietors (No.)	Ha/Prop	Parcels/Prop.	Average Ha/Parcel
Aveiro	277,240	953,597	102,728	3	9	0,29
Beja	1,027,856	85,408	26,078	39	3	12,03
Braga	273,020	576,920	68,935	4	8	0,47
Braganca	654,296	1,203,249	62,271	10	19	0,54
C. Branco	670,368	586,668	60,068	11	10	1,14
Coimbra	295,576	1,257,791	118,749	3	11	0,31
Evora	738,828	40,430	14,061	52	3	18,27
Faro	507,160	281,372	65,954	8	4	1,80
Guarda	549,616	698,792	87,197		8	0,80
Leiria	343,508	910,185	96,543	4	9	0,27
Lisboa	274,700	206,885	55,063	5	4	1,32
Portalegre	613,288	67,469	21,595	28	3	9,09
Porto	228,188	435,543	55,810	4	8	0,52
Santarem	668,924	463,035	84,345	8	5	1,44
Setubal	510,548	26,056	15,814	32	2	19,59
V. Castelo	210,838	776,042	76,042	3	10	0,27
Vila Real	423,820	837,927	71,956	6	12	0,50
Viseu	500,580	1,631,095	132,366	4	12	0,31
Total	8,768,354		1,215,575			

Source: F. Medeiros, *A Sociedade e a economia portugesas nas origems do salazarismo* (Lisbon: A Regra do Jogo, 1978), 20.

the period under study, 14,061 proprietors owned 738,828 hectares of land. Each proprietor owned 52 hectares of land distributed into 3 parcels that had an average size of 18.27 hectares. In contrast, in seven districts the number of parcels was larger, which indicates a greater fragmentation of property, and the average size of each parcel was less than an hectare. In Setubal, for example, during the period under study, 15,814 proprietors owned 510,548 hectares of land, and each owned 32 hectares of land distributed into 2 parcels. In Evora, 14,061 proprietors owned 738,828 hectares of land, and each owned 52 hectares of land distributed into 3 parcels. Similar situations existed in Beja and Portalegre. In contrast, in all the other districts the number of parcels was larger, which indicates a greater fragmentation of property, and the average size of each parcel was less than a hectare. In the district of Viana do Castelo, for instance, there were ten parcels per proprietor and the average size of each parcel was 0.27 hectare.

In the 1920s there were three distinct social groups in Portugal: the working classes (urban and rural, with the former limited to the cities of Lisbon and Pôrto); the latifundists and their allies, the financiers and industrialists; and the liberal urban bourgeoisie. Portuguese social formation (''society, the concrete complex whole comprising economic, political and ideological practices''; Heydebrand 1981, 81) at the time placed hegemonic control in the hands of the latifundists. They were the ruling fraction of the reactionary coalition, which was made up of them, of financiers, and of industrialists (such as Alfredo da Silva). The urban bourgeois middle class was too small, and consequently lacked the power to build the social structure and political system required for assuring capital accumulation and its own reproduction (Ginner 1982). The solution for the urban middle class was to join the reactionary coalition against the working classes, which were ultimately excluded "from any form of participation in the political sphere," as will be been shown later in this chapter and in the following chapters (Ginner 1982, 174). It has been aptly observed that when "a commercial and industrial class . . . is too weak and dependent to take power and rule in its own right . . . it throws itself into the arms of the landed aristocracy and the royal bureaucracy, exchanging the right to rule for the right to make money" (Moore 1966, 437).

In Portugal, the nonmodern sector was the ruling sector until the beginning of the 1950s, when it began losing power. Hence, the economy of the reactionary coalition had its base in agricultural activities that required a specific social organization. The reactionary coalition developed a political economy, and a concomitant society, "not in order to regiment and mobilize society in the interests of the more advanced sectors of capital, but to freeze the social structure in a way that maintained the hegemony of a backward and neo-feudal ruling class" (Lomax 1983, 110).

I have divided the period from 1926 to 1976 into five subperiods. This periodization is necessary to properly understand and explain how and why the model of capital accumulation implemented by the reactionary coalition was perpetuated (for almost half a century), transformed, and then abolished. The first subperiod covers the years 1928–1939 and deals with the implementation of the political economy of the reactionary coalition. The second period (1940–1944) analyzes the effect of World War II on the coalition's economic conditions. In the period from 1945 to 1959, I analyze the transformations (albeit in an embryonic stage), that the coalition's regime began experiencing. The fourth period, from 1960 to 1967, analyzes the continuation of the coalition's system in face of systemic contradictions and transformations. Finally, in the fifth period, 1968–1974, I analyze the causes of the transformation and fall of the political economy of the reactionary coalition.

The Political Economy of the Reactionary Coalition

The Model

Portuguese social scientists use the term *modelo económico* to refer to the economic plans, policies, and strategies of the regimes of Salazar and Caetano.[3] My usage of the term has a broader meaning. In my view, the political economy of the reactionary coalition was conceptualized and implemented to assure the production and reproduction of capital accumulation through the subordination and exploitation of the working classes. This subordination and exploitation were to be accomplished not only indirectly, via the objective nature of the capitalist mode of production, but also directly, via the implementation of coercive mechanisms of social control by the state. This is why a liberal capitalist society had been rejected by the nonmodern hegemonic sector since the beginning of the twentieth century, and why the political economy model of the reactionary coalition called for a particular type of social organization. The latter would assure capital accumulation and the exploitation of the working classes without risks, without demands from below.

While formally the model of the reactionary coalition was built on corporatist principles and organization that theoretically created a social atmosphere of class harmony (and thus prevented or reduced class exploitation), in reality "harmony" was created through coercive methods, and much accumulation and exploitation was accomplished via a feudalist modus vivendi and a mercantilist modus operandi, that is, a social formation characterized by ascriptive social status and profound social distance between the owning and nonowning classes, and via a state-supervised, guaranteed, risk-free accumulation of wealth.

Capitalism, private ownership of the means of production, and the free buying and selling of labor were alive and well in Portugal before and after the 1920s. But after the reactionary coalition seized power and implemented its system of political economy, the Portuguese capitalist mode of production was given specific parameters within which it was to be reproduced. Henceforth, it was not liberal-democratic capitalism but a particular subtype of capitalism. It was based on private ownership of the means of production; it was subject to ubiquitous and extensive management by the state; it was almost totally risk-free; and it assured the highest profits with the least possible costs. It was also a capitalist system that prevented economic development and made and kept Portugal the poorest country in Western Europe.

Since the reactionary coalition was interested in developing a political economy that guaranteed price stability, sound public finances, a positive balance of payments, controlled internal and external competition, and high profits and low costs, some of the mechanisms of the model were designed and implemented during the military dictatorship, that is, before the implementation of the Constitution of 1933, which made official the institutionalization of the Estado Novo.

The Operational Mechanisms of the Model

Lei de Condicionamento Industrial. The (Control of Industry Act), Decree no. 19,354, became law on January 3, 1931, two years before the establishment of the Estado Novo.[4] This important mechanism required prior state authorization for the establishment or the relocation of industrial plants, or for new investment in machinery and equipment designed to increase industrial activity. Initially, Decree no. 19,354 covered only eleven industries, but at the end of 1931 Decree no. 20,521 expanded the coverage of industrial licensing to all industrial activities. Moreover, while decrees 19,354 and 20,521 stipulated that the control of industrial activities was to be temporary, Decree no. 1956 of 1937 institutionalized and made permanent the mechanism of industrial licensing.

Specifically, the law stipulated the following: (1) Business enterprises had the right to contest the establishment of any new enterprise on grounds that the capacity of the country could not sustain a new enterprise in that sector and that there would be a loss of capital, a squeeze on raw materials, a rise in prices, and/or a drop in quality. (2) The expansion or the modernization of existing firms was to be strictly controlled; for example, firms in the textile industry were licensed for fixed looms or spinning machines. (3) A change in the location of a firm had to be approved by a commission consisting of representatives of that industry (Leeds 1984, 23–24).

Formal requests for changes in an enterprise, whether in size, quality or type of equipment, or location, were handled by the appropriate corporative organization or by the grêmio, the economic coordinating commission (or guild) of the relevant industry. When a new firm was established in a new industrial sector, it was given monopolistic concessions. In any case, the requests for changes submitted by companies were reviewed by the corporative officials who, as members of the particular industry, had vested interests in restricting competition.

The Control of Industry Act was an effective mechanism to constrain the development of liberal–democratic capitalism; prevent or delay modernization; restrict internal competition; and protect the interests of established monopolistic companies.

Such large discretionary powers of governmental officials in the licensing of industrial investment often strengthened the monopolistic position of existing firms, led to misallocation of capital resources, gave rise to claims of grave irregularities and deterred investment by foreign enterprises in the Portuguese economy. (Baklanoff 1978, 105)

The Control of Industry Act was affected by the changes and development of the capitalist mode of production (CMP). It was revised in 1945, 1964, and 1965. Changes in the Portuguese CMP also changed the beneficiaries of the Act. In the 1930s it protected both the nonmonopolist petite bourgeoisie and existing monopolistic firms. After World War II, however, it became an effective mechanism for the proliferation of the monopolistic groups.

Estatuto do Trabalho Nacional (National Labor Statute), implemented on September 23, 1933, as Decree-Law no. 23,048, was the reactionary coalition's mechanism responsible for controlling, silencing, and rendering submissive the Portuguese working class. Under its provisions the General Confederation of Workers (organized as the National Workers' Union in 1914 and renamed in 1919), was declared illegal and ordered to go out of existence. The law also prohibited strikes, lockouts, and any form of working-class activities and civil disobedience, such as public demonstrations. Conflicts between employers and workers were to be resolved in labor courts established under the statute. In addition, urban workers (and employers) were organized in a system of syndicates that were not allowed to expand beyond the district level. The statute also called for government approval of all syndicate officials, and direct state intervention in the internal affairs of the syndicates.

The statute was a mechanism of repression. It controlled the working class. It fragmented workers' cohesion by prohibiting their organization beyond the district level. It imposed on workers fascist syndicates directly controlled by the state. All this was done to guarantee the maintenance of a low level of workers' wages and, at the same time, a high level of capital accumulation via the conflict-free and risk-free expropriation of surplus value.

Price/Wage Control and Subsidies to Agriculture. The control of labor costs could not be limited to the implementation and maintenance of low wages. It had to cover prices, particularly food prices. Therefore the National Labor Statute included a table stipulating both wage and price levels. But the control of labor costs, designed and implemented to increase surplus value, had negative consequences. First, it forced food costs to be artificially low and made agricultural production difficult, if not impossible, without state subsidies. Thus the state had to compensate the farmers with subsidies. The latter, in turn, inhibited growth of agricultural production and caused almost total stagnation in the primary sector of the economy. Some of the state subsidies were not reinvested in farming activities but placed in banks, and thus were diverted to other economic activities. This diversion in turn contributed to the alliance between the main beneficiaries of state subsidies, the latifundists and the bankers/financiers. And, while low salaries produced high levels of surplus value, they also limited working-class purchasing power and, consequently, limited increases in productivity and in the expansion of the domestic market, particularly in industrial and consumer goods.

Control Aduaneiro. An additional mechanism of the political economy of the reactionary coalition was the system of protective tariffs, which remained in force until the 1960s. The implementation of tariffs against foreign producers protected the reactionary coalition from two enemies: foreign competition for Portuguese industry, and pressures to modernize in terms of technological expansion and democratic labor relations. The Control of Industry Act controlled internal competition, and protective tariffs controlled external competition. Foreign goods of course would enter Portugal, but they would be subject to import duties that would make their cost to several times higher than domestically produced goods. Even unavailable goods were subject to the high tariffs. It is obvious that the import substitution strategy implemented by the reactionary coalition was to maintain the status quo.

Acto Colonial. The Colonial Act and Native Statute of 1930 repealed the administrative decentralization and liberal reforms of the Republic and implemented a new and more centralized administrative structure that increased the control and exploitation of the colonies. Following the British colonial model, albeit within the limitations imposed by the level of economic development, the reactionary coalition employed the Colonial Act to increase the role of the colonies as a source of raw materials and as importers of farm or manufactured goods from the metropolis. (The Portuguese colonial empire is analyzed in Chapter 4.)

1928–1939: REPRODUCTION AND *IMOBILISMO*—THE ORTHODOXY OF THE REACTIONARY COALITION

Economic Conditions

During this period, the implementation of the political economy model of the reactionary coalition produced economic stagnation through policies and programs that reflected a greater concern with economic stability or assured capital accumulation than with economic development. Hence, programs designed to educate and train the Portuguese people, to encourage investment in industrial activities, and to modernize agricultural production were not undertaken. Instead, economic programs and activities were limited to the improvement of the infrastructure of continental Portugal (and to the buildup of the armed forces). The Estado Novo allocated funds to road and bridge construction, road repair, and similar projects. "The total network of Portuguese roads increased from 13,000 kilometers in the mid-1920s to 26,000 by 1950 and over 32,000 by 1970" (Robinson 1979, 129).

Economic Growth

During this period Portugal was already close to the bottom of the list of the least developed countries in terms of most of the standard economic indicators. Economic growth during this period was almost nonexistent. In fact the average annual rate of economic growth between 1914 and 1950 was below 3 percent (Murteira 1975). The economic condition of Portugal during this period was aggravated by the fact that important parts of the economy were in the hands of foreigners. Despite the reactionary coalition's moratorium on foreign investment (which isolated Portugal from Western Europe), and its rhetoric on nationalism, it did not nationalize any foreign enterprise. Therefore, wine production and exportation, cork production and exportation, mineral-extraction, public transportation, telephone service, and electric power remained under the control and ownership of foreigners, particularly the British. The latter were already playing an important economic role in the country: "Portugal was reduced to the status of an economic dependency of Great Britain by the end of the seventeenth century" (O'Brien 1974, 20).

The years 1928–1939 represent a period of introverted, controlled, and stable economic activities. It was also a period of economic stagnation and minimal economic growth. Even so, the reactionary coalition and its foreign allies were the main beneficiaries of (1) an abundant supply of cheap labor; (2) the absence of internal or external competition; (3) monopolization and protectionism in colonial markets. On the other hand, the Portuguese worker was forced at best to emigrate and at worst to live at a bare subsistence level.

1940–1945: PARTIAL SUSPENSION OF THE MODEL— WORLD WAR II

The War

During World War II the reactionary coalition was forced to consider de jure neutrality the best policy. Inasmuch as the coalition's ideological allies were the Axis, Portugal would not fight for democracy. On the other hand, Portugal's economic dependence on, and the old relationship with, England made it impossible to join its ideological Allies. Moreover, the coalition took advantage of its neutrality. England agreed not to ask it for military help and not to interfere with the Estado Novo after the war. Neutrality was the best policy for avoiding the possible physical occupation of continental Portugal and/or its overseas colonies. Portugal sold a great percentage of its wolfram production to Germany until June 1944, when, under the General Allied Trade and Surplus Purchase Agreement, of which it had been a member since 1942, it was forced to cease exporting wolfram to Germany.

But in spite of its neutrality, or perhaps because of it, Portugal did experience an externally caused, limited suspension of the reactionary coalition's model of political economy. This suspension must be seen as the seed of structural changes in Portuguese society that would soon emerge. Portugal's neutrality attracted individuals escaping from European economic uncertainties and Axis occupation; many of them brought their wealth with them. Most of those refugees stayed in Portugal for a short while before emigrating to England, the United States, or Latin America. Some decided to make Portugal their home. In either case their presence had an effect on the economic and social conditions of Portuguese society. The money they spent caused inflation and increased business activity. Some of those foreigners not only spent money but also invested in the economy and provided business ideas and deals to local industrialists and financiers.

Moreover, the neutrality transformed Portugal from essentially an isolated importing country into a country whose traditional exports, such as canned fish, textiles, wine, and minerals (wolfram), were in great demand. This new situation caused increases in the number of enterprises, in demand and supply in the internal market, and in the number of factories, as well as changes in the approach to and techniques of production. Moreover, Portugal's holdings of gold and foreign exchange rose substantially. "Strong foreign demand and high prices of the war years permitted a ten-fold increase in the gold and foreign exchange holdings between 1938 and 1947" (Pintado 1964, 122).

The Push for Industrialization

World War II and Portuguese neutrality were profitable to the bourgeoisie. Both caused an increase in foreign markets and in business deals, and helped to strengthen the slowly emerging linkage between industrial activities and banking (financial capital). Equally important, if not more so, were the push for industrialization favored by a small number of industrialists, and the recognition that the absence of heavy industry in Portugal, and difficulties in importing machinery and equipment, were barriers to the now desired industrialization. This push for industrial "takeoff," however, was to coexist for some time with an ideology that was agrarian, conservative, and traditionalist. In other words, although after the war Portugal began moving away from agricultural activities, ideologically and politically the political economy model of the reactionary coalition remained unchanged.

1945–1959: REPRODUCTION WITH TRANSFORMATION— THE EMBRYONIC STAGE

After World War II

In the years after the war, Portugal experienced change in two main areas. First, its outlook toward Europe in particular, and the outside world in general, began a slow and long process of change, in large part because the volume and value of Portuguese exports to Europe during the war had been greater than exports to the colonies. Second, there was a shift in power within the reactionary coalition. Specifically, at this time Portugal was moving away from "the earlier protectionism, . . . the notion of ruralism and the primacy of agriculture, and toward the first stages of [limited] large-scale industrialization" (Leeds 1984, 27). The initiator of this movement toward industrialization and the best-known member of the then embryonic modern sector of the reactionary coalition, was J. N. Ferreira Dias, an engineer and, more important, secretary of state for industry in the years immediately following World War II. Regarding the reactionary coalition's fear of industrialism, Ferreira Dias observed:

The idea of not creating industry so as to not stimulate social dangers seems to me divorced from common sense; it reminds one of the old joke about the sick person who dies from the cure. . . . It is childish to lose the benefits that industry can bring to all of us in exchange for the illusion that we can detach ourselves from the social development of the world. . . . Why be afraid of industry? In view of the social problems, as real as man himself, there seem to be two condemnable attitudes: to cover one's eyes so as not to see or to react in the style of Torquemada, in the insensate hope of making time move backwards. . . . Let us march with the times, let us flee from anachronisms. Let us improve the country through industry, let us improve the life of workers through salaries and social justice. . . . That a particular person draws away from this out of fear of losing money or of risking contact with socially dissatisfied people is understandable; but this attitude in official entities reminds one of the figure of the cowardly lion in *The Wizard of Oz*. (1946, 215–217; quoted in Leeds 1984, 28)

The reactionary coalition found a way of moving the country toward limited industrialization that reduced the risk of economic losses and increased the chances of economic gain, for the plan excluded any increases in salaries, betterment of social conditions, and improvement of workers' living conditions. A new law would be implemented to make the limited "takeoff" legal and official, without altering the role of the Estado Novo—controlling the workers and maintaining the status quo.

The New Law of Industrial Licensing

The Control of Industry Act of 1931 controlled and limited internal competition. Hence, while favoring established enterprises, it hindered the development of economic and industrial concentration and monopolization during the period 1930–1945, and protected the medium and petite bourgeoisie. The new law designed to move the country into industrialization was to change this. The new version of the Control of Industry Act was implemented in March 1945 as Law no. 2005, Lei de Fomento e Reorganização Industrial (Law of Development and Industrial Reorganization). While the new version was, like the old, a law of noncompetition, it no longer protected the medium and petite bourgeoisie; it was to become the mechanism for rapid development of monopoly and financial capital. Law no. 2005 was to control competition among the large monopolistic groups.

As for the idea of monopolies, let us observe the following: the principle of preserving competition whose utility is recognized as a stimulus to production and a means of assuring the stability of economic relations, even though it may be distasteful to some. But if the products are manufactured in small and dispersed units, badly equipped, without technology, with high production costs, there is no other solution but this: to have a few units capable of producing at low cost. If only one or very few possess the capital and technology to maintain an industry in terms of serving the collective interests, it would be absurd not to take advantage of them. (report accompanying Law no. 2005; Leeds 1984, 28)

Regarding the activities of the state, the new law stated:

The state will participate in the capitalization of firms directly or through its institutions of credit when it is judged indispensable to assure the success of the enterprise. This participation will not normally exceed that of the private sector, and when the State is involved directly, its portion will be transferred to private entities as soon as the position of industry and the defense of its interests permits. (Law 2005, Sec. VII; Leeds 1984, 26)

Table 1.6
Economic Performance: Average Annual GNP Expansion in Portugal, Spain, and Greece, 1953–1957

Portugal	4.5
Spain	6.9
Greece	6.0

Source: V. Xavier Pintado, *Structure and Growth of the Portuguese Economy* (Geneva: EFTA, 1964), 19.

It is important to realize that while originally the political economy model of the reactionary coalition was created and implemented to protect the interests of the latifundists, the hegemonic segment of the coalition, beginning with the 1945 Law of Development and Industrial Reorganization the same model was used to facilitate the expansion of the emerging hegemonic segment, large-scale industrialists and monopolistic groups. Thus all the mechanisms of the original model remained in force to guarantee and facilitate capital accumulation and the exploitation of the Portuguese workers. Moreover, the changes in the Portuguese capitalist mode of production, during and after World War II, and the movement toward limited industrial takeoff, occurred in a context of coexistence with an agrarian and traditionalist ideology. The only really new characteristic of the revised model was that it no longer protected the medium and petite bourgeoisie. In fact, in the years to come, these two groups would experience much proletarianization as a result of monopolistic absorption.

Economic Performance

In spite of the effects of World War II, and the new law of industrial licensing, the economic performance of Portugal between 1945 and 1959 was poor. The average annual rate of expansion of the gross national product was 4.5 percent. Comparing Portugal's economic performance with that of Spain and Greece during the period 1953–1957 (see Table 1.6) shows that Portugal lagged behind.

The poor economic performance was caused by the political economy model of the reactionary coalition. Moving toward industrialization alone, without changing the economic, political, and social structures of the country (the social relations of production), without the abolition of the corporative system, without democratization and the opening up of the country, made economic development difficult to accomplish. For example, between 1954 and 1959, the average annual rate of increase of industrial production was 6.5 percent. But the rate of increase for the primary sector of the economy was only 1 percent. Second, the industrial configuration of Portugal at the time was characterized by a multiplicity of small firms using inefficient methods of production and obsolete equipment, and by the development of large monopolistic groups engaged in capital-intensive industrial activities such as steel production (Siderurgia Nacional) and oil refining (SACOR).

Reproduction and Transformation: The Beginning of Contradictions

From 1945 to 1960 Portuguese society was characterized by contradictions. On the one hand was the hegemonic control of the latifundists, their rural and traditionalist ideology, and the protection of nonproductive and anachronistic agriculture. On the other hand was the initiation of industrial development. But this development took place within traditional socioeconomic and political structures. More specifically, in terms of forces of production, Portugal was moving forward, albeit at a very slow pace. But in terms of relations of production, the country was not moving at all, because ideological and political power was still in the hands of the reactionary coalition and, more important, because the same ideological and political structures had been utilized by the industrial and financial bourgeoisie. Moreover, the initiation of economic development was characterized by contradiction; the new law of industrial licensing facilitated economic concentration and placed large-scale monopolistic groups and small and medium entrepreneurs at opposite poles. During this period, the political economy model of the reactionary coalition was maintained and reproduced. But because of the contradictions, the model also was transformed.

1960–1967: REPRODUCTION, CONTRADICTION, AND TRANSFORMATION—THE BEGINNING OF THE FALL

The Opening of the Country

The poor performance of the Portuguese economy forced the reactionary coalition to change the policy of economic autarky and isolation from Western Europe. In the late 1950s the coalition was forced to admit that, in terms of most economic indicators, the introverted economy was keeping the country below all the other European and Mediterranean countries except Turkey. In the 1920s, and still in the 1950s, Portugal was Western Europe's poorest nation. By that time, technocrats familiar with the arguments of Ferreira Dias and representing the large, somewhat progressive industrial monopolistic groups, called for the opening up of the country to both new capital and new competitiveness, which required a change in the protectionist mechanisms of the political economy.

The European Free Trade Association (EFTA)

Portugal become a charter member of EFTA in 1960 and a member of the General Agreement on Tariffs and Trade, the World Bank, and the International

Table 1.7
Portugal's Major Trading Partners, 1960 and 1972 (percent)

Trading Partner	Exports		Imports	
	1960	1972	1960	1972
Overseas territories	25	15	14	9
EFTA	21	41	20	24
EEC	22	21	38	32
Other Western Europe	4	3	4	4
United States and Canada	12	12	8	11
Rest of the world	16	8	16	20
Total	100	100	100	100

Sources: For 1960, Associação Industrial Portuguesa, *Guide to Investment in Portugal* (Lisbon: AIP, 1968), 15. For 1972, derived from Bank of Portugal, *Report of the Board of Directors 1973* (Lisbon, 1974), 295–296, as quoted in Eric N. Baklanoff, *The Economic Transformation of Spain and Portugal* (New York: Praeger, 1978), 132.

Monetary Fund in the early 1960s. In view of the undeveloped condition of the Portuguese economy, EFTA, in a special provision outlined in Annex G, of the Stockholm Convention, gave Portugal ten years to catch up with the industrialization level of Western Europe.

The level of Portuguese industrial development, the size of her units of production, and the fact that a good deal of her manufacturing industry had been created behind a protective tariff barrier meant that Portugal was not in condition to fulfill the general obligations of the Stockholm Convention. It was, indeed, in recognition of this that the Stockholm Convention accorded Portugal the status of a "young economy." (Pintado 1964, 198)

Accordingly, Portugal's protective tariffs would be removed in a more gradual process than usual, and its products could enter member countries duty-free.
     The membership in EFTA liberalized investment policy,

which enabled investors, mainly foreign, to build up an export-oriented industry based on low wages . . . parallel to this expansion in foreign investment, there was an expansion in the investment activity of the Portuguese economic elite partly in cooperation with foreign industrialists. (Kohler 1982, 174)

In the first few years after Portugal joined EFTA, its exports to EFTA countries increased by more than 13 percent per year (see Table 1.7). In fact, "EFTA's share of Portuguese exports nearly doubled from 21 percent in 1960 to 41 percent in 1972" (Baklanoff 1978, 132). The opening up of Portugal and the increasing importance of EFTA are shown in Table 1.8.
     In addition to its effect on export, the entry into EFTA had other, equally important consequences. First, it breached the isolation of Portugal from the rest of the world. Second, it made some key technocrats, who were followers of

Table 1.8
Growth of Portugal's Exports, 1960–1972

EEC	6.7
EFTA	18.7
United Kingdom	13.6
United States	7.4
Rest of world*	
Total	8.5

*Rate of growth not indicated.

Sources: Presidência do Concelho, *IV plano de fomento, 1974–1979* (Lisbon, 1974), 75–76, tables VIII and XV, quoted in Eric N. Baklanoff, *The Economic Transformation of Spain and Portugal* (New York: Praeger, 1978), 133.

Ferreira Dias—Xavier Pintado, Pereira de Moura, and modernizing, progressive, and Europeanist monopolists such as António Champalimaud—more aware of the system of industrial control's detrimental effects on the country's economic modernization and development. Third, it increased the relationships between Western European and Portuguese "modern" class members.

The latter consequence increased conflicts of interest "between those areas of the economy that had traditionally been based on the colonies and those that leaned more towards the European markets" (Kohler 1982, 175). As Table 1.7 indicates, continental Portugal's exports to overseas colonies fell from 25 to 15 percent between 1960 and 1972, and imports from the colonies also decreased. An additional consequence was the further development of the contradiction characterizing the Portuguese situation: on the one hand a modernizing, developing country with a colonial empire, and on the other hand a country with a backward, oppressive, protectionist, traditionalist, and reactionary economic, political, and social structure.

The African Wars

Continental Portugal was faced with outbreaks of guerrilla warfare in Angola in 1961, in Portuguese Guinea in 1963, and in Mozambique in 1964. The subsequent cost of maintaining the empire forced the reactionary coalition to open the country even further to foreign investment, which became quite large by the second half of the 1960s. Extensive penetration of foreign capital was a second and much larger crack in the isolation of Portugal. "Behind the facade of social and political immobilism under the loosening grip of an aged Salazar, Portugal knew deep and lasting changes during the 1960s" (Pintado 1964, 7).

The outbreak of war on three fronts in the African colonies forced the Estado Novo to increase the military budget substantially. In 1960, defense and security took 28.7 percent of public expenditure. By 1968 the wars in Africa were absorbing 44.3 percent of Portugal's budget, a heavy cost.

This increase in public spending in turn increased personal income, which caused an increase in internal demand for consumer goods without productive growth; an increase in economic production; and inflationary pressures. These changes were in contradiction with the political economy model of the reactionary coalition, which favored economic stability without inflation. Moreover, since defense expenditures reduce the funds available for domestic investment (i.e., economic development), the reactionary coalition was forced to raise taxes, which affected the poorer workers most severely (between 1970 and 1975, income taxes rose 53 percent, and indirect taxes increased by 74 percent), and to borrow from abroad. This decision was a sharp deviation from the autarkic posture that the reactionary coalition held for almost fifty years. A few examples of foreign loans made to Portugal between 1962 and 1965 follow.

In 1962 a consortium of U.S. banks lent 600 million escudos; the Kreditanstalt, 1 billion escudos; the U.S. Export-Import Bank, 2 billion escudos to finance the construction of the Tagus River bridge; the West German Bank for Reconstruction, 37 million dollars.

In 1963 two loans were made by the World Bank, totaling 12.5 million dollars to finance the production of electric energy; a loan by the South African Reserve Bank; (for twenty years at 2 percent) of 153 million escudos; a loan by Seligman & Cie. and the Banque Française de Commerce Extérieur of 109 million escudos to finance the construction of the Tagus River bridge. (A second loan of 53 million escudos was extended in 1964.)

In 1964 Portugal received a loan of 10.9 million dollars from the U.S. government to purchase wheat (five years, at 4 percent); a loan of 7.5 million dollars from the World Bank for the production of electric energy in the Douro region; a loan of 597 million escudos from the U.S. Export-Import Bank to finance construction of the Tagus River bridge.

In 1965 a Swiss financial company lent 34.78 million dollars for industrial financing in Angola (seven–eleven years, at 5.5 percent); and the World Bank lent 15 million dollars to finance production of electric energy in Portugal (twenty years, at 5.5 percent; eight U.S. banks and one German bank participated in this loan).[5]

The outbreak of war brought the metropolis and the colonies closer. On November 8, 1961, Decree-Law no. 44016 was implemented. Its purpose was to create "an integrated, multicontinental state and a common escudo currency" (Baklanoff 1978, 106). In addition, after the outbreak of the wars, the flow of private and public capital from continental Portugal to the colonies increased substantially; and the colonies, particularly Angola and Mozambique, became attractive for investors in Germany, the United States, Sweden, Switzerland, England, and Japan. To save the empire, the reactionary coalition implemented a new policy of economic and social betterment of life in the colonies, and at the same time opened the empire to foreign investors.

In order to save the colonial empire, the reactionary coalition subordinated the socioeconomic development of the country to the African wars, initiated linkages between domestic and foreign capital, and opened the country to direct

Table 1.9
Foreign Direct Investment in Portugal, 1963–1969 (millions of escudos)

Year	Amount
1963	124
1964	284
1965	673
1966	735
1967	616
1968	565
1969	615

Source: Banco de Portugal. Reproduced in Carlos Almeida and Antonio Barreto, *Capitalismo e emigração em Portugal* (Lisbon: Prelo, 1976), 49.

and indirect foreign investment. In doing so, it expanded the contradictions that characterized the socioeconomic structure, and initiated its own fall.

Foreign Investment

In 1959, foreign investment in Portugal accounted for less than 1 percent of the country's gross capital formation. In 1965, 20 percent of the total investment in the private sector was foreign. And by 1970, foreign investment accounted for 27 percent of the country's gross capital formation (Baklanoff 1978, 137; Costa 1975, 140). As indicated above, the primary reason for the opening of the country to foreign investment was the cost of the African wars, but the following factors also attracted foreign investment to Portugal: (1) the cost of both skilled and unskilled labor was the lowest in Europe—30 to 40 percent lower than in Central and Northern European industrial countries, according to literature on investment opportunities published by the Banco Português do Atlântico (n.d.); (2) by establishing production facilities in Portugal, nonmembers of EFTA could export goods duty-free to the EFTA (a market of over 100 million consumers) because Portugal was an EFTA member; (3) the Estado Novo passed laws that assured the transfer of interest, dividends, and capital gains, and the repatriation of capital. Such transfers were guaranteed under Decree-Law no. 46412 of April 28, 1965. Between 1961 and 1971, 22.6 million contos (1 conto equals 1,000 escudos, and in 1971 1,000 escudos equaled U.S. $34.78), representing profits, interest, and royalties, left Portugal. The figure for the period 1943–1960 was 900,000 contos. Finally, the political economy model of the reactionary coalition which was beginning to be outdated, assured not only political stability but also the absence of labor disputes, which were outlawed. Within a short period of time, foreign investors gained control of many sectors of industrial activities.

Table 1.9 reveals that direct foreign investment rose from 124 million escudos in 1963 to 735 million in 1966. The decline in 1967 was caused by restrictions

Table 1.10
Percentage of Foreign Capital in Portugal, by Sector, 1970–1971

Sector	Foreign Capital
Pulp and paper	43
Rubber	72
Chemicals	48
Crude oil derivatives	100
Minerals, nonmetallic	43
Metallurgical and machinery	38
Electronic and electrical machinery	81
Transport equipment	62

Source: Derived from Ramiro da Costa, *O Desenvolvimento do capitalismo em Portugal* (Lisbon: Assírio & Alvim, 1975), 142.

imposed in the United States and in Great Britain, combined with a depression in Europe.

The data in Table 1.10 show that by 1970, foreign investors had assumed a dominant position in some industrial sectors of the Portuguese economy. The investors were mainly from the United States, Germany, England, Sweden, and Belgium.

The lion's share of foreign direct investment came from the EEC. West Germany was the major national source of total investment during [1970–1973], accounting for about 26 per cent of the total; the United Kingdom was the second most important source (16 per cent of the total); and the U.S. investors ranked third, with 15 per cent of the total. . . . According to U.S. State Department sources, accumulated direct U.S. investments, representing about $200 to $250 million, were third in magnitude behind those of the United Kingdom and the Federal Republic of Germany. (Baklanoff 1978, 137)

Economic Production and Economic Growth

Through public spending, the colonial wars caused an increase in economic production. The army consumed greater quantities of consumer goods and military equipment, and the colonial markets expanded because of greater demand for goods and services, greater economic activity and growth, and greater foreign investment. Moreover, the wars initiated both consumer and capital goods production. In 1974, just before its independence, Angola attained a GNP of U.S. $3 billion and a per capita income of about U.S. $500, quite high for sub-Saharan Africa. All this had an effect on the Portuguese capitalist mode of production. The economic stability was shattered, and 1961 marked the beginning of an economic expansion that lasted until 1970. The annual average rate of increase of the GNP was above 6 percent. The rate of growth from 1914 to 1950 had been 3 percent, and between 1950 and 1960, above 4 percent but below 5 percent (Murteira 1975, 530).

Table 1.11

Origin of Portugal's GDP at Factor Cost, 1961 and 1973 (millions of escudos, 1963 prices)

Sector	1961 Mil. Escudos	%	1973 Mil. Escudos	%	% Change 1961/1973
Primary	17,370	23.8	20,408	12.7	18.0
Agriculture, Forestry, Fishing	16,908	23.2	19,590	12.2	16.0
Mining	462	.6	818	.5	77.0
Secondary	26,843	36.8	81,213	50.7	203.0
Manufacturing	21,779	29.8	65,052	40.6	199.0
Electricity, Gas, water	1,728	2.4	5,409	3.4	213.0
Construction	3,336	4.6	10,752	6.7	222.2
Tertiary	28,767	39.4	58,723	36.6	104.0
GDP	72,980	100.0	160,344	100.0	119.7

Sources: National Statistics Institute, derived from OECD, *Economic Survey: Portugal* (Paris, July 1970), 50, table B, and OECD, *Economic Survey: Portugal* (Paris, November 1976), 49, table B, both quoted in Eric N. Baklanoff, *The Economic Transformation of Spain and Portugal* (New York: Praeger, 1978), 120.

The data in Table 1.11 reveal the significant ways in which the Portuguese economy changed. Gross domestic product (GDP, or total output) grew by 120 percent in real terms; the secondary sector increased by more than three times; the tertiary sector doubled; but the primary sector, mainly the agricultural sub-sector, increased by only 18 percent. Manufacturing production in 1973 was three times greater than in 1961 (Baklanoff 1978, 121). As was mentioned above, the average annual rate of GNP growth for the decade 1960–1970 was 6 percent. Some sectors of the economy, however, experienced greater growth, as can be seen in Table 1.12.

Between 1960 and 1973, the secondary sector averaged a growth rate of 9 percent annually. The primary sector lagged behind with a rate of 1.5 for 1960–1970 and 0.7 for 1970–1973, which demonstrated its historical low productivity. The tertiary sector kept pace with a rate just about equal to that of the GNP.

In causing the economic rate of growth indicated above, the colonial wars eventually had a second and no lesser consequence: They brought to the surface the anachronistic nature of the reactionary coalition's political economy model, and the fast-growing contradiction between the forces of production and the relations of production. For example, in 1963, two years after Portugal joined the EFTA and two years after the outbreak of wars and the opening up of the country, Salazar's minister of economy, Luis Teixeira Pinto, succeeded, not without opposition from protectionist interests, in passing legislation that some-what liberalized the system of industrial licensing. But in 1965 Decree-Law no.

Table 1.12
Growth of Portugal's GDP, by Sector, 1960–1970 and 1970–1973

Sector	1960-1970	1970-1973
Primary	1.5	0.7
Agriculture	1.4	0.1
Fishing	0.5	2.0
Mining	6.2	6.0
Secondary	9.2	9.0
Manufacturing	8.9	9.0
Construction	8.1	8.0
Electricity, gas, and water	9.0	9.0
Tertiary	5.9	7.1
Total	6.1	7.0

Source: Presidência do Concelho, *IV plano do fomento, 1974–1979* (Lisbon, 1974), vol. 1, 55–56, table I. Quoted in Eric N. Baklanoff, *The Economic Transformation of Spain and Portugal* (New York: Praeger, 1978), 121.

46,666 introduced the National System of Industrial Licensing and extended it to the new industrial enterprises not only in the metropolis but in the colonies as well.

Although Decree-Law no. 26,509 of April 1936 already covered the colonies in terms of exploitation of raw materials, the 1965 law covered the opening or installation of new capital goods industries. To the reactionary coalition and the bourgeoisie, the opening up of the colonies to foreign investment was one thing; to lose both control and raw materials was another. Moreover, the economic expansion that Portugal experienced in the decade of 1960–1970 "corresponded to the utilization of the then (weak) structural socioeconomic potentialities, and in no way to an alteration in the actions of the public officials regarding new avenues for development" (Almeida and Barreto 1976, 51).

Such potentialities played an important role in producing economic growth in capital-intensive, not labor-intensive, industries. Employment failed to increase "by as much as 1/2 of 1% per year" (Robinson 1979, 4). The economic system was characterized by fragmentation, backwardness, and industrial dualism. Of the forty thousand manufacturing firms that existed in the 1960s, 75 percent employed four or fewer workers. Only 12 percent of industrial companies employed more than two hundred workers. There were also regional asymmetries. Most industrial production and capital investment was concentrated in the coastal regions. The merchandise trade deficit increased during the period 1960–1973. Portugal become increasingly dependent on international capitalism.

The Agriculture Problem

The agricultural sector of the economy lost its privileged position and became a serious problem to the country as a whole. As Table 1.12 indicates, the primary

Table 1.13
Portugal's Foreign Trade in Agricultural Products, 1967–1971 (thousands of escudos)

Year	Imports	Exports	Difference
1967	7,604,719	6,886,630	-718,089
1968	8,124,236	6,034,744	-2,089,492
1969	8,707,989	6,966,137	-1,741,852
1970	9,330,898	7,964,435	-1,366,463
1971	10,569,482	8,263,753	-2,305,729

Source: INE, *Estatísticas agrícolas* (Lisbon, 1971). Quoted in Ramiro da Costa, *O Desenvolvimento do capitalismo em Portugal* (Lisbon: Assirio & Alvim, 1975), 106.

sector, essentially agriculture, lagged behind the other sectors in performance. There are several reasons for this. Portuguese agriculture is characterized by a strong predominance of small farms. About half of the existing farms have an area of less than one hectare, and almost nine out of ten are no larger than five hectares. In the northern part of the country the holdings were excessively fragmented and too many were noncontinuous, which made integrated farming and rational crop rotations impossible. In the southern part of the country, the area of large estates, on the other hand, holdings tended to be continuous and nonfragmented.

But the size of farms was not the only problem. The sector failed to modernize its methods of production. Backward techniques in the exploitation of the land contributed to the poor performance. Immobilism was the prevailing condition of the primary sector until the fall of the reactionary coalition's Estado Novo. That immobilism was never questioned, and hence no agrarian reforms were developed and implemented. And while productivity was low, high profits were guaranteed by the abundant and very cheap labor force and other features of the political economy. Instead of land reform and modernization of methods of production, there was much investment in financial and speculative activities, and a linkage between latifundists and financiers. Two serious consequences arose from this backward and immobilist agriculture: (1) the exodus of the rural proletariat and semiproletariat, as well as of small and medium farmers (their population of 1.25 million in 1960 was reduced to 895,000 in 1970); (2) increased importation of agricultural products (see Table 1.13).

THE EXPROPRIATION OF SURPLUS VALUE: INCOME, WAGES, EMIGRATION, REMITTANCES, AND TOURISM

In order to properly explain this section, it is necessary to repeat several observations. First, Portugal rejoined the rest of the world, particularly Western Europe, early in 1960. Second, the African wars made foreign capital, investments, and penetration of the country welcome. Third, the secondary sector of the economy (industry) replaced the primary sector as the main contributor to increases in the GNP and economic growth. Fourth, all of this rendered the political economy model of the reactionary coalition anachronistic and contradictory, and caused ubiquitous changes. But, although modified in some ways, the economy was not changed until 1974 because, while it was originally conceptualized and implemented to serve and protect the interests of the latifundists, later it worked as well in the service of the industrial bourgeoisie. The use of the model by the new ruling class fraction explains why the shift from the primary to the secondary sector occurred without institutional or superstructural changes. A very good illustration of this is the distribution of national income and the control of wages. The latter made possible handsome profits for latifundists as well as for industrialists.

Income

The distribution of income was extraordinarily uneven. In 1967, only 2.3 percent of the population had an annual income of at least sixty thousand escudos (from 1962 to December 1971, one escudo equaled U.S.$0.035; hence, 60,000 escudos equaled U.S.$2,100). And in 1973, 7 percent of Portuguese families had an annual income below eighteen thousand escudos, and 11.3 percent had an income between eighteen thousand and thirty thousand escudos. Moreover, in 1973, 30 percent of the families lived below the poverty line in terms of being unable to satisfy basic human needs (Silva 1982). Table 1.14 shows the number of families with an income of at least sixty thousand escudos by district. From this table we see that 6.5 percent of the families in the Lisbon district had an annual income of at least sixty thousand escudos, and in the Vila Real district only 0.3 percent of families attained that income level. Moreover, in Portugal as a whole there were twelve thousand to fifteen thousand families that had an annual income above two hundred thousand escudos (Sousa 1969).

Labor's share of national income was 39 percent in 1950, 45 percent in 1969, and 51 percent in 1973. The share in most nations is 60 to 70 percent (Moura 1969, 22). In 1970, at an Industrial Policy Colloquium, the secretary of state for industry, Rogerio Martins, shocked the attending industrialists when he observed, "Wage increases should not only accompany productivity increases, but normally tend to surpass them."

Wages

The political economy model of the reactionary coalition made the Portuguese worker the worst-paid worker in Western Europe. In most European countries the average worker's wages were three to five times higher than in Portugal. Table 1.15 compares the average hourly industrial wage in various European countries in 1963.

The reactionary coalition's control of the cost of labor satisfied several conditions of the economy. In addition to guaranteed widespread expropriation of

Table 1.14
Families in Portugal with Income of at Least 60,000 Escudos, 1960

Districts	Total No. Families (a)	No. Families With Income at Least 60,000 (b)	Percent of Families With Income at Least 60,000
Aveiro	132,387	1,777	1.3
Beja	76,164	478	0.6
Braga	134,216	1,232	0.9
Braganca	58,928	209	0.4
C. Branco	89,539	819	0.9
Coimbra	124,364	1,550	1.2
Evora	63,062	761	1.2
Faro	94,972	824	0.9
Guarda	78,985	294	0.4
Leiria	111,122	918	0.8
Lisbon	432,807	28,051	6.5
Porto	304,177	10,054	3.3
Portalegre	56,413	587	1.0
Santarem	137,819	1,400	1.0
Setubal	112,791	1,750	1.6
V. do Castelo	69,259	279	0.4
Vila Real	80,380	257	0.3
Viseu	125,451	522	0.4
C. Portugal	2,282,836	51,762	2.3

[a]Number of families according to the 1960 census.
[b]A relation is admitted between number of families with incomes of at least 60,000 escudos and the number of people paying complementary tax.

Sources: Labor Development Board, *The Division of Income in Continental Portugal*; INE, *Statistics on 1967 Dues and Taxes*. Reproduced in Banco Português do Atlântico, *The Portuguese Market* (n.d.).

Table 1.15
Average Industrial Hourly Wages, Selected European Countries, 1963

Country	Average Hourly Wage in Escudos	Average Hourly Wage in U.S.$
Sweden	37.12	1.30
Norway	30.22	1.06
United Kingdom	25.61	0.90
Switzerland	24.17	0.85
Austria	15.54	0.54
Portugal	5.28	0.18

Source: V. X. Pintado, "Niveis e estruturas de salarios comparados" (1967), quoted in Francisco Rafael et al., *Portugal, capitalismo e Estado Novo* (Lisbon: Publicações Afrontamento, 1976), 69.

surplus value and the maintenance of a plentiful supply of labor, it guaranteed low levels of inflation, economic and social stability, and low-cost exports. With the beginning of the 1960s low labor cost attracted foreign investment and tourism. But low wages limited the purchasing power of workers, imposed constraints on the domestic market, and were responsible for extremely high rates of emigration. "Although Portugal has a population of nine million (1964), average income per head is so low ($270 in 1961), that in terms of total demand it corresponds to less than two and a half million average European consumers, and to less than two million EFTA consumers" (Pintado 1964, 13).

Another critic of labor cost control observed:

One cannot speak of the small size of our market (in a demographic sense) as a principal cause of our industrial limitations and our poverty. In terms of population, the Swiss, Swedish, Belgian, and Norwegian markets are smaller. What really is small and decisive in our market is the excessively weak purchasing power of our population. . . . The explanation for the mediocrity of our industry should be sought in the very system in operation at the present; in a combination of limiting conditions such as . . . institutions favoring lucrative capital, policies of containing salaries. . . . This conditioning necessarily generates a sharply asymmetrical distribution of wealth and a weak propensity to invest. (Almeida 1961, 49; quoted in Leeds 1984, 36)

In terms of total cost of production, in most industries the weak purchasing power was the result of the wide gap that existed between labor cost and total cost (see Table 1.16). Labor represented less than one-tenth of the total production cost in the food, beverage, tobacco, oil refining, basic metals, and leather goods industries. Even in the dangerous mining and quarrying sector, the cost of labor was still below 50 percent of total cost.

The cost of labor was also determined by geographic location and, of course, by sex. In 1969, the average wages in Lisbon were twice as high as those in the northern districts of Braga, Portalegre and Viseu. And the cost of female labor was much lower than of male labor (see Table 1.17).

In 1964, the level of expropriation of the surplus value from the average proletarian was two:eight, which means that the workers were paid for what they produced in two hours, and the remaining six hours of their labor/productivity were appropriated by their employer (Costa 1975, 162). In the case of the Portuguese *criada* (servant or maid), the level of expropriation was much higher. In 1961 the hourly average wage for a maid was 2.5 escudos (U.S.$0.09). A maid who lived in was paid 300 escudos per month (U.S.$10.50). For that amount she worked seven days a week, starting at around 6:30 in the morning, usually for more than twelve hours a day (Fryer and Pinheiro 1961, 78). The Portuguese *criada*, typically a country woman, was without a doubt the most exploited worker in Portugal until 1974.

Portuguese industrialization was based on the sacrifice of the laboring classes (low wages, high price levels for consumer goods), weak state intervention with regard to redistribution

Table 1.16
Structure of Costs in Portuguese Industry, 1957–1959 (percent)

	Labor	Materials	Electricity	Fuels & Lubricating Oils	Depreciation Allowances	Taxes
Mining/quar.	45	28	4	7	13	3
Food	7	85	1	2	4	3
Beverages	9	73	1	2	10	5
Tobacco	4	46	0	0	1	48
Textiles	16	68	2	2	9	3
Cloth/footwear	21	72	0	0	4	2
Wood & cork	14	78	1	2	3	2
Furniture	29	64	1	1	5	2
Chemicals	11	73	4	2	8	3
Oil refining	6	63	0	6	9	17
Basic metals	6	81	4	1	7	1
Metal products	23	64	2	2	8	2
Nonelec. mach.	22	67	1	1	6	2
Elec. machinery	26	65	1	2	6	1
Transport equipment	33	57	1	2	6	1
Paper	14	66	2	7	10	2
Printing & publish.	33	54	1	1	10	2
Leather goods	8	87	1	1	3	1
Rubber	15	70	2	3	8	3
Nonmetallic minerals	29	38	6	15	10	2
Other	18	69	2	1	8	2
Building & construction	26	58	0	2	3	1
Electricity. gas	14	11	0	4	67	3

Source: INE, *Inquérito industrial e estatístico das sociedades* (Lisbon, n.d.), quoted in V. Xavier Pintado, *Structure and Growth of the Portuguese Economy* (Geneva: EFTA, 1964), 147.

Table 1.17
Average Daily Wages for Nonskilled Workers in Portugal, 1965

	Highest Average: **Lisbon**		Lowest Average: **Vila Real** (a)	
	(in Escudos)	(in U.S.$)	(in Escudos)	(in U.S.$)
Total	42.00	1.47 (b)	25.00	0.88 (b)
Men	48.00	1.68	28.00	0.98
Women	27.00	0.95	14.00	0.49

(a) A district in Northern Portugal
(b) Calculated on the basis of 1 Escudo = 0.035 US$

Source: Derived from Carlos Almeida e Antonio Barreto, *Capitalismo e Emigração em Portugal* (Lisbon: Prelo, 1976), 61.

(of wealth), be it direct or indirect, through public investments and expenditures of a "social" type, such as education, housing, health, social security, and rural advancement. It was a capitalist process, albeit with the state intervening to an important extent, but in the sense of helping the private sector, and not compensating for or correcting the latter's abuses and shortcomings in a humane perspective. (Moura 1969, 26; quoted in Robinson 1979, 157)

It was the material living conditions of the Portuguese worker, conditions for which the reactionary coalition was historically responsible, that produced an "anticipatory socialization to an emigratory solution to life problems." The workers' solution was neither political activity nor religious involvement, but *heterotopian*, a hope "oriented to an 'elsewhere', an extra-national substitute opportunity structure" (Martins 1971, 85).

Emigration

Portuguese emigration is not a new phenomenon. Its explanation is not, however, found in the Portuguese culture but in the economic and sociopolitical situation of Portuguese society. It is there that we find the "push" factor for the extremely high levels of emigration. During the period under study (1926–1976), the political economy could not, and did not, make possible a decent standard of living for the rural and urban working populations. Quite the contrary; it was based on the sweat and blood of the workers.

Between 1926 and 1967, 1,326,233 workers left Portugal in search of a decent standard of living elsewhere (Almeida and Barreto 1976, 176). And "two out of every three workers leaving the Portuguese agricultural sector" between 1966 and 1975 "found employment outside the country" (Baklanoff 1978, 129). In 1966 alone, 131,000 workers left Portugal.

Historically, the "elsewhere" or "extra-national substitute opportunity structure" was Brazil, Argentina, other Latin American countries, and, later, North

America. Beginning in the mid–1960s, Western Europe, particularly France and West Germany, became the "elsewhere." In 1967, 64 percent of all the legal emigrants went to France, while only 3.5 percent went to Brazil. By then, France had become the major importer of Portuguese labor. In 1970 there were an estimated 1.2 million Portuguese emigrants in the European Economic Community, and from 1966 to 1973 industrialized Europe absorbed 74 percent of the Portuguese emigration. North America (United States and Canada) received 18 percent during 1966–1974, and 33 percent in the following two years.

With the exception of Ireland, Portugal has registered the highest net population loss, more than 2 million people from 1864 through 1973. The rate of emigration has accelerated since the end of World War II, nearly 64 per cent of all emigration (1,409,222 people) taking place between 1960 and 1973. (Keefe et al. 1977, 95–96)

Portuguese emigration was both legal and illegal. A legal emigrant had a passport, a visa issued by the authorities of the country of destination, and an employment contract. An illegal emigrant had no documents. The existence of *emigração clandestina* was caused by (a) official control of emigration and (b) the difficult and arbitrary process of obtaining a passport. In the late 1960s, Portugal signed emigration agreements with France, Germany, and other countries. The official process and recruitment of emigration was under the jurisdiction of the National Emigration Board. A third reason for illegal emigration was the avoidance of military service and the African wars. In 1963, 1964, and 1965, 16,256, 37,280 and 23,350 workers, respectively, left the country illegally (Almeida and Barreto 1976, 185). Prior to 1963, Portuguese emigration was mostly from the primary (agriculture) sector of the economy. But after that year, emigration from the secondary sector increased substantially (see Table 1.18).

Emigration from the secondary sector—technicians and other skilled workers—was not ignored, as rural emigration had been. The Portuguese Association of Industries surveyed its members, and found that 18 percent of the companies had been seriously affected by the shortage of labor caused by emigration, and 40 percent had been somewhat affected. In order to put a moratorium on, or to reduce, the exodus of skilled workers, Portuguese employers had to do what they had not done for many years: raise wages and improve benefits. Portuguese emigration played an important role in the Portuguese economy. First, it was without a doubt a very effective "safety valve for open and disguised unemployment, particularly in the rural areas" (Baklanoff 1978, 130). Thus, in absorbing large numbers of Portuguese workers, the industrialized countries of Europe and North America were engaged, albeit not for philanthropic reasons, in "employment-availability" assistance to Portugal (Hume 1973).

Moreover, such assistance saved the expenses of "building schools, housing, and other infra-structure that would have been required if emigrants had stayed home" (Robinson 1979, 10). Instead of seeking and obtaining the extensive foreign capital assistance necessary for real industrialization and genuine mod-

Table 1.18
Emigration from Portugal, by Sector of Economic Activity, 1957–1967 (percent of total labor force)

Year	Primary	Secondary	Tertiary
1957	39.1	15.7	10.8
1958	33.1	18.1	10.5
1959	31.3	17.0	9.1
1960	32.8	11.2	7.6
1961	33.5	14.4	8.4
1962	29.9	18.1	8.5
1963	28.1	27.3	6.7
1964	28.4	31.0	6.9
1965	25.8	30.2	7.7
1966	27.2	22.2	6.4
1967	24.9	14.5	6.5

Note: Includes individuals age 10 or older; does not include illegal emigration or emigration to colonies.
Source: Carlos Almeida and Antonio Barreto, *Capitalismo e emigração em Portugal* (Lisbon: Prelo, 1976), 214.

ernization, which would have expanded both capital-intensive and labor-intensive markets, the reactionary coalition used emigration to solve the problem of domestic unemployment and underemployment. Thus, ultimately, the real recipient of "employment-availability" assistance was the maker of the situation requiring the assistance: the reactionary coalition.

Second, the reactionary coalition and the Portuguese bourgeoisie benefited from the "exportation of cattle" in a very direct way, via the emigrants' remittances, which came to constitute a vital source of external funds and played an important role in the financial stability of Portugal.

Remittances

While historically workers' remittances always played an important role in the Portuguese balance of payments, their importance and value increased substantially after the early 1960s. Workers' remittances become the greatest source of foreign exchange, and the largest amount in the invisible earnings account. The visible trade deficit of U.S.$182 million in 1964 was covered by U.S.$198 million from workers' remittances and tourism, and the trade deficit of U.S.$444 million in 1968 was covered by U.S.$489 million from workers' remittances and tourism. Table 1.19 shows the makeup of the Portuguese balance of payments and the volume and increase of private transfers.

Just prior to the coup of April 25, 1974, the amount of emigrants' remittances "exploded to U.S.$1.1 billion on average in 1972–73, equivalent to over one-half of the value of Portuguese merchandise exports or about 10 percent of

Table 1.19
Continental Portugal's Balance of Payments, 1967–1969 (million escudos)

	1967 (1)	1968 (2)	1969 (2)
Current transactions	- 871	+ 1,361	+ 1,738
Trade balance	+ 9,564	- 8,705	- 10,743
Current invisibles	+ 10,435	+ 10,066	+12,481
Tourism	+ 5,376	+ 3,893	+ 2,659
Transport	- 1,419	- 1,056	- 1,226
Insurance	- 92	- 140	- 164
Capital earnings	- 68	- 162	- 128
Other	+ 645	- 17	- 63
Private transfers	+ 5,993	+ 7,548	+ 11,277
Capital transactions	+ 2,797	+ 459	- 1,673
Short-term	- 598	- 2,019	- 1,838
Private sector	- 598	- 2,019	- 1,838
Public sector			
Medium and long-term	+ 3,395	+ 2,478	+ 165
Private sector	+ 2,993	+ 1,995	+ 8
Public sector	+ 412	+ 483	+ 157

(1) Revised figures   (2) Temporary figures

Source: Bank of Portugal, *Annual Report, 1969.* Reproduced in Banco Totta & Açores, *Data on the Portuguese Economy, 1970.*

national income" (Baklanoff 1978, 130). Workers' remittances then exceeded the "value of total agricultural output" (Cabral 1977).

Tourism

As is shown in Table 1.19, tourism was an important source of foreign currency thanks to the low cost of labor in Portugal. In the 1960s, tourism accounted for the second highest amount in the invisible earnings account. In fact, from 1964 to 1967 tourism revenues exceeded workers' remittances (see Table 1.20).

By the 1970s, remittances and tourism revenues almost equaled the total value of all merchandise exports. Portugal had become dependent on the "invisibles" for imports not only of materials, energy, and equipment but even of food. About half of the nation's food supply was imported (Holland 1982). As is shown in Table 1.20, there was no restructuring of the agricultural sector during the rule of the coalition.

The magnitude and importance of remittances and tourism is also seen in Portuguese reserve holdings. In late 1973, the Central Bank's reserves at the official gold price totaled 2,839 billion dollars. But, since the commercial value of the gold was three times the official value, the reserve holdings were actually

Table 1.20
National Income from Tourism and Emigrants' Remittances, 1958–1969 (millions of escudos)

Year	Tourism	Emigrants' Remittances
1958	735	1,552
1959	715	1,913
1960	678	1,868
1961	890	1,489
1962	1,450	1,704
1963	2,142	2,371
1964	3,480	2,679
1965	4,721	3,378
1966	7,476	4,181
1967	7,403	6,267
1968	5,786	7,902
1969	4,792	11,812

Source: Carlos Almeida and Antonio Barreto, *Capitalismo e emigração em Portugal* (Lisbon: Prelo, 1976), 97.

three times higher and represented about twenty-three months of 1973 imports (Murteira 1974, 532). For the OECD countries the average was 3.5 months of imports. We have here a very good example of the mercantilist nature of the model of political economy of the reactionary coalition!

With such good sources of revenue, however, came consequences that contributed to further disequilibriums in the economy. Increases in disposable income caused increases in demand for consumer goods, which in turn caused increases in imports, since domestic production was limited. This state of affairs, combined with military expenses, caused inflation that after 1965 become quite severe. Since the economy had no provision for inflation, such disequilibriums and contradictions indicated the imminent fall of the system.

1968–1974: MONOPOLIES, MULTINATIONALS, CAETANO, AND TECHNOCRATS

Monopolies

Origins

The Portuguese oligopoly emerged in the latter part of the nineteenth century, and developed and expanded during the First Republic. With the fall of the First Republic and the seizure of power by the reactionary coalition, the oligopoly was forced to accept a temporary moratorium on increased centralization and concentration of economic activities. After World War II, however, the reactionary coalition was forced to begin moving away from the ruralist philosophy and toward industrialization. With the implementation of the New Law of Industrial Licensing of March 1945, the coalition removed the moratorium on increased centralization and concentration of economic activities. The new law was the mechanism for rapid development of monopoly and financial capital.

Other capitalist countries, despite often ruthless anti-trust legislation, have failed to resist the trend towards larger concentration of industrial power. Portugal actually encouraged the process. Industries in which monopolies or oligopolies already existed, such as cement, beer, tyres, and fertilizers, were protected from even the possibility of fresh competition. Salazar used the banks consistently and deliberately to encourage a few private empires, protecting them both from small businessmen and (until the 1960s) from the encroachment of foreign investment. (The Insight Team 1975, 57)

Identification of the Monopolies

Until the fall of the reactionary coalition in April 1974, Portugal was run by forty-four families. Real economic and politic power was in their hands. However, power was not distributed symmetrically among them but was skewed toward a core of fourteen families who increased their power during the period of 1968–1973 (Santos 1977). The families that constituted the core were the following: (1) Melo; (2) Espírito Santo; (3) Champalimaud; (4) Quina; (5) Mendes de Almeida; (6) Queirós Pereira; (7) Figueiredo (group Burnay); (8) Feteiras; (9) Bordalo; (10) Vinhas; (11) Albano de Magalhães; (12) Domingos Barreiro; (13) Pinto de Magalhães; (14) Brandão de Miranda. The remaining thirty families were dependent on the core group, particularly for access to new large projects, but were relatively autonomous (Santos 1977, 72).

The monopolistic economic groups consisted of two main subgroups. The monopolistic core was constituted of seven large financial groups: (1) CUF (Companhia União Fabril); (2) Espírito Santo; (3) Champalimaud; (4) Banco Português do Atlântico; (5) Borges & Irmão; (6) Banco Nacional Ultramarino; (7) Fonsecas & Burnay (Santos 1977, 72; Martins 1975, 35). The seven groups controlled the Portuguese economy directly and indirectly via the Estado Novo. Below this monopolistic core was a subgroup that, although lacking economic power at the national level, was monopolistic at the regional and/or sectorial level: (1) Feteira-Bordalo; (2) Brandão Miranda; (3) Manuel Vinhas; (4) Comundo; (5) Albano de Magalhães; (6) Domingos Barreiro; (7) Banco Intercontinental Português (BIP) (Jorge de Brito); (8) Pinto de Magalhães; (9) Banco da Agricultura; (10) SACOR; (11) Sociedade Central de Cervejas; (12) Mendes de Almeida; (13) SONAP; (14) Entreposto. Some interlocking did occur, however, with some of the latter groups penetrating the monopolistic core. The first six members of the subgroup participated in the Banco Português do Atlântico, a member of the monopolistic core (Santos 1977, 72).

Economic Concentration and Power

Until the fall of the reactionary coalition, economic concentration and power were located in the monopolistic core, which was involved in every aspect of the Portuguese economy. CUF, the largest group of the core, was founded in 1898 as a soap factory in Lisbon, and had expanded its operations into chemical products, textiles, tobacco, food products, mining, cellulose and paper, construction and maintenance of vessels, metallurgical and metallomechanical operations, oil refineries and petrochemicals, electrical products, banking, insurance, the merchant marine, real estate, hotels, night clubs, restaurants, casinos, and supermarkets.

In 1973, CUF comprised more than 100 firms and had more than 10 percent of the social capital of all firms in Portugal. It was equivalent to 449 companies in volume of capital, to 286 companies in level of revenue, and to 152 companies in number of employees. CUF owned a large bank (Totta e Açores) and the largest insurance group, Imperio-Sagres Universal, (formed by three insurance companies). CUF's holding company, Sociedade Geral Financeira, was responsible for the financial activities of the group. Also part of the group were the Norma Co. (management), the Profabril Co. (engineering), the Sogestil Co. (stock market activities), and the Empresa Geral de Fomento (planning, control of investments, and financial evaluation of all companies of the group). CUF also had major interests in Guinea, Mozambique, and Angola.

The second largest group was Espírito Santo, which had a strong position in the financial sector. It originated in 1920 when José Maria Espírito Santo Silva founded the Banco Espírito Santo, which later merged with the Banco Comercial de Lisboa. In 1973 the group owned the largest commercial bank, Banco Espírito Santo & Comercial de Lisboa. The group also owned the second largest insurance company, Tranquilidade, and had successfully entered the industrial sector. Through family members, Espírito Santo controlled twenty companies. The group was very active in the economies of Angola and Mozambique. It owned the Sociedade Agrícola do Cassequel in Angola, and the Sociedade Agrícola do Incomati in Mozambique, both involved in sugar production. In Angola the group grew and processed coffee, and extracted and refined oil. It was one of the three large stockholders of SACOR, the largest oil refinery in continental Portugal. Espírito Santo was associated with North American capital. It owned about a third of the capital of Portuguese Firestone, was associated with North American capital in other companies, and was the official representative of Chase Manhattan Bank in Portugal.

The Champalimaud group monopolized the cement and steel industries, and controlled a significant portion of paper and pulp production. In 1970, the group's two major companies controlled 75 percent of total sales in the cement industry. The group had its origins in the Casa Sommer, founded in the early 1900s by Henrique Sommer. In 1973 the group owned twelve large industrial companies, two of which were in Angola and Mozambique. It also owned a large bank, Pinto & Sotto Mayor, and five insurance companies, two of which were in Angola and Mozambique. The group occupied third place in terms of financial activities. In 1954, the group was given permission (*alvará*) to open a steel mill in continental Portugal; Siderurgia Nacional (National Steel) became a reality in

1961. In 1971, Siderurgia Nacional accounted for two-thirds of all sales of iron and steel. The group also acquired steel and iron production companies in Angola.

The Banco Português do Atlântico was prominent in the financial sector. It was the third largest bank in terms of volume of deposits and commercial portfolio. Its origins were in the banking house founded in 1919 by Cupertino de Miranda. In the early 1970s, the group owned a medium-size insurance company (Ourique) and controlled seventy companies. The latter were active in oil refining, cement production, cellulose production, brewing, tourism, movie theaters, advertising, and constructing and renting parking lots. In Angola and Mozambique, the group owned a bank and companies active in brewing, cotton and textiles, and hydroelectric production. Unlike the Espírito Santo group, which originated in the banking system and later entered the secondary sector, and also unlike the CUF and Champalimaud groups, which originated in the secondary sector and later entered the banking system, Banco Português do Atlântico entered both sectors simultaneously (Martins 1975, 44).

The group Borges e Irmão had its origins in the banking house of António Borges e Irmão, founded in 1884 in the city of Pôrto. In the early 1970s, the group controlled forty companies engaged in insurance, investments, tires, chemical products, housing construction, textiles, pharmaceuticals, metallurgy, advertising, tourism, hotels, and daily newspapers in the cities of Lisbon and Pôrto. It also controlled a fishing fleet and was active in the former colonies. In both Angola and Mozambique, Borges e Irmão had a subsidiary, the Banco de Crédito Comercial e Industrial, and controlled oil production in Angola. The group was associated with General Tire and Rubber through MABOR, a tire company founded in 1940 by the chief executive officer of the group, the Count of Covilha.

Banco Nacional Ultramarino was a monopolistic group with its base in the bank itself, one of the largest in continental Portugal. The focus of its activity was the *ultramar*, or former colonies. It was the issuing bank (the government's distributor of currency) in Mozambique, Guinea, Cabo Verde, and São Tomé e Principe. In Angola and Mozambique, Banco Nacional was also active in mining, agriculture, and insurance. In continental Portugal, the group was active in insurance (controlling the company Fidelidade), the merchant marine, tourism, and manufacturing. It was associated with English capital through its interest in the Anglo-Portuguese Bank of Mozambique, and with Danish capital through its interest in SECIL, a cellulose company controlled by Danish interests in continental Portugal.

The Fonsecas e Burnay group was based in the bank of the same name. It was formed in 1967, when the Banco Fonsecas, Santos e Viana merged with the Banco Burnay. The former owned several companies in continental Portugal, including the Sociedade Estoril, which had been granted the government concession to operate the rail line running from Lisbon to Cascais. The Banco Burnay had been the representative of the Société Générale de Belgique, which prospected for diamonds and oil in the former African colonies. CUF had an interest in this group through ownership of its stock. The group was associated with

Table 1.21
Structure of Portuguese Companies, by Level of Social Capital, 1939–1973
(percent)

Company Size	Social Capital (contos)	1939 1	1939 2	1959 1	1959 2	1968 1	1968 2	1973 1	1973 2
Very small	<10	22.1	0.3	24.5	0.3	14.5	0.1	8.3	.03
Small	11-100	54.5	5.5	51.9	3.4	47.6	1.6	45.6	1.1
Below average	101-1000	20.6	60.0	19.8	9.7	27.6	9.4	32.1	5.8
Average	1001-10,000	2.5	2.5	3.1	14.4	8.5	18.2	11.6	17.7
Above average	10,001-50,000	0.3	15.2	0.5	17.3	1.2	17.0	1.8	19.2
Large	50,000-100,000	0.03	11.1	0.1	9.6	0.2	10.0	0.3	9.1
Very large	>100,000	0.01	5.4	0.1	45.3	0.2	43.7	0.3	47.1

1= Companies
2= Social Capital
1 conto = 1,000 escudos

Source: Américo R. dos Santos "Desenvolvimento monopolista em Portugal (fase 1968–73): Estruturas fundamentais," *Analise Social* 13 (1977), no. 49:80.

ITT. In association with Standard Elétrica, the group undertook real estate projects. The group was the sole representative of Chrysler and the owner of Chrysler de Portugal. It also was associated with French capital.

The move toward industrialization begun with the implementation of the New Law of Industrial Licensing of March 1945 produced monopolistic capitalism and a tremendous concentration of economic power. "In 1971 it was calculated that 168 companies, many of them interlinked or belonging to the same group, or 0.4 per cent of all the companies existing in Metropolitan Portugal, held 53 per cent of the total capital" (Robinson 1979, 145).

Table 1.21 indicates the development of economic concentration, in terms of the number of existing companies and levels of social capital, between 1939 and 1973. In 1939, 97 percent of the companies in the three low levels of social capital (very small, small, and below average), companies with a social capital of no more than one thousand contos, controlled 66 percent of social capital. In 1959, however, 96 percent of the companies at the same three levels controlled only 13.4 percent of the social capital. By 1973, 2.4 percent of the large monopolistic companies (above average, large, very large) controlled 75.4 percent of the social capital. Such accelerated concentration of capital caused the proletarianization of the petite bourgeoisie. In 1959, there were 6,386 small companies, with social capital up to ten contos. In 1968 that number had been reduced to 4,810, and by 1973 it was 3,577 (see Table 1.22).

Table 1.22
Degree of Social Capital Concentration* in Portugal, 1939–1973

1939	1959	1968	1973
0.196	0.751	0.788	0.877

*The measurement of concentration was arrived at in the following manner:

d = percentage total capital in the three high levels
percentage total companies in the three low levels.

Source: Américo R. dos Santos, "Desenvolvimento monopolista em Portugal (fase 1968–73): Estruturas Fundamentais," *Analise social* 13 (1977), no. 49: 81.

Multinational Corporations

Causes of Their Appearance

With the opening of the country to foreign investment, Portugal witnessed an emergence of business enterprises that were partially or totally owned by multinational corporations. By 1973 there were 270 such companies (Martins 1975; quoted in Santos 1977, 75). Portugal offered the most favorable tax rates in Europe to private enterprises; taxation on profits, including all local taxes, did not exceed 38 percent of profits. Portugal also offered three additional attractions: (1) an absence of labor disputes and unions that translated into no strikes, walkouts, and other labor disruptions; (2) opportunities for tax evasion and fraud; (3) absence of sophisticated customs controls, which facilitated under/overinvoicing (Santos 1977, 73).

Finally, the most favorable investment attraction was the guarantees offered to the multinationals, and other foreign investors, under Decree-Law no. 46412 of April 28, 1965. This law assured "the free transfer of interest, dividends and capital gains obtained with lawfully imported capital, as well as total repatriation with no limitations to such capital" (Banco Português do Atlântico n.d., 2).

Objectives and Plans

Although all multinationals entered the Portuguese economy because of its favorable and beneficial attractions, their objectives and plans varied. In terms of their articulation within the Portuguese economy, Santos (1977) has identified four groups of multinationals.

The first group consists of multinationals that came to Portugal with the objective of exploiting the internal market and planned to stay. By 1973, this group consisted of 150 companies, the majority of them branches of a parent company. These companies brought with them technological expertise that they applied to import-substitution production. Among the firms are Société Financière des Mines, Air Liquid, ICI, International Paints, Hoechst, Abbott, Pfizer, Lever, Nestlé, Ford, General Motors, Fiat, and Renault.

The second group of multinationals came to Portugal to exploit the external market through the international division of labor. They planned to remain in Portugal only as long as profits could be maximized. They stayed one to two years, and then relocated to more favorable parts of the world. By 1973, there were ninety-five companies in this group, the great majority producing ready-made articles and employing large numbers of female workers. They included Melka, Algot, Maconde, Blue Bell, Grundig, Phillips, General Instruments, Texas Instruments, and Siemens.

The third group of multinationals came to Portugal to assure the importation, distribution, and packaging of raw materials, pharmaceutical products, chemical products, and technology under the supervision of the parent company in their country of origin. In 1973, there were fourteen companies in this group, including ICI, Shell, Bayer, BASF, Roche, and Ciba-Geigy.

The fourth group of multinationals came to Portugal to speculate in real estate transactions linked with tourism and the hotel industry. The twenty companies in this group included Leon Levy, Costain, and Grão-Pará.

With one exception, the penetration of multinationals into the Portuguese economy did not produce monopolistic groups comparable with the national groups in terms of size and diversification. The exception was ITT, which came to Portugal with economic and political objectives in terms of articulation with the internal productive market. In 1973, ITT controlled six companies and was negotiating the purchase of others. It owned Standard Elétrica, a chain of hotels, Oliva-Metallurgic Industries, and Oliva, Rabor, and Imprimarte (Santos 1977, 75). Beginning in the early 1960s, when foreign capital penetrated the Portuguese economy, first indirectly and later directly, the model of political economy of the reactionary coalition become an increasingly anachronistic barrier to capitalist trade in multinational markets. Within seven years the reactionary coalition's model still existed, but only de jure, for de facto it was already dead. The penetration of international capitalism into the formerly isolated Portuguese society took the power to control the economy away from the reactionary coalition, and consequently rendered the corporatist system meaningless. Portugal was experiencing a systemic crisis when, in September 1968, Salazar, the competent 'organic intellectual' of the reactionary coalition suffered an incapacitating stroke which terminated the forty years of loyal service to the coalition. With the economic and politic systems on the verge of collapse and the colonial wars continuing, the nation was going to have a new prime minister, the first since 1928.

Caetano, Technocrats, Opposition and Fall

President Américo Tomás, a member of the coalition's old guard (he had been elected in 1958, and reelected in 1965) appointed sixty-three-year-old Marcelo

Caetano, a longtime loyal member of the inner circle of the reactionary coalition, president of the Council of Ministers (prime minister). Caetano's involvement with the reactionary coalition dated back to the creation of the Estado Novo. At the age of twenty-three, Caetano had been a legal adviser to the Finance Ministry, and one of the framers of the Constitution of 1933. Before his appointment as prime minister, he taught and practiced law, and from 1959 to 1962 he had been the rector of Lisbon University.

Faced with a systemic crisis that was threatening the existence of the Estado Novo, Caetano realized that reforms had to be implemented to save the economic-political system he had helped to build, and in which he believed. Like his predecessor, Caetano was anti-parliamentary, anti-democrat and anti-liberal. As prime minister, his favorite motto was "Evolution with continuity." Caetano's government, which lasted from 1968 to 1974, can be divided into two periods: 1968–1971 and 1972–1974.

The first period is referred to as the period of "liberalization" because of the implementation of political and social reforms. During this period Caetano made known his intentions to replace the Estado Novo with a more liberal Estado Social, and implemented policies to liberalize and modernize the system and to solve the systemic crisis. Some of the measures were simply cosmetic; others were more daring and far-reaching. Among the former are the changing of the name of the secret police (PIDE) to General Security Directorate (DGS); of the National Union (UN, the political party of the reactionary coalition and the only existing party) to Popular National Action (ANP); of the Propaganda Secretariat to the Information and Tourist Board; and of the Censorship Board to the Previous Examination Board. Caetano also allowed the return of the bishop of Pôrto, who had been forced to leave the country in 1958 for having criticized the regime. Caetano also prevented (temporarily) the deportation of Mario Soares, a longtime opponent of the regime.

Caetano began pleasing the liberal sectors of the bourgeois class, in particular the new group of technocrats, who favored political pluralism, and began giving hope to the working class, when he permitted opposition candidates to run for the National Assembly in November 1969. Several liberals not bound to the policies of the UN/ANP were elected to the Assembly. Caetano also permitted reforms in the organizational control and structure of labor unions. Regulations implemented in 1968–1969 allowed nongovernmental, democratic control and organization of unions.

But perhaps the most far-reaching measure of liberalization and modernization implemented by Caetano was bringing a new group of technocrats into government. He appointed Dr. Valentim Xavier Pintado, the economic adviser to the Banco Português do Atlântico and a critic of the introverted economic policies of Salazar as secretary of state for commerce, and Dr. Rogério Martins as secretary of state for industry. He also appointed Rui Patricio, his godson, as foreign minister; Baltasar Rebelo de Sousa as minister of corporations, health and welfare; Dr. Veiga Simão, a Cambridge-trained nuclear physicist, as minister of education; João Salgueiro as secretary of state for planning; and Maria Teresa Lobo as under secretary for health and welfare. Moreover, Caetano allowed the technocrats to form an opposition–reform group, Sociedade de Estudos de Desenvolvimento Econômico e Social (SEDES, Society for the Study of Economic and Social Development.

Founded in 1970 by a group of young technocrats, many of whom were members of the Popular Democratic Party, SEDES was a group that represented, implicitly or explicitly, the interests of the "modern" segment of the ruling class (of which they were members), as well as a movement in opposition to the Estado Novo. The group "included leading representatives of the liberal bourgeoisie, above all intellectuals who were striving for a reform of the political system from within" (Kohler 1982, 182; Blume 1977). SEDES sought social change that would permit the incorporation of Portugal into the industrial and democratic world of modern Europe. Its members wrote articles for daily newspapers and held public meetings on a variety of economic, political, and social topics.

SEDES spoke on behalf of the liberal business community and the technological intelligentsia that sought a more modern and more efficient capitalist society, and was an ardent supporter of market economy and political pluralism, for it embraced the ideology of equal opportunity for all members of the population. As government officials, the technocrats implemented far-reaching measures. They eliminated price controls, lowered trade barriers, attracted more foreign investment, and reformed the domestic credit system. Rogério Martins, the secretary of state for industry, was instrumental in the promulgation, in 1972, of a new Industrial Development Law, more in tune with the "modern" sector (Baklanoff 1978, 113).

Caetano's period of liberalization eventually encountered problems. After forty years of labor's conforming to the rules imposed by the reactionary coalition, in 1968 and 1969 the country experienced mass labor organization and the outbreak of industrial disputes and strikes. The immensely costly colonial wars continued; inflation, and industrial and trade deterioration, were increasing; and the liberal reforms had displeased the reactionary coalition. The latter first showed its dissatisfaction by the resignation of Franco Nogueira, an *ultra* member of the old guard who had been foreign minister under both Salazar and Caetano, and was the chief executive officer of the Espírito Santo group.

Although Caetano brought the young technocrats to his government, they constituted only one of "four broad clusters of interests" in his governing coalition. The other three were the "ultraconservatives," the "integralists," and the "federalists" (Graham 1975, 40). The "ultras" were the hard-liners, members of the old guard, "rationalizers of the old order," defenders of the society built by the reactionary coalition. Of the four clusters of interests, theirs was the one "with the longest lineage as a recognized set of interests within the New State" (Graham 1975, 40). They fought for minimal change in the economic–political–social system of continental Portugal and for the retention (also minimal change) of the colonial empire.

The "integralists," formed after the outbreak of the colonial wars, argued that the colonial system no longer worked. They favored "economic, social, and institutional changes with far-reaching implications for established interests in the Portuguese state" (Graham 1975, 40).

The "federalists" also favored maintenance of the Portuguese colonial system, but differed on how this could be accomplished. They believed that Portugal could continue to be a multicontinental state only if massive internal development was implemented in the overseas provinces and if the provinces were given increased autonomy in their affairs.

The young technocrats were members of the fourth cluster, the "developmentalists" or "Europeanists." They favored integration into Europe and concomitant systemic changes. And they advocated the termination of the colonial empire through a negotiated settlement. To them, the future of Portugal was in Europe, not in Africa.

The liberalization period of Caetano's government began slowing down in 1971 and came to a full stop when President Tomás decided, at the age of seventy-eight, to seek election to another seven-year term. Since he was a member of the old guard, an *ultra*, his reelection would signal a rejection of Caetano's liberal measures. On July 9, 1972, Américo Tomás was reelected president with 616 of the 669 electoral college votes. The still-powerful *ultras* had won. With the reelection of Tomás, liberalization measures were replaced with increasingly repressive actions. Government control of labor unions, which had been reestablished in 1970, was increased when, in 1972, collective bargaining was suspended for two years, and the forces of social control of the reactionary coalition (the secret police [PIDE/DGS] and the Guarda Nacional Republicana [GNR, Republican National Guard]) again became active in strikebreaking and control of demonstrations caused by intense labor unrest. In 1973, the government fired civil servants for taking part in a peaceful demonstration against the colonial wars.

Despite the efforts of the *ultras* to save their model of political economy and the colonial empire, the task was by then impossible. Portugal's problems were the results of irrevocable structural contradictions and profound stagnation. The consequences of the latter had been mitigated by workers' remittances. Hence, the colonial empire could not be saved; and the economic system, declining as it had been for some time, was about to collapse. In 1973, at the conclusion of the Free Trade Agreement between Portugal and the European Economic Community (EEC), the introverted political economy model of the reactionary coalition collapsed. On April 25, 1974, the political regime of the reactionary coalition ended.

NOTES

1. "Portugal não é país comercial nem industrial . . . fas-se um grande mal ao país tentando transformar em fabril uma industria que verdadeiramente só pode ser agrícola e preparam-se acaso para o futuro crises industriais que não têm por certo tão fácil e

pronto remedio como as agrárias'' (Anselmo de Andrade, *Portugal econômico, teorias e factos* (Lisbon, 1918), 343; quoted in Amaro 1982, 1000). My translation.

2. ''As desordens do industrialismo manifestaram-se ultimamente nas exigências dos operários, no espírito de dissipação das grandes massas populares, no disinteresse pela dura conservação das cousas e dos meios de trabalho'' (Campos 1923, 94; quoted in Medeiros 1978, 115).

3. See for example, Murteira (1974) and Moura (1969).

4. Even before 1931, there had been three decrees regulating important national industries: Decree no. 12051, July 31, 1926; no. 14945, October 28, 1927; no. 15581, May 19, 1928 (Rafael et al. 1976, 3).

5. ''Recent Economic Developments in Portugal,'' *Staff Papers*, 13, no. 2 (July 1966); Associação Portuguesa das Empresas do Ultramar, ''The Growing Economy of Portugal'' (New York: 1968), quoted in Almeida and Barreto (1976, 47–48).

2

Seizure of Power

HISTORICAL BACKGROUND

Less than ten years into the twentieth century, the monarchy in Portugal found itself in precarious circumstances. The house of Coburg-Braganza faced two serious problems. First was the condition of Portugal's finances, which had deteriorated because of foreign debt that had climbed to 210 million escudos. The second problem was the monarchy's capitulation to the Ultimatum of 1890.[1] The Portuguese people were much grieved by the extravagance and licentiousness of King Carlos (who was assassinated on February 1, 1908) and later of his son, King Manuel II (who died in 1952). More important, the monarchy ceased to serve the interests of the landowners and of the rural and urban petite bourgeoisie of Lisbon and Pôrto.

On October 5, 1910, the armed forces seized power, overthrew the monarchy, and established republicanism in Portugal. A provisional government was organized under Dr. Theófilo Braga, a cultural historian and leading Republican idealogue, although the Partido Republicano Português (PRP, Portuguese Republican Party) was a minority movement with its strength among the lower-middle and working classes. The latter, however, were not directly active in the political system because the Portuguese parliamentary republic of 1910–1926 was made up of elite elements. Urban middle-class lawyers, intellectuals, journalists, and bureaucrats were overrepresented in the Republican regime. Very few members of the parliament had experience in public administration.

The Portuguese First Republic was formally implemented with the Constitution of 1911, which provided for a parliamentary system of government and a president chosen by the parliament. The new constitution guaranteed individual civil rights and "provided the basis for the creation of an egalitarian society" (Keefe et al. 1977, 49).

In reality, however, parliamentary rule was based on a rather restricted class pluralism. The accepted political actors were selected from the upper and upper-middle classes, which were rather small. The Republican liberal bourgeoisie, which was composed essentially of urban middle-class professionals, was never willing to "incorporate the peasantry, the proletariat and other forces into a legitimate sphere" (Ginner 1982, 184).

Nevertheless, albeit in a paternalistic way, the First Republic was willing to attempt to solve many of the existing social problems. The activities of the PRP included improvement of workers' living standards; an eight-hour workday; guarantee of the right to strike; social welfare legislation; agrarian reforms; programs to combat the high rate of illiteracy; programs for developing technical education; development of profitable colonialism; an antimonarchical stance; abolition of all titles of nobility; armed forces reform; anticlericalism; and abolition of religious education (through the Separation Law of 1911).[2]

This policy not only raised taxes for the rich but also caused some of them to pay taxes for the first time. But it did not cause any significant change in the structure of Portuguese society. The social transformation from a monarchy to a republican parliamentary system did not widen the social and economic bases of the new regime. To the ruling fractions of the owning classes, the Republic was a concession to stop social agitation and to attempt to solve the systemic crisis that the previous liberal model seemed incapable of solving. The people were excluded from political participation during the monarchy and during the later parliamentary rule (Campinos 1975, 18). For example, under parliamentary rule, suffrage was limited to literate males over twenty-one. But only one in four was literate in 1910.

The composition of the [parliamentary] assembly shows some modifications of social categories represented, in contrast to the monarchy assembly, but not in any significant manner which demonstrates a change in the dominant social class: there is still the predominance of [public] functionaries, university graduates and rural proprietors. (Caetano 1967, 437; quoted in Campinos 1975, 18)

But although the activities of the First Republic representatives were not sufficiently radical to produce structural changes in Portuguese society, they were more than sufficiently radical in terms of the interests of the owning classes and the clergy.

Capitalists, landowners, foreign investors and high ranking bureaucrats felt their interests were threatened; the generals and colonels were disgusted by the idea of radical notions infiltrating the army; and the clergy of all ranks, from cardinal-patriarch of Lisbon to the village curate were horrified by a regime whose first acts were inspired by the most extreme anti-clericism. (Harsgor 1976, 2–3)

The first indication of the dissatisfaction of the dominant classes—landowners, financiers, and emerging industrialists—with parliamentary rule and their interest in forms of class domination that could guarantee the expropriation of surplus value and capital accumulation without the inconveniences of free competition, strikes, and other "subversive" activities, is found in the works of Antonio Sardinha (1889–1925), a defender of the "futurism of the past."

On April 8, 1914, Sardinha organized a nationalist movement called Integralismo Lusitano. It rejected parliamentary rule and favored the return to an "organic, traditionalist and anti-parliamentarian" monarchy in which the assembly would rubber-stamp legislation approved by a technical council and final approval would be exclusively by the monarch. Integralismo (much influenced by Charles Maurras of Action Française) and its suggestion for a "better" system of rule were incorporated, several years later, in the Movimento Católico Social Português and specifically in the Centro Acadêmico de Democracia Cristã (Academic Center of Christian Democracy).

But before they could organize the necessary forces to seize power, the dominant classes had to face World War I. In 1916, Germany invaded Angola and Mozambique, which forced the Democratic-Republican government to send thousands of soldiers to Africa and to ship an expeditionary force of forty thousand to Flanders. Defending the colonies and fighting in Europe had a very high cost. The Portuguese army suffered severe losses; the people experienced food shortages and inflation. The purchasing power of the escudo was reduced by half. The conservative wing of the Republican parliament, the Unionists, were not pleased with the overall situation, particularly since they had been against joining the war. In terms of lives lost and extraordinary expenditures, entering the war on the Allied side was a mistake that only increased people's disillusionment with the Republican rule. It also played an important role in the first successful attempt to abolish parliamentary rule.

On December 5, 1917, General Sidónio Pais led an uprising, seized power, arrested and deported the president, and appointed himself president-dictator. País had been influenced by Integralismo Lusitano. With País as military dictator, republican institutions were abolished, trade unions were banned, and a corporatist state was being considered. But País was assassinated in December 1918. After his death, the Constitution of 1911 was reinstated, free elections were held in 1919, and the Democrats returned to power.

But well before 1926, the republican model was no longer protecting the interests of the ruling owning class fraction, and was almost life-threatening to the petite bourgeoisie. Business groups such as the Associação Commercial de Lisboa (Commercial Association of Lisbon) and the Associação Industrial Portuense (Industrial Association of Pôrto) had been complaining for some time that the instability of the republican political system was detrimental to the economy. And a third group, the Associação Central de Agricultura Portuguesa (Central Association of Portuguese Farmers), which represented many latifundists, not surprisingly held the view that the Republican regime was causing great harm to the country. Furthermore, there was much disillusionment with the

Table 2.1
Strike Rate in Portugal, 1860–1929

	1860-1869	1870-1879	1880-1889	1890-1899	1900-1909	1910-1919	1920-1929
No. of strikes	0	15	12	38	91	391	127

Source: Philippe C. Schmitter, *Corporatism and Public Policy in Authoritarian Portugal* (Beverly Hills, Calif.: Sage, 1975), 13.

Republican regime among the working classes. They showed their dissatisfaction through strikes and an anarcho-syndicalist orientation. The strike rate in Portugal between 1860 and 1925 is shown in Table 2.1.

Although the number of factory workers was quite small, the deteriorating economic conditions and what appeared to be the inability of the Republican government to solve such conditions justified the high number of strikes, particularly between 1910–1919. The Confederação Geral dos Trabalhadores (CGT, General Confederation of Workers), became alienated from bourgeois politics and the democratic Republic (Robinson 1979, 6).

The urban petite bourgeoisie (originally the backers of the establishment of the Republic and of parliamentary rule) became opponents of the economic, political, and social situation. The First Republic's pro-labor legislation had become detrimental to the petite bourgeoisie. On October 14, 1924, many commercial establishments did not open in a one-day protest that contributed to the formation of a new organization, União de Interesses Económicos [UIE], Union of Economic Interests), whose membership was composed of managers and landowners. According to its members, the UIE was formed to combat "social subversion," meaning workers' strikes and labor demonstrations, and social unrest (Maxwell 1974, 17).

The capitalist mode of production was very much present in Portugal at the beginning of the twentieth century. The buying and selling of labor, the expropriation of surplus value, and the private accumulation of capital were occurrences of daily life. Nevertheless, Portuguese society, while no longer precapitalist, was not a capitalist society or a "fully 'bourgeois society.' "[3] The transition to industrialism had been prevented by both endogenous and exogenous obstacles. By 1926 Portugal had not experienced a "bourgeois revolution," a "revolution from above," or a "peasant revolution."[4]

The endogenous obstacle to the transition was the small size of the urban proletariat, the large size of the rural population, and the size of the commercial and industrial modernizing classes (which were too small to seize power and to rule). The exogenous barrier was the periphery–core dependent relationship (also referred to as "free exchange"[5]) that had existed between Portugal and England. These structural factors made it impossible for autochthonous development of a "fully 'bourgeois society.' " Thus the small commercial and industrial bourgeoisie, "exchanging the right to rule for the right to make money,"[6] had no option but to compromise. The result was the establishment of a coalition of an immobilist, patriarchal, and traditional landed aristocracy[7] with a weak ("but strong enough . . . to be worthwhile political ally") modernizing bourgeoisie.

The UIE is an example par excellence of a "reactionary coalition" in which the landed aristocracy holds power. Not long after its organization, Portugal suffered a long period of conservative authoritarian bureaucratic rule.[8] According to its rhetoric, the UIE was formed to "combat 'social subversion.' " In reality, its purpose was to abolish the parliamentary government and to replace it with a political system that guaranteed the extraction of surplus value and the simultaneous elimination of the inconveniences and risks of competition, strikes, and a "fully 'bourgeois society.' "[9]

The (limited) social transformations created under the aegis of the "paternalistic" conservative political order became too much at odds with it [class despotism]. A new solution had to be found that on one hand, allowed the continued legitimation of the inherited system of inequality . . . and on the other successfully destroyed [any] . . . movements of the left which began to challenge seriously the system. Such a solution . . . meant the end of the liberal bourgeois order as well as a redefinition of the political and economic functions of the state. (Ginner 1982, 184)

Although the First Republic was unstable (between 1910 and 1926 it had forty-six cabinets and eight presidents), by 1926, when it was overthrown, the art of politics had been learned and the economic storm had passed. "The 1926 revolution was timed to break out before public opinion could feel that the currency had become more stable, the budget more balanced and the public debt lowered" (Harsgor 1976, 29). Therefore, "authoritarian rule did not come to Portugal in the imminence of economic collapse" (Schmitter 1975, 29).

THE MILITARY DICTATORSHIP

Seizure of the State Apparatus

On May 28, 1926, the right-wing military agents of the reactionary coalition, inspired by Mendes Cabeçadas and led by General Gomes da Costa,[10] started the coup d'état in Braga, the heart of the conservative rural regions of northern Portugal. The armed forces, which had been neutral during the fall of the liberal constitutional monarchy, became an active political force in 1911 when the Republican Party attempted to weaken the military hierarchy by granting privileges to sergeants and noncommissioned officers. There was little or no opposition,[11] even in Lisbon, to the military seizure of power, and five days later parliamentary rule was ended and the sixteen-year-old democratic Republic was dead. Civilian state officials were replaced with military officers. The military dictatorship of the young lieutenants was established; and while it was to last only until 1928, it marked the first step toward the implementation of reactionary authoritarianism.

According to the rhetoric of high-ranking military officers, the seizure of state power, the *Pronunciamento*, was necessary to "save the country" from corrupt politicians. In reality, however, the intervention by the military agents of the reactionary coalition was warranted because the political formula of bourgeois parliamentary rule, especially the progressive legislation put forward by the Democratic Party, was at odds with the interests of the hegemonic class.

But one year after the revolution, the country was faced with a deficit of 670,000 contos (670,000 million escudos). On May 31, 1926, just after the establishment of the dictatorship, the country's floating debt amounted to £240,035; by July 1927 the debt had reached £1,575,015. Also, the domestic floating debt had risen from 1,282,142 contos in May 1926 to 1,631,964 contos by June 1927 (Araquistan 1928, 43). From 1925–1926 to 1926–1927, state expenditures rose by 40 percent and the budget deficit increased by 38 percent (Robinson 1979, 44). The increase in state expenditures and the concomitant worsening of public finances can be explained by the lack of experience in economic administration among the military officers who had replaced civilian officials, the "political weakness of the military," and the absence of any plans for running the country after the seizure of power (Martins 1968). The end result was that "After a year of [military] dictatorship, the Portuguese state was very much poorer than the year when the constitutional government was replaced" (Araquistan 1928, 47). The military had succeeded in seizing power but had been unable to develop a "coherent alternative" to the parliamentary rule it had abolished.

Failure of the Military Dictatorship

By 1928 it was obvious that the young lieutenants could not create a new and stable state (Wheeler 1978). Inasmuch as the public finances had worsened under their rule, they began to be perceived as politically and administratively incompetent. In an attempt to reduce dissatisfaction, General Carmona appointed General Sinel de Cordes as finance minister in April 1928. But Sinel de Cordes failed to solve the country's financial problems. In fact, during the 1928–1929 fiscal year, the military allocated 23.42 percent of the national budget to defense spending. Great Britain's allocation was 10.43 percent in the same period (Gallagher 1981a). So serious were its budget and financial problems that Portugal was unable to pay its debt to Great Britain, even after the debt was reduced to twenty-four million pounds (Kay 1970, 30).

The League of Nations Loan

In an attempt to solve the problem of the state's finances, the military searched for loans abroad. But, because of the social and political uncertainty in Portugal, only the League of Nations responded favorably to the Portuguese application for a loan of twelve million pounds. General Sinel de Cordes, the finance minister, went to Geneva to initiate formal negotiations, but the loan was never extended. The League would grant the loan only on certain conditions, which included "an inquiry into Portugal's state finances" and a study of the organization of the Bank of Portugal, that "amounted to establishing a receivership over Portuguese finances" (MacAdams 1952, 24). These conditions and stipulations were refused by the military in the name of nationalism.

The fiscal crisis contributed to the formation of factions within the military and increased the dissatisfaction within the owning class. While a small number of military officers were not against the move toward a "presidential bourgeois republic," the majority championed the creation of an authoritarian state, which had been favored by conservative latifundists and business groups for some time, and which would serve the interests of the reactionary coalition. The majority prevailed. Salazar was recalled from Coimbra to solve the state's fiscal crisis and to rejuvenate the economy in a way that almost guaranteed risk-free capital accumulation. With the return of Salazar, the military dictatorship of the young lieutenants was replaced with civilian authoritarianism.

THE "ORGANIC" INTELLECTUAL OF THE COALITION[12]

António de Oliveira Salazar

It is a commonly held view that Salazar was a deus ex machina who "emerged from nowhere to rescue the Portuguese nation" at a moment of serious and complex social, economic, and political troubles (Gallagher 1983, 85). Such a view is incorrect. The professor of economics from the University of Coimbra "did not just drift" into becoming the "organic" intellectual or the "thinking and organizing element" of the reactionary coalition. He himself had much to do with becoming the loyal servant.[13] In Salazar, the extreme right[14] found its perfect front (Saraiva 1974, 70).

Salazar was born in Vimieiro, a tiny village near the town of Santa Comba in Beira Alta province, on April 28, 1889. He was never the poor boy most biographers have said he was. His father was an estate manager and as such "belonged to a higher social stratum than Salazar's official biographers have admitted." Moreover, the family owned "at least three houses" (Harsgor 1976, 3). When he was eleven years old, Salazar won a scholarship to the Viseu seminary, where he stayed for eight years. He took minor orders but did not proceed with studies for the priesthood (Kay 1970, 11). In 1910, the year the Republic was proclaimed, Salazar entered the University of Coimbra to study law, economics, and public administration.

Salazar's philosophical background was Thomist, but he was also influenced by Pope Leo XIII and his *Rerum novarum* and Charles Maurras's Action Française (Kay 1970, 22). A further influence on Salazar was Pope Pius XI and his *Quadragesimo anno* (although Salazar did not remain loyal to the latter's work).

Salazar became an assistant lecturer in the department of economics at the University of Coimbra in 1917. At the same time he published "The Gold Agio: Its Nature and Causes (1891–1915)," "The Problem of Wheat Production," and "Some Aspects of the Commodity Crisis." In May 1918 he was awarded a doctorate (Kay 1970, 24). In 1921 Salazar was a founding member of the right-wing Centro Académico de Democracia Cristã and was elected to the parliament. After only a few days, however, he resigned his seat. "He never concealed his contempt for a parliamentary system in which the country's elite was not recognized and given a free hand" (Harsgor 1976, 4).

Salazar returned to his post as lecturer at Coimbra and began writing and publishing his views "in order to attract the kind of people whose backing he desired," and "to explain the ways in which the country's finances could be restored" (Harsgor 1976, 4). "He was a frequent contributor to journals concerned with social studies and especially the weekly *O Imperial*, directed by his friend, Manuel Goncalves Cerejeira, who later became Cardinal Patriarch of Lisbon" (Kay 1970, 23).

In 1921 Salazar attended a convention of commercial and industrial associations and presented his views on "cheap public management by cutting social services." In 1924 he was the "outstanding figure" at the Eucharistic convention at Braga. One year later he wrote *O bolshevismo e a sociedade* (Bolshevism and Society). By then he had become the spiritual leader of the Portuguese reactionary coalition.

When the military appointed Salazar as finance minister in 1926, just after the seizure of power, they were not, therefore, appointing an unknown professor from Coimbra. The view of Salazar as an unknown professor, while held by some students of Portugal, is incorrect.

[Salazar's name] was known. His provocative critiques of the economy had been widely publicized particularly his studies of the gold standard and wheat production. . . . His call for a government above party interests put him solidly on the [military] junta's wavelength. On the strength of his growing reputation and the advice to the generals by their friends . . . a small group of officers drove to Santa Comba to see him and to put pressure on him to accept [the appointment]. (Kay 1970, 38)

Salazar arrived in Lisbon on June 12, 1926, to assume office. He held the finance portfolio for five days. The most common and feasible explanation, in light of his return to Coimbra, is that in 1926 the military junta rejected his "conditions for doing the job." Salazar demanded "complete control over all spending, severe cuts in public expenditure, a share in all decisions affecting financial legislation" (Kay 1970, 39). In 1926, the military did not want to allocate that much power to a civilian, and it was not in a position to acquiesce to Salazar's demands. Moreover, if they were to rule, to return favors to those who had assisted them in the seizure of power, they had to be in full control of the state apparatus. This situation, of course, was to change, and the conditions proposed by the League of Nations forced the military to bring Salazar back to solve the state's financial crisis and to assure capital accumulation, through the subordination and exploitation of the working classes. Such a task was accomplished very successfully by António de Oliveira Salazar, who built the New State, which, although reactionary and authoritarian, and an instrument of class domination, did accomplish accumulation of surplus value through the subordination and exploitation of the masses of the people.

Moreover, Salazar provided the new regime and the power holders with two highly successful ideological mechanisms of repression. The first was the person of Salazar himself. The ideologues of the reactionary coalition manipulated the masses to perceive Salazar as the man of the country, the man for law and order. He was the embodiment of consensus. In time, both the bourgeoisie and, ironically, the proletariat (especially the rural proletariat of the northern part of the country) saw Salazar as the savior of the nation, for he had brought peace to the country. Hence, especially after 1928, the authoritarian regime was individualized, reduced to the person of Salazar; it became Salazarismo. The regime of the reactionary coalition became the regime of Salazar. Second, the appearance of a "monocratic" rule (the personalization of power in the person of Salazar) gave the regime an autonomy it never really had and, equally important, kept the real power holders, the ruling class, the coalition of latifundists, financiers, and industrialists, safely in the background.[15]

On April 27, 1928, Salazar became finance minister again. This time his conditions were accepted, and he received the power to control the financial activities and budgets of the various governmental services. Salazar was thus able to seize the reins of political power. This is not to say that his power was sufficient to make him autonomous, to make him a dictator. Salazar never ruled alone. He knew that above him were the military, the guardians of the reactionary coalition. That is why he exempted the armed forces from his sweeping budget cuts and financial regulations. Shortly after his reappointment, he began working "with a small group of devoted followers," some of whom had been his students at Coimbra University. The military dictatorship had entered its second stage, which has been referred to as "the rise of Salazar and civilian authoritarianism" (Wheeler 1978, 247).

In 1929 Salazar began making speeches in which he called for a new constitution that was to serve as the foundation of a new political order. In 1930, Salazar defined the institutional form of the new political order as an "authoritarian corporate republic." Some of the initial steps deemed necessary in order to bring "the corporate state to reality" were also made public at that time: (1) the abolition of all political parties and trade unions; (2) the implementation of total censorship; (3) the vesting of political power in the executive; (4) inculcation

of the concept *Deus, pátria e família* (God, country, and family).[16] The new
political order began to take shape in 1930. The vehicle instrumental in expediting
the process was the União Nacional (National Union).

The National Union

The National Union was established on July 30, 1930. Theoretically "all . . .
Portuguese citizens with no distinction of political affiliation or religious beliefs"
could be members. The only condition for membership was loyalty to the association's political activities. In practice, however, things were much different.
The National Union was not an association or a movement as it is usually defined;
it was a political party of "regime loyalists," of "situationists." The Union
was a civil and political association (read: party) established to give direction
and support to the seizure of power that commenced in 1926. And it remained
the regime's mouthpiece until 1974.

The Union became a vehicle for the realization of two important tasks that
needed to be accomplished if the Estado Novo was to emerge and be implemented. First, before 1926 the "right wing 'fascist' or integralist oriented"
group was both homogeneous and heterogeneous. The homogeneity lay in its
conservatism and economic interests (the owning class fractions), and in its
geographical location in (the northern and central parts of the country). The
heterogeneity lay in its associational ties. Ideologically, the political mosaic of
Portugal before the 1926 coup consisted of the following parties: (1) Conservative
Monarchists, (2) Integralists, (3) Legitimists, (4) Catholics (CADC), (5) Union
of Economic Interests, (6) Liberals, and (7) Nationalists.

Realizing that the Estado Novo could not become a reality in a political context
characterized by factionalism, Salazar used the Union as the instrument to ho-
mogenize the divided factions. To my mind, the National Union is a very good
example of Gramsci's "social group."

The supremacy of a social group manifests itself in two ways, as "domination" and as
"intellectual and moral leadership." A social group dominates antagonistic groups, which
it tends to "liquidate", or to subjugate perhaps even by armed force: it leads kindred
and allied groups. (Gramsci 1971, 57–58)

Equally relevant to the nature and role of the National Union is Gramsci's further
observations:

A social group can, and indeed must, already exercise "leadership" before winning
governmental power (this indeed is one of the principal conditions for the winning of
such power); it subsequently becomes dominant when it exercises power, but even if it
holds it firmly in its grasp it must continue to "lead" as well. (Gramsci 1971, 57–58)

The success of the Union, therefore, lies in having brought the country's heterogeneous political elites into an organizationally strong and ideologically united

hegemonic power bloc. One must keep in mind, of course, that the threat to business as usual caused by an incompetent military dictatorship, the ensuing financial conditions of the country, and the absence of a political order suitable to the maintenance of domination and accumulation of surplus value increased the likelihood of the Union's success.

The second task of the Union was determining the nature of the future New State. Having succeeded in creating "ideological cohesion" among the elite factions, and free of any real "autonomous political parties and oppositional interests," the Union could, and did, install and consolidate a new political order that would protect the interests of the bloc in power.

The greater the state elites' combination of organizational strength and ideological unity, the greater the possibility of installing the new regime. . . . The degree of ideological cohesion in support of the choice [of regime] and of the institutional strength of the coercive elite is an independent variable of considerable importance. For example, if the elite that assumes control of some key sectors of the governmental coercive apparatus is itself weakly organized and/or internally divided it may not be able to dominate the entire state apparatus, much less agree on [the nature of the state] to impose society. (Stepan 1978, 83)

It is therefore not surprising to find that Article 1 of Decree no. 21,608 (published in the government's official newspaper, *Diário do governo*, ser. I, no. 195, August 20, 1932) stated that the National Union was "a nonpolitical association, independent of the State," and was designed to assure social, economic, and political order. To accomplish this task, the Union's members would collaborate with the government in the development and implementation of public policies.[17] Interestingly, the decree was passed one month after Salazar had been appointed prime minister, the first civilian since the coup of 1926 to hold the position.

On November 23, 1932, Albino dos Reis, minister of the interior and member of Salazar's first cabinet (organized on July 5, 1932):

Outside the National Union we do not recognize [other political] parties. Within we do not accept [the existence of] groups. The N.U. is not an association of influentials, is not an association of electoral power blocs. . . . We have a doctrine and we are a force. As such it is our duty to govern; we have the mandate of a victorious revolution and the approval of the nation. (quoted in Campinos 1975, 489)

THE NEW STATE: POLITICAL RHETORIC

The Political Philosophy of the New State

At the base of the New State political rhetoric was the concept of harmony among all groups in society, but principally between capital and labor. Salazar and the ideologues of the reactionary coalition, particularly the founding members of the Integralismo Lusitano and some members of business groups in Lisbon and in Pôrto, argued that liberal democracy and capitalism produced class struggles, social conflicts, and cutthroat competition in the pursuit of selfish personal interests. Their state, the corporate state, would produce a society in which harmony would be the responsibility of every citizen. The corporate state and the concomitant society demanded the primacy of the interests of groups over the interests of individuals. Hence, life in Portugal would be organized under the principles of corporatism and social solidarity instead of under cutthroat competition in pursuit of selfish interests.

The corporate system produces a regime of social organization based on the grouping of men in accordance with the type of their natural interests and their social functions, and by necessity, as the claim to distinct political representation of such diverse groups.[18]

Social harmony would become a reality not because the state would abolish social classes and class differences, but because the new state would consider the different classes "harmonious" instead of "conflicting," and because the "corporate bodies" would provide the appropriate "channels of class articulation." What this means, of course, is that the new state would be anticapitalist, antiliberal, antiparliamentarian, and antimodern. But it would not be anticapitalism. However, the society of the New State was not a typical capitalist society, and there was much capitalism in Portugal; but it was a capitalism of many "legitimists" or "Junkers" as well as of few "Orleanists" (Marx [1852] 1977). That is, it was a system of economic production subordinated to the established ethos of the ruling landowning aristocracy and characterized by "patriarchal employer–worker relations." It was a system of much manufacturing but little "machinefacturing." It was a distinct type of capitalist mode of production.

In order to guarantee that social harmony would be accomplished, the ideologues of the New State argued that the fundamental units of the new social organization would be the family and the economic corporation. In the latter, employers and employees would work together, as a family, toward the common goal, the national interest.

The Political Structure of the New State

The Constitution of 1933

Although civilians had been running the state apparatus since 1928, the military dictatorship ended and civilian reactionary authoritarian rule began officially and legally with the adoption of the Constitution of 1933. The latter defined the Portuguese state as

a unitary and corporative republic founded upon the equality of all its citizens in the eyes of the law, upon free access for all the classes to the benefits of civilization, and upon the participation of all the constituent forces of the nation in its administrative life and in the making of law.[19]

The corporative constitution was approved in what most students of Portugal consider a rigged national plebiscite on March 19, 1933, and formally became the law of the land on April 11 of the same year.

Kay (1970, 49) shows the official results of the voting as follows:

For	719,364
Against	5,955
Abstentions	488,840
Registered voters	1,214,159

Fryer and Pinheiro (1961,116) show the numbers to be as follows:

For	580,379
Against	5,405
Abstentions	11,528
Total electorate	less than 600,000[20]

Fryer and Pinheiro (1961) observed that the results of the constitutional election were rigged by permitting only a small number of voters to cast "No" votes and by counting almost all the abstentions as "Yes" votes.

MacAdams[21] shows the vote on the constitution to be as follows:

Registered voters	330,258
Votes for the Constitution	1,292,864
Votes against the Constitution	6,190
Nullified votes	666
Not voting	30,538
Total	1,330,258

In spite of the contradictions in the above figures, and in the absence of rigorous official statistics, we know two things. First, the electorate was made up of adult males who were literate or who paid at least one hundred escudos annually in taxes, and of adult females who were literate, or who paid two hundred escudos in taxes, or had a secondary education. The result of such requirements was an electorate of between 1.2 and 1.3 million persons out of a total population of approximately 7 million. Moreover, the requirements effectively limited the franchise to male heads of households. In view of these limitations, the size of the electorate did not increase significantly in thirty years (1933–1965).

Second, historically, the majority of the electorate of the city of Lisbon did not vote because of little confidence in politics and because of apathy. In 1913, 61.8 percent did not vote. In 1915, the percentage of abstention was 48.2, and in 1918, it was 65 percent. And in 1919, approximately 80 percent of the voters did not cast their ballot (Mónica 1982). This pattern of nonvoting gives credence to the observation that in the constitutional election of 1933, almost all those who abstained were casting a "Yes" vote (Fryer and Pinheiro 1961, 116).

The Constitution of 1933 organized the Portuguese nation-state according to a corporatist model. The principal theoretical characteristic of the structure of the corporate state is that the legally recognized bodies or entities attempting to influence government policy are not political parties but corporations. This view rests on the belief that political parties are mechanisms of *individual* interest representation, while corporations are mechanisms of *collective* interest representation that place the interests of the nation above any group and above any individual. Hence the motto *Tudo pela nação, nada contra a nação* (All for the nation, nothing against the nation). Corporatism has been defined as "a system of government founded on the incorporation of the interests of the various corporations."[22] Schmitter defined it as

a system of interest representation in which the constituent units are organized into a limited number of singular, compulsory hierarchial order, and functionally differentiated categories, recognized or licensed (if not created) by the state and granted a deliberate representational monopoly within the respective categories in exchange for observing certain controls of their selection of leaders and articulation of demands and supports. (1975, 8–9)

The Corporative State

The corporative state was organized into an executive structure headed by a president and a premier. The former was elected by universal suffrage for a period of seven years.[23] Between 1933 and 1974 the three presidents were military men even though the constitution articles dealing with the presidency did not cite a military background as a prerequisite. General Oscar Carmona was in office from 1926 to 1951, General Craveiro Lopes from 1951 to 1958, and Admiral Américo Tomás from 1958 to 1974. Craveiro Lopes was replaced by the ruling coalition because he tried to be more than a puppet, a role played extraordinarily well by Américo Tomás. The coalition did not permit even interelite dissent.

The Head of State

Under the Constitution of 1933, any citizen who was thirty-five or older and had lived in Portugal without interruption, could become president of the Republic. Theoretically, the center of power was located in the office of the presidency. The president had the constitutional power to appoint the president of the Council of Ministers (the prime minister), and the rest of the cabinet upon the recommendations of the prime minister. The latter and the cabinet members were responsible only to the president, and thus were not under the constitutional authority of the National Assembly. The president was assisted in running the government by the Council of State, which consisted of the president of the Council of Ministers; the president of the National Assembly; the president of the Corporative Chamber; the president of the Supreme Court justices; the attorney general; and "ten . . . men of outstanding ability" who were appointed by the president.

In practice, however, the political structure of the New State was not based on a presidential form of government. Not only was the president outside (and somewhat above) the system of government, but the daily administrative and governmental responsibilities were handled by the prime minister and his cabinet. The political structure of the New State was characterized by

a strong executive form of government with almost all power formally vested outside and above the general governmental structure in the presidency of the republic. In practice, however, the president exercised his authority at the behest of the prime minister who was the most powerful element in the Portuguese political system. (Keefe et al. 1977, 198)

The National Assembly

The legislative branch of the New State was unicameral. Originally, the Assembly was made up of ninety deputies elected by citizen electors for a maximum of four years.[24] There were no constitutional qualifications for membership in the Assembly. The constitution specified that the National Assembly was to make, interpret, suspend, and revoke laws. Moreover, it was to guarantee the constitutionality of governmental acts, to authorize the government to collect taxes, to meet public expenditures, and so on.

Formally, the National Assembly was a powerful political body. It had the constitutional power to develop and approved legislative bills (called decrees), which, if signed by the president within a fifteen-day period, would automatically become law. If the president vetoed the decree and a two-thirds' majority of the Assembly reapproved it, the president could not impose a second veto but was forced to sign the decree into law.

The Corporative Chamber

Articles 102 to 106 of the Constitution of 1933 called for the creation of a Corporative Chamber (instead of a Senate) in addition to the National Assembly. Hence, the founders of the New State could claim that Portugal was indeed a corporative state. Formally, the Chamber was the official political body for interest representation. It was made up of twenty-four specialist sections responsible for representing the interests of economic, religious, and social groups.

Officially, the members of the Chamber, the procoradores, were representatives of local governmental bodies, municipalities, the administration, and industrial, agricultural, commercial, financial, cultural, and religious groups. But many procoradores were actually army officers, high-level bureaucrats, or well-known persons accepted by the regime. The task of the Chamber was to hold hearings on the various groups' activities and to report and to give *pareceres* (opinions) to the National Assembly. The sessions of the Chamber, which were not open to the public, were held during the three-month session of the Assembly.

An important characteristic of the Corporative Chamber was that it did not have any legislative power. It was merely a consultative political body, and its *pareceres* were strictly advisory. Hence, they were often ignored by the Assembly and by the Executive.

In 1934 a Corporative Council composed of certain ministers and two academic lawyers was set up. It appointed the administration's representatives in the chamber. A high proportion of the members of the Chamber [were] appointees, not elected. (Kay 1970, 55–56)

The Colonial Act

Inasmuch as Portugal had a vast and immensely rich empire, the reactionary coalition had to create political mechanisms to deal with overseas territories. Although some colonial legislation had been formulated in 1926 and 1929, the Colonial Act of 1930 set forth new principles for the administration of the colonies. According to the founders of the Estado Novo, in following these new principles the nation would "fulfill its historic mission of colonization in the land of discoveries." (See Chapter 4.)

The Colonial Act was the creation of Salazar while he served for a short period as minister of colonies in 1930. His work was followed by his successor, Armindo Monteiro. Generally, the Colonial Act stipulated that the administration of the colonies must be unified and under the control of the state, not of private companies. It also changed the classification of the overseas territories from "provinces" to "colonies." (A few decades later, the Estado Novo reversed the classification to circumvent the language of the United Nations Charter.) The change was made in order to abolish the measures taken during the First Republic to move toward greater financial and political autonomy for the overseas possessions. However, according to Marcelo Caetano, the reason was twofold: "[To bring] the colonies to closer communion with . . . continental Portugal, [and to declare] Portugal's intention to maintain and perpetuate the legacy of history."[25]

Some of the provisions of the Colonial Act were elaborated and expanded in subsequent legislation, such as the Overseas Reform Act of 1933 and the Organic Charter of 1933.[26] The Colonial Act was incorporated in 1951 into the political constitution "as an integral part of the law of continental and overseas Portugal." At that time the territories ceased to be classified as "colonies" and once more became "overseas provinces."

The Corporate Structure of the New State

The *Estatuto do trabalho nacional*[27] (National Labor Statute), Decree-Law no. 23,048 of September 23, 1933, was the foundation of the formal corporate structure of the reactionary coalition's political regime, and the mechanism for the elaboration of interest representation.[28] Theoretically, the National Labor Statute was designed to realize the principal aims of the New State: peace, cooperation, harmony, and solidarity between capital and labor, and the placement of the interests of the Portuguese nation above the interests of individuals and groups.[29] Under Article 5 of the statute, both labor and capital, individuals and groups, were expected to carry out their functions "with a spirit of peace and subordinated to the principle that the administering of justice [is] a state function."

In Section II, the National Labor Statute recognized the value of private enterprise and considered it the best means of social and economic progress (Article 4). But at the same time the statute stipulated that it was the responsibility of the state to coordinate and regulate the nation's economic and social life in order to establish an equilibrium between capital and labor, between production and consumption (Article 7). Labor unions, strikes, sit-ins and lockouts were outlawed (Article 8). The state recognized the individual right of private property (Article 12).

In Section III, the statute set forth, by means of a number of decree-laws and regulations, the corporate organizational structure of interest representation, with the corporations at the apex as the coordinating and supervising units of all the vertically subordinated organizations. The latter were functionally placed at three levels.

The primary elements of the corporate organization were, in ascending order, the following:

1. *Freguesias*. The lowest corporative unit was the parish, made up of families who lived in a given neighborhood area. The parish gave the head of the family an opportunity to have his interests represented at the parish and municipal level.

2. *Casas dos pescadores*. Associations of fishermen and their families.

3. *Casas do povo*. Rural "unions" of both employers and workers.

4. *Grêmios*. Guilds consisting of individual employers or firms engaged in a specific trade or industry; they were extended to the *casas da lavoura* (rural workers) and *grémios da lavoura* (rural employers).

5. *Sindicatos nacionais*. National syndicates composed of workers and employees, or members of liberal professions, engaged in a specific trade or industry. Subject to total state control.[30]

The intermediate or secondary elements were the following:

6. *Federações regionais* or *nacionais*. Regional or national federations made up of the syndicates and the guilds in a specific trade or industry.

7. *Uniões*. Unions made up of persons in connected and affiliated trades or industries already grouped in *grémios* (employers) and *sindicatos* (workers).

The third order element was comprised of

8. *Corporações*. Corporations made up of the federations and the unions, and organized according to occupation.

Theoretically, employers and workers sent representatives to the Corporative Chamber.

In addition to the three orders of elements, the state created, by means of Decree-Law no. 26,757 of July 8, 1936, "organizations for economic coordination" that would bring corporatism to economic production.

These organizations also were divided into three groups:

1. *Commissões reguladoras* (regulating committees), responsible for the control of imports

2. *Juntas nacionais* (national juntas), responsible for the development and control of exports and the expansion of foreign trade

3. *Institutos* (institutes), to supervise and extend official guarantee of the quality of exports

To strengthen its corporative base even more, the New State created two additional organizations: the Instituto Nacional do Trabalho e Providencia (National Labor and Welfare Institute), by Decree-Law no. 23,053, of September 23, 1933, and the Conselho Técnico do Comércio e da Indústria (Technical Council of Commerce and Industry), by Decree-Law no. 26,370, of September 24, 1936. The Council was supposed to guide and control the activities of the corporative organizations. It consisted of seven members, with the minister of commerce and industry as chairman. The Institute, under the direction of the assistant secretary of state for corporations and welfare, was responsible for assuring the enforcement of social laws and the integration of elements of production into the corporative order. Under the Institute, labor tribunals were set up for the arbitration of contracts and labor disputes, accident claims, insurance claims, wage levels, and so on.

THE NEW STATE: SOCIAL REALITY

Portuguese Corporatism

Corporatism in Portugal was the ruling reactionary coalition's response to the societal crisis created by the inability of the owning classes to create a stable system of bourgeois hegemony.[31] The ruling coalition chose corporatism over liberal democracy and socialism because the latter were not in their interests. In form, ideology, law, and rhetoric, the New State was a corporatist state based on a corporatist constitution. But in practice, the reality of Portuguese society from 1933 to 1974 was based neither on *corporatismo de associação* (societal corporatism) nor on *corporatismo de estado* (state corporatism). The former is "found imbedded in political systems with relatively autonomous multilayered territorial units; open, competitive electoral processes and party systems; ideologically varied, coalitionally based executive authorities" (Schmitter 1974, 105). On the other hand, state corporatism

tends to be associated with political systems in which territorial subunits are tightly subordinated to central bureaucratic power; elections are non-existent or plebiscitary; party systems are dominated or monopolized by a weak single party; executive authorities are ideologically exclusive and more narrowly recruited and are such that political subcultures based on class, ethnicity, language or religion are repressed. (Schmitter 1974, 105)

It has been observed, however, that the above definition of state corporatism is conceptually problematic because it has been used by various political elites that wanted "to penetrate and restructure associational patterns along corporatist lines," and because "extremely different policies" have been followed by regimes considered to be state corporatist (Stepan 1978, 73–74).

For my purposes, therefore, better analytic constructs are "inclusionary" and "exclusionary" corporatism. In terms of utilization of the state apparatus and public policy-making, inclusionary corporatism is used by "state elite[s] . . . attempt[ing] to forge a new state–society equilibrium by policies aimed at incorporating salient working-class groups into the new economic and political model" (Stepan 1978, 74). In the case of the exclusionary subtype, "The attempt to forge a new state–society equilibrium can rely heavily on coercive policies to deactivate and then restructure salient working-class groups."[32]

Clearly, inclusionary corporatism can easily be dismissed in regard to Portugal. This is not so with regard to exclusionary corporatism, because superficially one can argue that this subtype is applicable to the New State. But, while the exclusionary subtype may seem to apply to the reactionary coalition's political regime, it really is inapplicable because corporatism, properly speaking, did not exist in Portugal during the period 1933–1974.

The Absence of Corporatism

In reality the Estado Novo was not a corporatist state. Real state power was placed in the Executive and not in the Corporative Chamber, which was a consultative body. In fact, Salazar argued that "without a powerful executive there is no strong state."[33] Consequently, while under Article 5 of the Constitution of 1933 the Chamber had the responsibility of assuring equal participation in the social and political process to all societal elements, in reality it had no power.

Portuguese corporatism was hardly associative in character; it depended largely on the State. It was not pure because neither the corporations nor the corporative chamber had any legislative power. . . . In no way did it reconcile employers and workers. And it did not devote itself to the plight of the working man. (Lucena 1979, 68)

Not until 1956 did the Estado Novo decree the basic rules for the creation of the corporations. Oliveira Marques (1972, 296) lists the years in which the corporations were created: Agricultural, 1957; Industry and Commerce, 1958; Trade, 1958; Transport and Insurance, 1957; Credit and Insurance, 1957; Fishing and Fish Canning, 1957; Press and Graphic Art, 1959; Entertainment, 1959; Welfare, 1966; Science, 1966; Letters and Arts, 1966.

The Portuguese corporatist system "operated for twenty-five years (and in some cases even longer) without corporations," which means "without the nominal capstones of its organizational structure!" (Schmitter 1975, 11). Moreover, formally and legally the corporations were the highest-level mechanisms of equal interest representation both for workers and for employers, since it was in corporatism that guilds, syndicates, federations, and unions were gathered. In reality, however, this equal representation did not occur. The corporations were skewed toward representing the interests of employers.

It appears that all corporations' presidents were or had been employers. Interview contacts with supposed representatives of working class syndicates to governing councils indicated that those tended to be liberal professional lawyers, engineers, and managers who under Portuguese classification system were considered workers. (Schmitter 1975, 28)

The absence of corporatism can also be seen in the employers' associations (guilds) and the workers' associations (syndicates). In 1954 (twenty-one years after the imposition of the New State) "only 53 of 495 employer *Gremios* were obligatory. In 1967, only 91 of 559 were obligatory" (Schmitter 1975, 19). The situation was quite different for the syndicates. All labor organizations were compulsory from the beginning, and their structure and activities were regulated by the state. Even in dealing with the employers' guilds, their power was subordinated to state control and regulations. The syndicates became, for all practical purposes, instruments of government policy.

The absence of corporatism is also demonstrated by the *casas do povo* (unions of both rural employers and rural workers). In these unions the real interest representation was skewed toward the employers. The administrative bodies were

fully controlled by the latifundists who may intervene directly at all levels or indirectly through their more eminent clients. This intervention ranges from filling posts compatible with their rank from among the latifundists themselves to using their employees (*criados*, literally, "servants") for the humble posts. (Cutileiro 1971, 193)

Thus, instead of being corporative units or associations based on class and profession, the *casas do povo* were in reality single-interest units. "Landowners representing rural workers, were called on to bargain with landowners representing landowners'' (Schmitter 1975, 19). It was perhaps because of the one-sidedness of the *casas do povo* that as late as 1965 only one-fifth of rural inhabitants belonged to them. From 1933 to 1974 Portuguese corporatism was nothing more than a peripheral concept of political and social organization utilized minimally for ideological purposes, but always absent in the concrete, formation of the Portuguese society.

The Organic Statist State

An organic statist[34] political system was preferred not only by Aristotle and St. Thomas Aquinas (Stepan 1978, 29) but also by two individuals who had a great influence on the intellectual development of Salazar: Pope Leo XIII and Pope Pius XI (Kay 1970, 22). Both argued that ''Man's nature can only be fulfilled within a community'' of fellow human beings, and both conceived the state as having ''a moral *telos*'' (Stepan 1978, 29–30).

As the term ''statist'' indicates, organic statist political organization calls for a strong and ''interventionist'' state. But, at the same time, it imposes two ''normative principles'' on the legitimacy of the state's activities. First is the principle that the fundamental task of the state is the pursuit of the ''common good.'' Second is the principle of ''subsidiarity,'' conceptualized by Pius XI in his encyclical *Quadragesimo anno*.

It is a fundamental principle of social philosophy, fixed and unchangeable, that one should not withdraw from individuals and commit to the community what they can accomplish by their own enterprise and industry. So, too, it is an injustice and at the same time a grave evil and a disturbance of right order, to transfer to the larger and higher collectivity functions which can be performed and provided for by lesser and subordinate bodies. Inasmuch as every social activity should, by its very nature, prove a help to members of the body social, it should never destroy or absorb them.[35]

Portuguese corporatism was based on an ''organic'' state, and on ''organic'' structures such as corporations, the family, the parish, and professional associations. Liberalism's stress on individualism was rejected because the Aristotelian, Thomistic, and papal argument that man's nature is best fulfilled in a community, and not in isolation, was perceived to be a more valid argument. In reality, however, organic statism never existed in Portugal. The Estado Novo was never used for the common good, and the principle of ''subsidiarity'' was totally violated. The social teachings of Aquinas, Leo XIII, and Pius XI were betrayed; the Portuguese social reality was never characterized either by corporatism or by organic statism.

Exclusionary corporatism represent[s] a profound distortion of the ideal of social order posited in the abstract model of organic statism, in that the attempt to construct the political order by exclusionary policies results in the coercive deactivation of many groups, particularly labor. It represents a decrease, rather than an increase, of participation in the political community.[36]

The Nature of the State

The theoretical perspective informing this volume is that of class analysis and class conflict, especially as it illuminates the mechanisms of reproduction of the legitimation of economic and political orders, of their domination, and of the existing class inequalities. Hence, I am interested in viewing the state in its concrete forms, without ideological mystifications. In this section I first submit a rather limited review of Marxist theories of the state, then analyze the nature of the Portuguese Estado Novo. My analysis will be guided by Marx's dictum in the preface to the *Critique of Political Economy* that "in order to understand political forms," we must connect them to the "anatomy of civil society."

Marxists perceive the state in class societies as functioning (read: the mechanism) to reproduce a mode of production in which a specific class, the owning bourgeois class, is dominant by virtue of its ownership and control of the means of production. The state assures the maintenance of the necessary "general conditions for the reproduction of the wage labor/capital relation which is the heart of bourgeois societies" (Munck 1984, 206). The major functions performed by the state in capitalist societies are the provision of the general material conditions necessary for capital; regulating the conflict between labor and capital through co-optation and repression; and safeguarding the existence and expansion of the total national capital on the capitalist world market.[37] In capitalist societies the state is therefore an essential component of the relations of production. According to Engels, "The modern state, no matter what its form, is essentially a capitalist machine, the state of the capitalists, the ideal personification of the total national capital" (Engels [1878] 1969, 330). Moreover,

The state is therefore by no means a power forced on society from without; just as little is it "the reality of the ethical idea, the image and reality of reason," as Hegel maintains. Rather, it is a product of society at a certain stage of development: it is the admission that this society has become entangled in an insoluble contradiction with itself, that it is cleft into irreconcilable antagonisms which it is powerless to dispel. But in order that these antagonisms, classes with conflicting economic interests, might not consume themselves and society in sterile struggle, a power seemingly standing above society became necessary for the purpose of moderating the conflict, of keeping it within the bounds of "order"; and this power, arisen out of society, but placing itself above it, and increasingly alienating itself from it, is the state. (Engels [1884] 1972, 158–159)

While agreeing that the capitalist state serves the interests of the bourgeois owning classes, Marxists differ in their explanations of how the bourgeois state accomplishes its tasks. Jessop aptly observed that there is in Marxian theory "a variety of theoretical perspectives which co-exist in an uneasy and unstable relation," and that "it is this very plurality of viewpoints and arguments that provides the basis for the subsequent diversification of Marxist state theories'' (1982, xii).

The Instrumentalist Approach

To Miliband, the state is an instrument of elite interests. He argues that

In the Marxist scheme, the ''ruling class'' of capitalist society is that class which owns and controls the means of production and which is able, by virtue of the economic power thus conferred upon it, to use the state as an instrument for the domination of society. (1969, 22)

Miliband's central argument is that while the capitalist class does not govern, in reality it does rule. It does so because in a capitalist society, capitalism is considered to be in the national interest. This means that the well-being of economic institutions such as corporations and financial institutions must be maintained. Hence, the body politic in capitalist societies must serve the interests, the needs, of the capitalist class. Consequently, the state functions on the basis of the ''instrumental exercise of power by people in strategic positions'' who either manipulate state politics directly (direct instrumentality) or through the ''exercise of pressure on the state'' (indirect instrumentality; Gold et al. 1975).

The Structuralist Approach

Nicos Poulantzas (1969; [1968] 1974a) constructed a Marxist theory of the capitalist state using Althusser's structuralist epistemology. He argues that the class composition of those running the state apparatuses is of no importance to the nature of the state in capitalist societies. Instead, the structure of these societies that make the state the servant of the capitalist class is important. Social classes and the state are, according to Poulantzas, objective structures, and their relations must be taken as an objective system of regular connections. And in the system of objective structures, the agents (''men'') are, in the words of Marx, ''bearers'' of the structures. Because of these objective structures, the direct participation of the members of the ruling class in state activities and apparatuses is not the *cause*, but the *effect*, of the nature and workings of the system.

We must not, Poulantzas (1969) says, commit Miliband's mistake of taking social classes as ''groups'' and, more important, we must not reduce social classes to interpersonal relations. To investigate the problem of social actors as the origins of social action, in order to determine the motivation of conduct of the individual actors, may be ''good'' micro sociology, but it will not help us to understand the objective ''coordinates'' that determine the distribution of agents (''bearers'') into social classes. Instead, to understand such distribution, the theoretical starting point must be the claim that the relation between the bourgeois class and the capitalist state is an objective one. Thus, if in a particular society the functions of the state and the interests of the dominant class are in synchrony, it is a result of the nature of the system.

In the Poulantzas–Miliband debate[38] Poulantzas (1969) criticized Miliband for "the immediate examination of concrete facts" and for giving "the impression that for him social classes or 'groups' are in some way reducible to impersonal relations of the diverse 'groups' that constitute the state apparatuses." Miliband's (1970) reply took the form of a critique of structuralism. He stated that Poulantzas' exclusive stress on objective relations implied that

what the state does is in every particular and at all times wholly determined by those "objective" relations; in other words the structural constraints of the system are so absolutely compelling as to turn those who run the state into functionaries and executants of policies imposed upon them by the system. (1970, 53)

These structural constraints, according to Miliband (1970, 54), lead to "a kind of structural determinism or super-determinism which makes impossible a truly realist consideration of the dialectic between the state and the system."[39]

The Autonomy of the State

In view of the complexity of modern capitalist societies, Marxian political theorizing has given much consideration to the concept of state autonomy. Poulantzas ([1968] 1974a), drawing upon Marx's analysis of the separation of state and civil society under capitalism, points out the "characteristic autonomy of the economic and the political" that distinguishes capitalism from feudalism. In the latter political power was localized, and the lords were directly involved in the production process. In capitalism there is an institutionalized separation between political power and economic relations, even though the political sphere maintains the economic relations through legal and coercive arrangements.

Engels considered limited state autonomy to be possible.

By way of exception, however, periods occur in which the warring classes balance each other so nearly that the state power, as ostensible mediator, acquires, for the moment, a certain degree of independence of both. Such was the absolute monarchy of the seventeenth and eighteenth centuries which held the balance between the nobility and the class of burghers; such was the Bonapartism of the First and still more of the Second French Empire, which played the proletariat against the bourgeoisie and the bourgeoisie against the proletariat. ([1884] 1972, 160)

Both Miliband and Poulantzas agree that a certain (relative) level of state autonomy may be necessary for the survival of an established class society. Miliband pointed out that

The relative independence of the state does not reduce its class character: on the contrary, its relative independence makes it possible for the state to play its class role in an appropriately flexible manner. If it really was the simple "instrument" of the "ruling class" it would be fatally inhibited in the performance of its role. (1970, 57)

Dissatisfied with the orthodox Marxist view of the state simply as a repressive instrument of the economically dominant ruling class, Poulantzas ([1968] 1974a) took up the task of demonstrating that the state was not just a tool of bourgeois dominance. Instead of being a reflection, at the superstructure level of the capitalist society, of the economic base, the state, Poulantzas believed, was autonomous. It was a specific and relatively autonomous regional structure "with its own effects on the reproduction of a society divided into classes" (Jessop 1985, 54). According to Poulantzas, we could, therefore, "constitute the political as an autonomous and specific object of science" ([1968] 1974a, 29).

There are two types of state autonomy, according to Hamilton: instrumental and structural. By "instrumental" autonomy she means the "freedom" that the state has "from direct pressures by dominant class fractions and interests." "Structural" state autonomy refers to forms of state "action against the real interests of the dominant class, which would ultimately result in a basic structural change through which the existing mode of production, and with it the dominant class, would be superseded by a new one" (Hamilton 1982, 23). More specifically, she defines structural state autonomy as "the ability of those who control the state apparatuses to use it for ends other than, and particularly contrary to, those of the dominant class" (Hamilton 1982, 12).

Theda Skocpol's theoretical work on state autonomy, which goes beyond "relative autonomy," is a strong defense of "structural" state autonomy. Thus, Skocpol challenges the Marxian theory of the class nature of the state. She has clearly shown her views about the autonomy of the state:

Whatever the variation in its historical form, the state as such is seen as a feature of all class-divided modes of production; and invariably, the one necessary and inescapable function of the state—by definition—is to contain class conflict and undertake other policies in support of the dominance of the surplus-appropriating and property-owning class[es]. (1979, 27)

Consequently, she argues further, the state is not treated "as an autonomous structure—a structure with a logic and interests of its own not necessarily equivalent to, or fused with, the interests of the dominant class in society or the full set of member groups in the polity" (1979, 27).

Skocpol criticizes classical Marxist theories (and neo-Marxist structuralists) for making it "virtually impossible even to raise the possibility that fundamental conflicts of interest might arise between the existing dominant class or set of groups, on one hand, and the state rulers on the other." Hence, she points out, the state is not seen "as an organization for itself" (1979, 27). More recently she has argued that "states . . . may formulate and pursue goals that are not simply reflective of the demands or interests of social groups, classes or societies. This is what is usually meant by the 'state autonomy'." And she castigates "virtually all neo-Marxist writers of the state" for having retained "deeply embedded society-centered assumptions" (Skocpol et al. 1985, 5–9). In Skocpol's work we have a structural view of the autonomy of the state. To her, the state is an autonomous actor, capable of acting for itself.

Thus, Skocpol's model of the state is not anchored in Marxist theory but in a Weberian notion of the state as a power subject, as a third actor, a free agent. So, although the state reproduces capitalist relations of production, it does so independently of any conscious class interests. Following her views, the state in a capitalist society is not necessarily a capitalist state but an independent (political) power in the middle of two groups: the bourgeoisie and the proletariat. And the state favors bourgeois interests because it depends on capital accumulation for its survival (Carnoy 1984, 251, 259).

Skocpol's theory of the state also contains excessive neoinstitutionalism, for she "makes political institutions themselves (and everything else) so important that she courts the danger of falling into an ex-post-facto empiricism that is atheoretical and explains nothing" (Carnoy 194, 220). She ignores the fact that

there are "structural constraints" which no government, whatever its complexion, wishes, and promises, can ignore or evade. A capitalist economy has its own "rationality" to which any government and state must sooner or later submit, and usually sooner. (Miliband 1977, 72)

The State in Peripheral Societies

For proper understanding of the nature of the state, we must consider both its relation to internal class configurations and its function in the reproduction of a particular social formation, and its external relations. This is especially warranted when one is studying a peripheral or dependent society. Marx wrote on the external relations of India and Ireland, and developed two views of colonialism. He considered (incorrectly) that penetration by British capital was advantageous to India. In Ireland, however, he and Engels saw the same penetration as destroying the economy of England's first colony. British colonization was causing the underdevelopment of the Irish economy. To Lenin imperialism was a logically necessary phase of the capitalist mode of production, the stage born out of the crisis of profitability.

More recently, the world systems views of Frank (1978, 1980), Amin (1973, 1976, 1980), and Wallerstein (1974) postulate that the underdevelopment of dependent countries is the result of the international division of labor and of the external relations between dependent/peripheral countries and core/metropolis countries. Furthermore, Frank's dependency theory argues that in peripheral societies the state "is an essential instrument for the administration of the dependent role of these economies in the international division of labor and the capitalist world process of capital accumulation" (Carnoy 1984, 188). And the state in these peripheral societies is more independent of local owning classes, because of the asymmetry of power between the internal and external bourgeoisies.

World systems approaches have been criticized for basing their analyses on the process of circulation and not on the analytically prior process of production. In so doing, they neglect particular internal class configurations and struggles, and end up being ahistorical and mechanistic.

A theory of dependency that relates the dependent state more to the internal class struggle is Cardoso and Faletto's "historical–structural" theory. Their approach "emphasizes not just the structural conditions of social life, but also the historical transformation of structures by conflict, social movements, and class struggle" (1979, x). They argue that the interests of external bourgeoisies are imposed on society by local dominant groups "not precisely because they are foreign, but because they may coincide with the values and interests that the groups pretend are their own" (1979, xv). Echoing the historical–structural approach, Hamilton states that

while peripheral formations are, to a much greater extent than those of the core, shaped by external forces, it is their internal situation—the level of development of productive forces, the relative strength of contending classes, etc.—which generally determines the response of a given formation to external influences and in fact whether these influences will become dominant in shaping that social formation. (1982, 19)

"Normal" and "Exceptional" States

According to Poulantzas ([1968] 1974a; [1970] 1974b; [1975] 1976), there two main state forms: the normal and the exceptional. The normal "corresponds to conjunctures in which bourgeois hegemony is stable and secure" and class domination is imposed through "constitutionalized violence." The exceptional state "corresponds to a crisis of hegemony," and class domination is imposed through "the increased use of physical repression and open war against dominated classes" (Jessop 1985, 94).

An Exceptional State: The Bureaucratic-Authoritarian State

The exceptional state predominates in dependent societies because in these societies electoral rights are suspended, political parties are prohibited, and direct repressive mechanisms are put into practice. The bureaucratic–authoritarian state is therefore an exceptional state. But, in my view, the concept of the authoritarian state put forth by Linz (1970) and O'Donnell (1973), and applied to Spain and Latin America, respectively, are analytically inappropriate when considering the Portuguese Estado Novo.

Linz conceptualizes authoritarianism as a political regime/system

with limited, non-responsible, political pluralism, without elaborate and guiding ideology (except for some points in their development) and [in] which a leader (or occasionally a small group) exercises power within formally ill-defined limits, but actually quite predictable ones. (1970, 252)

I find Linz's concept totally inapplicable to the Portuguese case (and to any other case of authoritarian rule) for two reasons. First, his concept is thoroughly ideological. It implies that the Spanish authoritarian regime was a limited or near democracy, under peculiar circumstances. Linz is saying that while there was no fully developed pluralism in Spain, there was limited, interelite pluralism. Hence, the Spanish state was only partially an exceptional state. Second, Linz commits the serious error of underestimating (at best) or ignoring (at worst) the repressive characteristics so essential to authoritarian regimes.

I also find inappropriate to the Portuguese case the concept of the bureaucratic–authoritarian state that has been used to explain the new regimes in Latin America. O'Donnell's (1973, 1978, 1979) structuralist and functionalist concept of bureaucratic–authoritarian regimes causally links the emergence of such regimes to the structural requirements of highly modernizing or modernized dependent capitalist states. This characteristic restricts O'Donnell's concept of such states and makes it analytically inappropriate to the Portuguese case.[40] The Portuguese reactionary coalition installed an exclusionary political regime for reasons not connected to economic development. On the contrary, the coalition wanted to arrest the development of competitive liberal capitalism. We must keep in mind how different Portugal was from other Southern European and Latin American countries. Never a colony, it was nevertheless dependent on Great Britain. At the same time, until 1974 it possessed a vast colonial empire.

In my view, there was in Portugal, from 1933 to 1974, a reactionary bureaucratic–authoritarian state; I define such a state as a type of political regime that, although distinct from both democracy and totalitarianism, is characterized by the absence of pluralism, even interelite pluralism, and by the degree and extent of physical repression against the dominated classes.

Formally the New State was a corporatist state, but in reality it was created and implemented to protect the interests of a reactionary coalition against the common enemy, the workers. The New State was imposed from above because of the internal struggles between the owning classes and the working classes.

The Constitution of 1933 stated that every Portuguese citizen had the inalienable right to free expression and association. But, at the same time, the constitution stipulated that "special laws" would govern the exercise of freedom of speech. Article 22 stated:

Public opinion is a fundamental element of the policy and administration of the country; it shall be the duty of the state to protect it against all those influences which distort it from the truth, justice, good administration and the commonwealth. (Keefe et al. 1977, 137)

Furthermore, the constitution stipulated that individuals caught in criminal acts "against the safety of the state" could be imprisoned without formal charges. According to one observer, the "protective" clauses of the constitution were "more in evidence than the substantive proposition of freedom" (Kay 1970, 56). The real nature of the New State as an instrument of class domination is also discernible in some of the decree-laws. The legislation regarding the workers' syndicates made membership in them obligatory and, inasmuch as the syndicates' charters were granted by the state, reduced these labor organizations to agencies of the state designed and used to control the workers. Moreover, the legislation restricted the syndicates to the district level, prohibited the formation of territorial workers' federations, and required state approval of all candidates for the various offices of the organizations. "The Portuguese variety [of fascism] does not admit syndical liberty, assigning the functions of representation and professional discipline in each district to only one authorized syndicate" (Caetano 1967, 437; Campinos 1975, 18).

Employers' *grémios* (guilds), industrialists' associations, and chambers of commerce were not required to be part of the corporate structure. Hence, these associations could maintain some degree of independence because they were not controlled and supervised by the state. This meant, of course, that the allocation of privileges and the systematic satisfaction of interests were rather one-sided. Ginner observes that the real Estado Novo was

From the start entrusted with the preservation of the interests of the reactionary coalition. . . . [It] paved the way for further capital accumulation and the development of capitalism in accordance with the wishes of the ruling class. . . . It neutralized the working class and other threatening groups (such as dissident intellectuals and students) so that internal peace was assured. Usually, the reactionary coalition—landowners, industrialists, financiers—controlled the state through the army whose highest echelons were amply rewarded. (1982, 190)

CONCLUSION

The creation and implementation of the New State can be explained in the following manner. In Portugal during the 1920s there were three distinct social groups: the working class (urban and rural, with the former limited to the cities of Lisbon and Pôrto); the latifundists and their allies (financiers [bankers] and industrialists); the urban and rural petite bourgeoisie and the liberal urban bourgeoisie. The latter was small,[41] and thus lacked the power to build the social structure and political systems required to assure capital accumulation and its reproduction. Hence, the solution was to join the reactionary coalition against the working class. But, inasmuch as the power centers were located in the landed aristocracy, the modus vivendi was based on the primacy of the agricultural and rural ethos. The liberal urban bourgeoisie, the "modern sector," although part of the coalition, was not strong. And, as Organski pointed out,

if the country is too modern and the modern sector too powerful, why should modern elites already in full control compromise with the non-modern sector? If, on the other hand, the positions are reversed, why should the non-modern elites compromise? (1965, 28–29)

Portuguese society was not characterized by organic harmony between capital and labor, in voluntary associations, and in equal participation in the political process of policy formation. Rather, there was a system of class control and domination monopolized from above by the Estado Novo. The Estado Novo was never a corporatist or an organic state. It never put into practice the principle of "organic statism" because its task never was the pursuit of the common good. And it never had a "moral *telos*." The reactionary bureaucratic-authoritarian Estado Novo became "one of the most oppressive monopolistic of state capitalistic systems and it came to favor employer interests at the expanse of labor" (Wiarda 1979, 100).

The reactionary coalition did not secure *hegemony* via the Portuguese people's consent. Instead, the coalition imposed the new social formation from above, and secured control through coercive and oppressive mechanisms.

NOTES

1. The Portuguese expeditions of 1888–1890 into the regions west of Lake Nyasa and into the Manica district, and the publication of the *mapa côr-de-rósa* (pink map) through which Portugal claimed control of the whole interior of Africa, gave rise to a serious confrontation with Great Britain. The Portuguese expeditions and territorial claim involved territory that had been assigned by the British government to the newly founded South Africa Company. On January 10, 1890, the British sent the Portuguese an ultimatum protesting the expeditions. The Portuguese monarchy withdrew many of the claims it had made.

2. For many, if not the majority, of the Republicans, the Portuguese Catholic Church—perhaps even Catholicism—was their number one enemy, whose influence in the political and social spheres had to be broken. Their feelings were not without justification. Historically, the Roman Catholic Church in Portugal had been extremely conservative and always on the side of traditional power brokers. During the civil war of 1832–1834, between the Liberals (King Pedro) and the Traditionalists (King Miguel), the church was a strong supporter of the latter. In 1834, after the defeat of King Miguel, the government expropriated church property, purged the church hierarchy, and abolished religious orders. (Regarding the expropriation of church property, see note 7.)

3. According to Giddens, " 'Capitalist Society' may be said to exist when, as some Marxists have put it, capitalism becomes 'hegemonic'. . . . While the existence of capitalist society presupposes a high level of industrialization, the reverse does not hold. Strictly speaking, therefore, there is a very significant distinction between 'capitalism' and 'capitalist society' because, since the latter involves industrialism, it is of comparatively recent creation, while the former is not" (1973, 142).

4. Portugal had not taken any of the three "routes to modern world" conceptualized and elaborated by Moore (1966), which provides a more robust alternative to Rostow's "economic take-off" (1960) and Huntington's "expanded participation" (1968).

5. Pereira (1971) presents a good, extensive, and empirically substantiated argument that British expansionary economic interests blocked the nonagricultural growth and modernization of Portugal.

6. Moore (1966, 437), paraphrasing Marx and Engels.

7. This landed aristocracy was the beneficiary of the 1834 liberal constitutional monarchy from which it was drawn. In that year, after the defeat of the Traditionalists, much church property was expropriated by the government. "Intended to raise funds to pay

the debt of the civil war, the lands and buildings of 500 religious houses were sold at auction at prices below their market value to approximately 600 new owners who used government credits to make their purchases. The sale of church property resulted in a shift in the ownership of more than one-fourth of all land and created a new class— wealthy landowners'' (Keefe et al. 1977, 44).

8. The concept of the reactionary coalition is borrowed from Moore (1966, 437).

9. Moore (1966, 434) points out that agrarian elites will use "political mechanisms," while market-oriented elites will use "market mechanisms" for the extraction of surplus.

10. In July 1926, Gomes da Costa was relieved of his duties and exiled to the Azores by General António Fragoso Carmona, who on March 28 was "elected" president of the Republic by a "dubious plebiscite"; his term was to be five years, but he remained in the presidency for twenty-three years. He died in office in 1951.

11. On February 3, 1927, General Sousa Dias, commander of a garrison in the northern city of Pôrto, revolted against the coup of May 28. In Lisbon, naval and police units followed suit. But the military dictatorship was determined to keep control. It used heavy artillery and air power to stop the rebels' "attempt to go back to the Democratic Republic." After six days of fighting, with 120 persons dead and 650 wounded, the military dicta- torship was victorious (Robinson 1979, 42).

12. Gramsci observed that "every social group [read: class] coming into existence on the original terrain of an essential function in the world of economic production creates together with itself, organically, one or more strata of intellectuals which give it hom- ogeneity and an awareness of its own function not only in the economic but also in the social and political fields . . . an elite . . . must have the capacity to be an organizer of society in general" (1971, 5).

13. Generally speaking, I am not interested in the level of analysis of methodological individualism. Nevertheless, I must consider and argue that Salazar is an extraordinarily good example of Gramsci's "organic intellectual." For example, this peculiar bourgeois intellectual explains reality with and for a peculiar bourgeoisie. It is in this context, and not in the individualistic or idealistic context, that I pay attention to Salazar in the Portuguese conjuncture under study.

14. Martins (1968, 301) postulates that "in a relatively modern sense" the extreme right "may be dated in Portugal to 1914," when "the first journal of the new 'counter- revolutionary movement', the *Integralismo Lusitano*, started publication."

15. Amaro (1982). Some students of Portugal make the analytical mistake of seeing the Portuguese situation of 1928–1974 in terms of Salazarismo. According to Bruneau, "It would be difficult to argue that Salazar was controlled by any particular class. . . . Salazar alone ruled. He was . . . autonomous from all groups, and thus owed minimal obligations to them" (1984, 19).

16. Gallagher (1983, 345). Originally coined by Salazar, *Deus, pátria e família* became an effective slogan of the reactionary coalition.

17. "The National Union 'É uma associação sem caracter de partido independente do estado e destinada a assegurar, na ordem cívica, pela colaboração dos seus filiados, sem distinças de escola política ou de confissão religiosa, a realização e a defesa dos principios consigurados . . . ' " (quoted in McAdams 1952, 102).

18. O sistema corporativo é o regime de organização social que tem por base o agrupamento dos homens segundo a communidade dos seus interesses naturais e das suas funções sociais, e por necessário coroamento a representação política e distinta desses diversos organismos (Caetano 1943, 7).

19. Constitution of the Republic, (1933), Art 5.

20. This number represents less than 10 percent of the total population, which, according to the 1930 census, was 6,825,833. Kay (1970) argues that 600,000 for the total electorate is too small.

21. McAdams (1952, 26) cites the figures presented in Omar Emeth, et al., *El Portugal de hoy y su gobierno* (Santiago, Chile: Nascimiento, 1934), 43.

22. *Grande enciclopédia portuguesa e brasileira*, vol. VII (Lisbon and Rio de Janeiro: Editorial Encyclopedia Limitada, n.d.), 734; quoted in McAdams (1952, 7).

23. After 1958 (and very likely because of the success of the political campaign of the opposition candidate, General Humberto Delgado, a former coalition member; see Chapter 5) the Assembly changed the system by amendment of Article 72 of the constitution; the president was now elected by an electoral college composed of the members of the National Assembly, the Corporative Chamber, and the representatives chosen by the municipal and provincial councils.

24. The constitution was revised in 1945, 1959, and 1973, expanding the membership of the National Assembly to 120, 130, and 150, respectively. In the last expansion, 116 deputies represented continental Portugal and 34 represented the colonies.

25. João Ameal, "Mostruário do império," in *O mundo português*, vol. I (Lisbon: 1934), 99–100, quoted in Duffy (1961, 279).

26. The latter was modified in 1935, 1937, and 1945. It was replaced by the Organic Law in 1955.

27. The National Labor Statute was influenced by, if not based on, the Italian Labor Charter, as Marcelo Caetano pointed out: "The Italian School undoubtedly influenced the beginnings of Portuguese corporative policy, as can be observed in the Constitution and in the National Labor Statute. This law by its nature, structure and objectives corresponds to the Italian Labor Charter, from which it took some points of doctrine and organization" (Caetano 1938, 28, quoted in McAdams 1952, 121).

28. The constitution, Art. 16, states: "Imcube ao Estado autorizar, salvo disposição de lei em contrario, todos os organismos corporativos, morais, culturais, ou econômicos, e promover e auxiliar a sua formação."

29. The National Labor Statute, Art. 1, provides: "A nação portuguesa constitutes uma unidade moral, polítiéa e econômica, cujos fins e interesses dominão os [interesses] dos indivíduos e grupos que a compoêm."

30. In 1947, "These syndicates were organized on an industrial basis as follows: Mines & Quarries 7; Food & Tobacco 32; Lumber & Related Products 21; NonMetallic Minerals 10; Textiles 25; Nonprecious Metals 14; Electricity 1; Paper Industry 7; Furs 13; Chemical Products 5; Manufacturing 6; Building 23; Transportation & Commerce 63; Commerce & Insurance 47; General Services 20; and Miscellaneous Services 17" (Instituto Nacional de Estatística, *Estatística de organização corporativa* [Lisbon, 1947], 7; cited in McAdams 1952, 125).

31. I strongly disagree with the "culturist" analysis of the Portuguese case. This mode of analysis argues that corporatism, the dependent variable, was the result of Portuguese cultural characteristics, the independent variable. According to this argument, endogenous historical–structural situations, such as economic, political, and social conditions, and exogenous variables, such as foreign capital penetration, have not affected the "stronger and more deeply-ingrained corporative tradition characteristic of all Portuguese regimes, regardless of their self-imposed labels" (see Wiarda 1974a, 79; 1976). In my view, Wiarda shows a limited understanding of social structure and is unaware that the origins

of cultural traditions must be explained, and that by themselves cultural traditions explain nothing.

32. Stepan observes that "Both inclusionary corporatism and exclusionary corporatism employ policies that, if successfully implemented, restrict the autonomy of the groups they encapsulate. In no sense is the word 'inclusionary' meant to imply liberal, democratic, or socialist policies" (1978, 74).

33. António O. Salazar, "Não há estado forte onde o poder executivo o não é," in his *Discursos e notas políticas*, vol. I (Coimbra: Coimbra Editora, 1934), 81.

34. Stepan states that "the term Organic-Statism needs some clarification. 'Organic' refers to a normative vision of the political community in which the component parts of society harmoniously combine to enable the full development of man's potential. 'Statist' is used because of the assumption . . . that such harmony does not occur spontaneously . . . but requires power . . . and occasionally restructuring of civil society by political elites" (1978, 26–27).

35. Quoted by Pope John XXIII, *Mater et Magistra* (Christianity and Social Progress), in *The Social Teachings of the Church*, Anne Freemantle, ed. (New York: New American Library, 1963), 228–229; cited in Stepan (1978, 36).

36. Stepan states that "no concrete inclusionary attempt satisfies entirely the pure organic-statist model either" (1978, 81).

37. E. Altvater "Notes on Some Problems of State Intervention," *Kapitalstate*, 1 (1973): quoted 100; in Munck (1984, 206).

38. The debate appeared in *New Left Review* (1969–1970).

39. In Poulantzas' later works there was a retreat from structuralism and a recognition that structural causality has no subject. As an Althusserian structuralist, Poulantzas argued in his early work that a society was a system of objective processes and structures. Later, he realized that Althusser's functionalist epistemology reduced persons to simple "bearers" of these structures, and saw that such a reduction excluded any possibility of real class struggle in history and rendered historical–structural change an impossibility. In other words, Poulantzas became aware that social structures do not produce themselves but are the product, albeit not in an idealistic and voluntaristic manner, of the actions of human agency.

40. In his latest writings O'Donnell is less structural–functionalist, and gives more consideration to internal situations within Latin American dependent states.

41. In 1930, 56.5 percent of the active working population was in the primary sector. In 1940, the percentage was 49.3. Moreover, as late as 1957, 93.6 percent of all industrial enterprises were small, having no more than twenty workers.

3

Class Domination

From 1926 to early 1974, Portuguese society was under the control of the state, the mechanism that guaranteed and protected the interests of the ruling reactionary coalition. And, although a corporative constitution was approved in a national plebiscite on March 19, 1933, society was controlled through coercion, not consent. The state's development and implementation of coercive and repressive mechanisms guaranteed the maintenance of the reactionary coalition's hegemony. Acting on behalf of the coalition, the Estado Novo

created a police state not in order to regiment and mobilize society in the interests of the more advanced sectors of capital, but to freeze the social structure in a way that maintained the hegemony of a backward and neofeudal ruling class. (Lomax 1983, 110)

To assure its domination, the ruling coalition placed ''greater confidence in the use of force than in the existence of consensus as the source of social order'' (Mónica 1978, 39). Hence, for forty-eight years social order in Portugal was achieved through the mechanisms of repressive state apparatuses. The latter had to be developed and implemented because, from the moment the military seized power in 1926, the state was ''entrusted with the preservation of the interests of the reactionary coalition'' (Ginner 1982, 190).

THE REPRESSIVE STATE APPARATUS

The Armed Forces

Notwithstanding the common practice of reducing the Estado Novo to the person of Salazar, of individualizing the total economic–political–social formation into Salazarismo, the agents of the real power holders before and during the Estado Novo were the armed forces. On behalf of the reactionary coalition, the military had been active in various governments during the Republic. Between 1919 and 1926, "twelve out of twenty-six cabinets" were "presided over by army or navy officers." Moreover, the armed forces, and therefore the reactionary coalition, were well "represented in the cortes (parliament)" (Bruce 1975, 37). In 1926, the armed forces seized power and ruled, de jure and de facto, until 1933.

On the surface, the corporative Constitution of 1933 put an end to the military dictatorship and introduced the new and lasting bureaucratic-authoritarian civilian regime with Salazar at the helm. But, beneath the surface, the position and role of the military remained unchanged. The generals, most, if not all, of whom belonged to the conservative right wing, stood as the guarantors of the exercise and maintenance of the reactionary coalition's hegemony. Article 81, section I, and Article 82, section I, of the Constitution of 1933 indicate clearly that the civilian bureaucrats, including Salazar, were formally subordinated to the military.

Article 81 stated:

It shall be the business of the President of the Republic: (1) to appoint the Chairman of the Council of Ministers, Prime Minister, and the ministers, secretaries and under secretaries of state from among Portuguese citizens and to release them from their offices.

Article 82 stated:

The acts of the President of the Republic must be countersigned by the Prime Minister and by the competent Minister or Ministers; otherwise they shall be legally non-existent. . . . *The following do not need countersigning* (1) *The appointment and dismissal of the Prime Minister*, (2) Messages sent to the National Assembly, (3), Message of resignation of his post. (Emphasis added.)

The president of the Republic had the constitutional power to appoint and dismiss the chairman of the Council of Ministers and the ministers (Bruce 1975, 37–38). Until 1974, the president of the Portuguese Republic was always a military officer. But the armed forces were never active rulers. Their function was to guard and to protect the rule of the reactionary coalition. Thus, I find it analytically inappropriate to state, as Nolte does, that "at the bottom the Estado Novo [was] simply a military dictatorship which was lucky to find an outstanding civilian who simultaneously strengthened and transformed it" (1966, 14–15).

The Paramilitary Forces

The Guarda Nacional Republicana (GNR)

In addition to the armed forces, the reactionary coalition had paramilitary forces at its disposal. These forces effectively maintained the status quo through violent control and repression of the working class.

The most notorious paramilitary force was the GNR. Formed in 1913 to replace the monarchy's Civil Guard and to protect the young Republic, it later become the protector of the Estado Novo and a heavily armed force known for charging on horseback into public demonstrations. Both the Cortes (Parliament) in São Bento, Lisbon, and the Presidential Palace in Belém, Lisbon, were protected by the GNR. Career officers from the armed forces were assigned on a regular basis to duty in the GNR. This practice indicates the power of the military. Its activities and supervision of the regime were not limited to its various branches; the paramilitary forces were also under its control. The GNR's lowest ranks were drawn mostly from the interior and poor parts of the country. To them, the GNR guaranteed living conditions far superior to those of poor urban and rural workers. Thus, indirectly, the GNR contributed to the movement of peasants into the petite bourgeoisie.

In the early years of the Estado Novo, the GNR was very active in breaking up rural workers' demonstrations and strikes; its forceful intervention resulted in hundreds of arrests and in the death of some workers. Catarina Eufebia, a twenty-nine-year-old rural worker, was shot down at close range by First Lieutenant Carrajola in May 1954. Rural workers Alfredo Lima and José Adelino dos Santos also were shot by GNR troops (Duarte 1962, 9–21).

During the reactionary coalition's regime, the GNR consisted of several battalions stationed in barracks throughout Lisbon, on its outskirts, and in the cities of Pôrto, Coimbra, and Évora. In rural areas, their presence was ubiquitous.

The Polícia de Segurança Pública (PSP)

The Public Security Police (PSP) were under the direct control of provincial governors until 1953, when they were reorganized as a paramilitary force under the jurisdiction of the minister of the interior. The PSP was a heavily armed force; its members always carried a service revolver and a nightstick made of rubber, and when they were on duty outside the police districts, the officers wore helmets and carried light machine guns. The PSP regularly used its mobile assault units when cooperating with the GNR in breaking up civil disturbances and labor disputes.

There were PSP units in each of the country's twenty-two districts, in the Azores, and in the Madeira Islands. Armed forces officers were assigned to duty in the PSP, as they were in the GNR, and special military units took part in PSP training programs. During the regime of the reactionary coalition, the PSP was a ruthless paramilitary force well known for its expertise in crowd control. To break up civil disturbances in Lisbon, they used water cannons that sprayed a special blue dye which marked the participants for easy identification and subsequent arrest.

The Legião Portuguesa

The Portuguese Legion, founded on September 30, 1936 (two months after the outbreak of the Spanish Civil War), was under the jurisdiction of the war minister, who at the time was Salazar. Under the command of an army officer, Botelho Moniz, the Legion in the 1940s was active in strikebreaking operations. While officially the Legion members were volunteers between the ages of eighteen and fifty, in reality some types of government and civil employment required joining the Legion. In the 1950s and 1960s, this was true in the fishing industry, which was under the control of Commander Henrique Tenreiro (later admiral), who was also the president of the executive committee of the Legion. Tenreiro was one of the wealthiest and longest-term beneficiaries of the coalition's regime.

From 1936 to 1945 the Legion had over 120,000 members whose training was conducted by military officers. It included special elite units such as the Motored Shock Force (also called the Anti-Communist Force), the Immediate Intervention Group, and a naval brigade under the command of Henrique Tenreiro (Kayman 1987, 190). Legionnaires served in the Spanish Civil War on the side of Franco, and "some 8,000 [of them] died . . . fighting Franco's cause" (Ferreira and Marshall 1984, 12). Armed forces officers, particularly those who fought in Spain, proudly displayed the Legion decoration on their uniforms. It has been aptly observed that the Legion was "a kind of reactionary coalition's SA" (Fryer and Pinheiro 1961, 126).

OTHER INSTRUMENTS OF CLASS DOMINATION

Censorship and Other Prohibitions

Censorship

The oldest repressive instrument of the reactionary coalition was censorship. It was first imposed shortly after the seizure of power by the military in May 1926. Under a decree of July 1926, the military dictatorship assumed the power to stop publication of newspapers found guilty of reporting inflammatory news on three different occasions. Eventually the system of censorship was expanded to cover all forms of mass communication.

Decree no. 13564, of May 6, 1927, prohibited the showing of films considered to be immoral by the reactionary coalition, and banned all public debates regarding matters of human sexuality (Mónica 1978, 78). The book *A vida sexual* (Coimbra, 1901) could not be sold to the public. It was available only to the medical profession upon written request (Fryer and Pinheiro 1961, 89). This in spite of the fact that the author of the book was Egas Moniz, a well-known neurologist and the only Portuguese Nobel Prize laureate.

Under Decree no. 22,469, of April 11, 1933, censorship committees were created to operate a system of prior censorship. To the reactionary coalition such a system was "indispensable to a labor of reconstruction and moral cleansing." The committees were to be nominated by the Estado Novo. According to Article 3 of the April decree, "The only purpose for the censorship will be to prevent the perversion of . . . public opinion in its function as social force. . . . " And that censorship would function "to defend public opinion from any factors which may misguide it against truth, justice, morality, good administration and the common good, and to prevent the fundamental principles of the organization of society from being attacked" (Robinson 1979, 56).

Decree no. 23,203, of November 6, 1933, defined the following as "crimes of rebellion committed by the press: "attacks on the established system of government or on members of government; inciting workers to strike; spreading rumors deemed prejudicial to the regime." Salazar observed, "Newspapers are the spiritual food of the people and like all foods, must be controlled" (Robinson 1979, 56).

Periodicals were subject to prepublication censorship. The imprint *Visado pela Commissão de Censura* (Passed by the Censorship Committee) appeared conspicuously on all newspapers and magazines. Foreign periodicals could not be censored, but certainly could be removed from circulation if they contained "matter whose disclosure would not be permitted in Portuguese publications" (Fryer and Pinheiro 1961, 186).

Books were not subject to prepublication censorship, perhaps because the reactionary coalition assumed they were less accessible to the people. After publication, however, books were examined, and if they were considered prejudicial to the regime, were removed from circulation and impounded. The authors and publishers were subject to fines and imprisonment. An example of this was the banning of Aquilino Ribeiro's novel *Quando os lobos uivam* (When the Wolves Howl). Because the novel described the policies of the reactionary coalition critically and negatively, Ribeiro was accused of discrediting the state. Other writers and intellectuals experienced the constant presence of the censor in their lives. Alves Redol, the late Communist novelist, compared the system of censorship to "intellectual solitary confinement. They never allowed me to write down what I wanted to say" (Robinson 1979, 57).

In July 1969, while being interviewed by Portuguese journalists regarding the system of censorship, Marcelo Caetano, the new prime minister, stated that there were no plans to abolish the system. "After 43 years of existence, the Portuguese population and generations of journalists born during its enforcement are used to the regime of censorship." He added, "If it [censorship] were abruptly abolished, that would only cause confusion not only among the people but also among the members of the press themselves."[1]

Other Prohibitions

In addition to censorship, the reactionary coalition imposed other repressive mechanisms to assure the reproduction of capital accumulation and the passive obedience of the Portuguese people. Political parties (other than the União Nacional, the party of the coalition) were prohibited, and free workers' unions and syndicates were abolished and replaced with syndicates conceptualized, implemented, and controlled by the coalition through the corporative constitution (see Chapter 2).

Furthermore, the reactionary coalition enacted laws covering public employment. These laws required loyalty oaths and background checks as conditions of employment. Law no. 1901, of May 21, 1935, required that every military and civilian employee of the state submit a notarized affidavit attesting to non-membership in secret societies or clandestine organizations, such as the Communist Party. And Decree-Law no. 25,317, of May 1935, stated that state employees demonstrating "a spirit of opposition to the fundamental principles of the political constitution, or who do not guarantee cooperation in achieving the higher aims of the state, will be suspended, retired, or dismissed" (Robinson 1979, 57).

Many public employees, military and paramilitary personnel, civil service bureaucrats, officials of the Estado Novo, and teachers and university professors refrained from questioning the legitimacy of the reactionary coalition's political regime because of the risk of losing their jobs and facing other sanctions. And if one became a known dissenter and adversary of the regime, the chances of securing public employment would be nil, because the background check would yield negative information. Thus, through the state labor market, the reactionary coalition very effectively controlled about half the population.

Professionals were not allowed to practice their profession if they were found to be involved in clandestine political activities against the regime. A medical doctor would be denied membership in the Ordem dos Médicos (Medical Association) if he/she had lost his/her "political rights" because of involvement in illegal political activities against the state. And medical doctors without membership in the Ordem could not practice medicine. Similar conditions applied to other professions.

Ideology

The Rural–Agrarian Ethos

While the reactionary coalition ruled for almost fifty years through the imposition of violent coercion and repression, ideological manipulation was also an instrument of class domination. From the first days of the regime, an aspect of the official ideology was what has been referred to as "agrarian fundamentalism" and "national agrarianism." The first term refers to "the view that agriculture was the 'sacred' way of life, the others being 'profane.' " The second refers to "the view that Portugal was essentially an agricultural country" (Martins 1971, 64–67).

The Republic of 1910–1926 had attempted to transport Portugal from the rural villages to urban centers, as a first step toward moving the country forward. The reactionary coalition reversed the direction, and took the country to the rural villages, to the past where neofeudalism reigned. Under the official orthodoxy, rural life was glorified and the cities perceived as the "opium" of the people (Mónica 1978, 142). "Worse, much worse than the emigration to Brazil; worse, much worse than emigration to Spain or France—is the emigration of the male to the factory" (Pimenta 1935; quoted in Mónica 1978, 140). Inasmuch as the hegemonic fraction of the reactionary coalition consisted of the latifundists, who needed an assured supply of hired labor, the Estado Novo, on behalf of the coalition, was the defender and guarantor of the rural ethos.

The Corporative Constitution

The corporative Constitution of 1933 was an instrument of ideological control and manipulation of the Portuguese people, particularly of the proletariat. At the base of the political ideology of the New State was the concept of social cooperation and harmony. The corporate state would produce a society in which social harmony would be the responsibility of every citizen. Life in Portugal would be organized under the spirit of cooperation and social solidarity instead of competing selfish interests. And the New State would create "corporate bodies" to be used as appropriate and harmonious "channels of class articulation."

Deus, Pátria, e Família

The Portugal of the reactionary coalition was a Catholic country. *Deus, patria, e Família* (God, country, and family) was coined by Salazar and became a mechanism of ideological domination. It was used for the inculcation of values such as respect and love for God, the country, and the family. It gave credibility to an aspect of the official orthodoxy: that Salazar ruled the nation by the grace of God. Salazar himself observed that "The foundation of political power, or the origins of sovereignty . . . are found in God. . . . This doctrine excludes, therefore, the social contract argument and the democratic principle of the origins of political power, which places the locus of power in the people and not in God."[2] And Marcello Caetano observed,

In general, the revelation of divine selection of a man to govern a determined nation, would be his emergence in rather difficult circumstances, followed by a series of surprising successes which, in removing the existing difficulties from the people, can only be explained as divine favor and grace. (Caetano 1967; quoted in Campinos n.d., 149)

Under Law no. 1,941 of April 11, 1936, "In all primary public schools there shall be placed, behind and above the teacher's chair, a crucifix to symbolize the Christian education set forth by the Constitution'' (Mónica 1978, 149). The Republic of 1910 had considered the church an element of the monarchy, and hence introduced anticlerical reforms and secular rationality. The reactionary coalition brought back religion.

Ideologically, individual interests were subordinated to the common good. Individuals and groups were considered to be mere elements of the nation and, hence, subordinated to the objectives and realization of the national interest. Under Article 71 of the constitution, sovereignty resided in the nation. Following Mussolini, who said ''Everything for the State, nothing against the State,'' Salazar stated, ''Everything for the Nation, nothing against the Nation.'' The nation was made transcendent, and the reactionary coalition used the idea of the ''primacy of the national interest'' for its own benefit.

Salazar affirmed that the nation was not the sum total of the individual citizens, as in liberal states, but ''an undefinable essence of the Portuguese historical community, through the centuries, in the form of a material and moral inheritance. We owe everything to it [the nation], and we conform to its superior interests'' (d'Assac 1964, 184; quoted in Campinos n.d., 22). Salazar also stated that ''Who is not patriotic, can not be Portuguese'' (Campinos n.d., 22).

The corporative Constitution of 1933 considered the family as the ''primary unit of social interaction.'' Section III, Article 12, stated:

The State shall ensure the formation and protection of the family as the source of the maintenance and development of the race, the first elementary basis of education, discipline and social harmony; and, by its association and representation in the parish and the town, the foundation of all political and administrative order. (Keefe et al. 1977, 132)

The family—as the foundation of all political order—was supposed to be active in the national government through the *juntas de freguesia* (parishes), which consisted of heads of families within officially designated geographic areas. Theoretically, the parish elected representatives to the national government. In reality, however, during the regime of the coalition, the Portuguese family had no participation in the government, which remained quite remote from its own foundation.

António de Oliveira Salazar

The statement of Marcello Caetano (1976) regarding the ''divine selection of a man to govern a determined nation'' shows how the official orthodoxy presented Salazar to the population. Salazar ruled by the grace of God. In his writings, Salazar always manifested divine providence, the people were told. The simple man of the country, the former seminarian, was also viewed as ''*O Bemfeitor da Patria*'' (the benefactor of the nation).

Thus the Estado Novo was personalized in Salazar. The state was Salazar, and he was the state. Accordingly, Salazar alone ruled. ''He was . . . autonomous from all groups." It has been observed that "Because Salazar formed it and guided it for all but six years of its existence, the regime was clearly a system of personal rulership."[3] In reality, however, Salazar never ruled alone, for the Estado Novo was the political system and the social organization of a class, or of a segment of a class, objectively and socially located in the Portuguese social formation of the times. The ideological practices of the reactionary coalition submitted an imaginary world to the people.

Social Inequality

Social Stratification

The nature and structure of Portugal's social stratification formed an effective mechanism of class domination. Before and during the coalition's rule, this structure of inequality changed very little. "In 1890 approximately 84 per cent of the Portuguese society could be classified as lower class, about 15 per cent middle class, and 1 per cent upper class" (Payne 1973, 574). The small size of the upper class reflected the extremely high level of concentration and centralization of economic power.

The upper class was comprised of latifundists; financiers; leading industrialists and other businessman; higher echelons of the officer corps, the civil service, academe, the Catholic hierarchy, and prominent members of the liberal professions (Martins 1971, 65).

Social classes were distributed as shown in Tables 3.1 and 3.2. The data in both tables show clearly that between 1950 and 1970, the working class was the largest in Portuguese society. In the years studied, the working class numbered almost 75 percent of the total economically active population, a good indicator of the economic and social backwardness of the country. The rather high number of nonproductive workers (mostly rural females, working in the cities as maids, servants, and cleaning women) was indicative of the absence of economic development. Moreover, the data also show that in 1950 the proletariat was essentially agrarian. However, after 1950 the rural proletariat was reduced substantially because of the structural transformations that Portugal experienced. On the other hand, the blue-collar proletariat increased substantially (by 214,000 between 1950 and 1960, and by 103,000 between 1960 and 1970). This fraction represented almost one-fourth of the statistical universe in 1950, and more than one-third in 1970. The bourgeoisie, always a minority, was also essentially agrarian in 1950. The agrarian bourgeoisie was 60 percent of the bourgeoisie in 1950, 40 percent in 1960, and 20 percent in 1970 total class. The bourgeoisie fell from 8 percent of the statistical universe in 1950 to 3 percent in 1970. The petite bourgeoisie was essentially rural, made up of semi-independent owners of small lots of land mostly in the northern part of the country. This characteristic explains why this class experienced the least transformation. These changes in

Table 3.1
Social Classes in Portugal, 1950–1970

Classes and Fractions	1950	1960	1970
Active population	3,196,482	3,315,639	3,163,855
Undefined activities and occupations	98,301	28,832	136,760
Statistical universe	3,098,181	3,286,807	3,027,095
Bourgeoisie	247,169	203,343	91,060
Agrarian	142,582	79,422	18,485
Industrial	46,142	55,507	21,225
Commercial	48,549	48,492	30,450
Undefined fractions	9,896	19,921	20,900
Working class	2,198,531	2,422,377	2,200,140
Proletariat	1,646,545	1,801,287	1,532,180
Rural proletariat	929,560	870,099	498,455
Blue collar	716,985	931,188	1,033,725
Non-productive workers	551,986	621,090	667,960
New middle class	17,320	18,860	39,515
Petite bourgeoisie	635,161	485,965	468,040
Small farmers	465,510	485,965	468,040
Craftsmen	83,061	71,075	103,545
Commercial	65,899	63,195	91,940
Undefined fractions	20,691	21,992	32,833

Source: A. Marques and M. Bairrada, "As Classes sociais na população activa portuguesa, 1950–1970," *Analise Social* 18, nos. 72–75 (1982): 1279–1297.

the class structure played an important role in the coup of 1974, and in the transition to democratic rule.

It has been aptly observed that the regime of the reactionary coalition was a "classicist dictatorship," and that "the political elite of a classicist dictatorship will not be composed of plebeian or socially marginal individuals" (Martins 1971, 64). This "classicist" dictatorship was comprised of a small elite whose perpetuation was the responsibility of the Estado Novo. Under the Constitution of 1933, corporative bodies (in name only), regulating economic activities, were created on the basis of class. The paramount criterion for their organization was class position. In urban areas, the bourgeoisie was organized into *grémios* (guilds), while the urban proletariat was organized into *sindicatos* (syndicates). The rural bourgeoisie was organized into *grémios da lavoura* (landowners' guilds), while the rural proletariat was organized into *casas do povo* (houses of the people). This organizational segregation benefited the bourgeoisie and harmed the working class, the majority of the people.

Ascribed Social Status

During the regime of the reactionary coalition, social status was ascribed; it was based on birth, on one's family background. Again, the Estado Novo was responsible for its perpetuation. "In the north or in the feudal pastures of the

Table 3.2
Social Classes in Portugal, 1950–1970 (percentages)

Classes and Fractions	1950	1960	1970
Statistical universe	100	100	100
Bourgeoisie	8.0	6.2	3.0
Agrarian	4.6	2.4	0.6
Industrial	1.5	1.7	0.7
Commercial	1.6	1.5	1.0
Undefined fractions	0.3	0.6	0.7
Working Class	71.0	73.7	72.7
Proletariat	53.1	54.8	50.6
Rural	30.0	26.5	16.5
Blue collar	23.1	28.3	34.1
Non-productive workers	17.8	18.9	22.1
New middle class	0.6	0.6	1.3
Petite bourgeoisie	20.5	19.5	23.0
Small farmers	15.0	14.8	15.5
Craftsmen	2.7	2.2	3.4
Commercial	2.1	1.9	3.0
Undefined fractions	0.7	0.7	1.1

Source: A. Marques and M. Bairrada, "As Classes sociais na população activa portuguesa, 1950–1970," *Analise Social* 18, nos. 72–74 (1982): 1293.

Alentejo [the region south of the river Tagus] the peasants will still doff their hats to you if you are respectable enough to wear a collar and tie" (*The Economist*, February 26, 1972, 9). The ideological orthodoxy viewed social class, and concomitant power, prestige, and status, as the effects of a divinely institutionalized social structure. Social equality was against God's will, it was against nature, and it was impossible to achieve. It was argued that "Good thinking required a prolonged mental exercise and a preparation foreign to the inferior classes; consequently, for a child born into the latter, it would be extremely difficult to experience upward mobility" (Mónica 1978, 137). Ideologically, the coalition dichotomized the configuration of class divisions between *nós* (us) and *eles* (them) or *o povo* (the people); and *o povo* was a "vast undifferentiated ascriptive mass" (Martins 1971, 64).

Discourse

Ideological control and manipulation also appeared in the language, in speech patterns. The "you" forms of address in Portuguese are *o senhor/a senhora*, *voce*, and *tu*. In practice, their use indicated social distance, social hierarchy, and subjugation. The class cleavages between the elite (*eles*) and the people (*o povo*) was easily discernible. An army officer, a civil engineer, or a medical doctor would use the familiar *tu* when addressing a soldier, a worker, or a patient. The latter would use the formal *o senhor* or *vossa senhoria* (which showed high respect), or *o senhor dotour*. Speech therefore assigned people to their respective social places. A middle-class housewife would call her maid

Maria, while the maid would address the housewife as Dona Maria. Discourse was a component of the ideological mechanisms used to subjugate the people; it "interpellated" them as naturally subordinated subjects.

The Education System

In 1970, 50 percent of the Portuguese population was illiterate, Portuguese society was essentially agricultural, and the landed aristocracy was the hegemonic center of the reactionary coalition. To the coalition, the literacy of the Portuguese population was neither necessary nor desirable, and was actually dangerous. Consequently, the Estado Novo reversed the direction the First Republic had given to education, and encouraged educational stagnation. Instead of education, the coalition wanted indoctrination (Mónica 1978, 39). Decree-Law no. 27,279 declared:

Elementary primary education would betray its mission were it to continue to place a sterile rationalist encyclopaedism, fatal to the moral and physical health of the child, above the practical and Christian ideal of teaching well how to read, write and add up, and how to practice the moral virtues and a lively love of Portugal. (Robinson 1979, 58)

To ensure that this decree was enforced, the reactionary coalition created two additional mechanisms of control of education. First, it implemented the practice of *livros unicos* (approved textbooks), which was applicable to all levels of the educational system. Hence, students read what the coalition wanted them to read. Second, in October 1936, the coalition founded the Mocidade Portuguesa (Portuguese Youth), under the leadership of a young coalition member, Marcelo Caetano. Under the jurisdiction of the minister of national education, the movement was initially a compulsory organization for students at all levels. Its purpose was to "stimulate the integral development of their physical capacities, the formation of their character and devotion to country, through the feeling for order, the taste for discipline and military duty" (Robinson 1979, 58).

Portuguese Youth replaced an earlier movement, the Acção Escolar Vanguarda (Student Vanguard), which the coalition had organized in 1934. The belts of the members' uniforms had a metal buckle with the letter S on it; while the S stood for *servir* (to serve), most people, including the students, thought it stood for Salazar. The movement adopted the Roman, or Nazi, salute.

Since the reactionary coalition rejected the notion of social equality, and argued that hierarchic social strata were in agreement with the natural order of things, this view influenced its conceptions of the role of education. Thus, education was not perceived as an avenue for social mobility, for admission into the professions, for the training of gifted minds. Social status was ascribed. Education was, above all, a mechanism of indoctrination (Mónica 1978, 133). Salazar stated categorically that "in a naturally stratified society, education has little or no bearing on greater equality" (Salazar 1939, 30–31; quoted in Campinos n.d.,

Table 3.3
Education Expenditures, Selected Countries

Country	Percentage of GNP	
Belgium	(1970)	4.8
England	(1969)	5.6
France	(1970)	3.5
Greece	(1970)	2.2
Italy	(1970)	4.3
Norway	(1970)	5.9
Spain	(1970)	2.4
Yugoslavia	(1970)	5.4
Portugal	(1967)	1.4

Source: Hugo Blasco Fernandes, *Portugal através de alguns números* (Lisbon: Prelo, 1976), 80.

133). The view that education had no bearing on equality explains why the reactionary coalition spent a very small portion of the country's GNP on education (see Table 3.3).

The organization of secondary education reflected class divisions. The system was bifurcated into lyceums and technical schools. The former were "ante-chambers" to the universities, while the latter were vocational/technical educational institutions. The system was inefficient and therefore had high dropout rates. During the reactionary coalition's rule, education was beyond the reach of the majority of the population. The average family could not afford not to have their children employed as early as possible. Going to school had to be replaced with going to work, usually at the age of ten or eleven. This explains the paradoxical fact that the number of individuals with university education was greater (slightly) than the number of individuals with high school education. In the early 1960s, 84 percent of university students came from the two highest social strata, which at the time constituted only a little over 10 percent of the population (Miranda 1969, 158–165).

Portugal had a large working class and a small, weak middle class. This class distribution had a detrimental effect on the nature and organization of the tertiary level of education. Because of such distribution,

The Universities never lost the monopoly of training for the higher professions and . . . [were] able to maintain their aristocratic ethos, their scholastic, pedagogical and archaic cultural mentality. They . . . therefore . . . acted as agents of cultural immobility rather than social mobility. (Martins 1971, 79)

Comparative data clearly indicate that tertiary-level education was a privilege for a very few. Table 3.4 shows that, with the exception of Brazil, Portugal had the smallest number of students per 100,000 inhabitants in 1970. Table 3.5 shows the access to university education among OECD member countries; Portugal had the lowest. Tertiary education was out of reach for most young people.

Table 3.4
Number of Tertiary-Level Students per 100,000 Inhabitants, Selected Countries

Country	Number of Students	Country	Number of Students
Spain	653	Norway	1,290
France (1969)	1,212	Sweden	1,547
Greece (1969)	857	Chile	802
Italy	1,280	Peru	918
Belgium	776	Uruguay	662
W. Germany	834	Venezuela (1969)	718
Yugoslavia	1,272	Brazil	464
Poland	1,008	Argentina	1,128
		Portugal	520

Figures are for 1970 except where otherwise indicated.
Source: Hugo Blasco Fernandes, *Portugal através de alguns números* (Lisbon: Prelo, 1976), 76.

Table 3.5
Access to Tertiary-Level Education, OECD Countries
(percentages of cohorts)

Country	Year	Percentage
Spain	1972	27.1
France	1971	30.0
Greece	1965	9.8
Italy	1973	28.2
Belgium	1970	28.5
W. Germany	1970	15.8
Norway	1970	27.5
Sweden	1972	31.1
G. Britain	1970	21.3
Denmark	1972	34.3
Portugal	1970	6.6

Source: Hugo Blasco Fernandes, *Portugal através de alguns números* (Lisbon: Prelo, 1976), 65.

This is indicated more clearly in Table 3.6, which indicates access to tertiary education according to socioeconomic status (SES). According to the data in Table 3.6, in the United States, in 1958, a young person from high SES had a five times greater opportunity to attend a university than a person from low SES. In Yugoslavia, in 1965–1966, the ratio was four to one. But in Portugal, in 1963–1964, a person from high SES had a 129 times greater opportunity to attend a university than a person of low SES.

The Church and the State

The First Republic (1910–1926) was antichurch and implemented legislation detrimental to the Portuguese Catholic Church. Church property was confiscated,

Table 3.6
Access to University Education According to Socioeconomic Status, Selected Countries

Country	Year	High SES	Low SES
Austria	1965-66	40	1
Belgium	1966-67	8	1
Denmark	1964-65	16	1
France	1964-65	30	1
W. Germany	1964-65	48	1
Greece	1964-65	8	1
Ireland	1961	20	1
Italy	1964-65	34	1
Japan	1961	30	1
Luxembourg	1964-65	65	1
Norway	1964-65	7	1
Spain	1962-63	87	1
Sweden	1960-61	26	1
England	1961-62	8	1
U.S.A.	1958	5	1
Yugoslavia	1965-66	4	1
Portugal	1965-66	129	1

Source: Hugo Bilasco Fernandes, *Portugal através de alguns números* (Lisbon: Prelo, 1976), 84.

religious orders were abolished, and the church educational and welfare services were terminated. The official position of the Republic vis-à-vis the church in Portugal was one of strong anticlericalism. The church was identified with the monarchy and was seen as a cause of the country's social problems.

The reactionary coalition, however, reversed the policy of the Republic, replacing anticlericalism with Christianity and Catholicism. The coalition accepted and favored the expansion of Christian beliefs and morality. Portugal, in the eyes of the coalition, was, and always would be, a Catholic country.

High church officials were accepted into the coalition's power structure. Cardinal Cerejeira, the patriarch of Lisbon during the coalition's regime and a powerful figure in the church, was a longtime friend of Salazar. Their friendship went back to the days when they were seminarians. In 1920 both men had been active in politics through membership in the Centro Académico de Democracia Cristã. (In spite of its title, the Center was more sympathetic to monarchic than to democratic causes.)

The church became the "third power base" of the reactionary coalition, the first being the latifundists and financiers, and the second the armed forces (Bruce 1975, 33–34). Clerics, especially village priests, functioned as noncoercive agents of social control. They maintained the status quo by preventing the development of class awareness and the formation of working-class representative bodies. According to the census of 1940, there were twice as many priests as medical doctors in Portugal (Mónica 1978, 70). The church legitimated and reproduced the coalition's ideological orthodoxy until the fall of the coalition in April 1974.

The State Police

The reactionary coalition's secret police were undeniably the most effective and reliable instrument of class domination and subjugation. Officially, the secret police were frontier guards and protectors against foreign infiltration. In reality, however, they were the guarantors of continous capital accumulation and the protectors of the Portuguese capitalist system; their function was to defend the system, and to act in the "Service of Order" (Martins 1971, 329). Actually their function was "to control or neutralize any group or persons who threatened the status quo" (Wheeler 1983).

Consequently, the real enemies of the secret police were not foreigners; they were the workers (the vast majority of the Portuguese population), the Portuguese Communist Party, and other opponents of the coalition. On behalf of the latter, the secret police routinely engaged in domestic spying. During the reactionary coalition's rule, they were ubiquitous yet inconspicuous and remote—and greatly feared. People did not hold political conversations in public places for fear that a *bufo* (spy or informer) might be listening. At one time, it was estimated that there was one *bufo* for every ninety-one Portuguese citizens (Robinson 1979, 55). The *bufos* were the eyes and ears of the secret police, and thus they made the secret police the key instrument of social control and class domination (Gallagher 1979). Among the people, the worst thing one could be called was *bufo*; ostracism and physical injury would likely follow.

The reactionary coalition's secret police operated under various names (see Table 3.7). After 1932, secret police were directly under the control of Salazar. He was visited daily by PIDE's director (from 1932 to 1944 the director was Captain Agostinho Lourenço, who later became director of Interpol). PIDE employed approximately three thousand full-time agents and more than twenty thousand *bufos*. Its Vigilance and Defense section was responsible for keeping records on political figures, on current and former prisoners, and on civil and criminal felons; investigatory work, which included surveillance and background checks; maintaining liaison channels with the other paramilitary forces of social control, including the espionage sector of the Portuguese Legion; and administering five prisons, three in continental Portugal (Aljube, Caxias, and Peniche), and two in the Atlantic islands (a fort in the Azores and a concentration camp in the Cape Verde Islands; Wheeler 1983).

Headquartered in Lisbon, PIDE had offices in the principal cities of Pôrto, Coimbra, Beja, Évora, Faro, and Portimão. There were also offices in the Madeira and Azores Islands and in the colonies. In the latter, PIDE was very active during the war period 1960–1974.

The secret police supervised the Conselho de Segurança Nacional (National

Table 3.7
Portugal's Secret Police, 1926–1974

Date	Decree	Title
12/16/1926	no. 12,972	Policia Secreta de Lisboa (Secret Police of Lisbon)
1927	_____	Policia Secreta do Porto (Secret Police of Porto)
1929	_____	Fusion of the autonomous PSL and PSP.
7/28/1931	no. 20,152	Policia Internacional Portuguesa (PIP; Portuguese Secret Police). Created special section for domestic spying.
1/23/1933	no. 22,151	Policia de Defesa Politica e Social (PDPS; Police for Political & Social Defense). Replaced special PIP section for domestic spying.
8/29/1933	no. 22,992	Policia de Vigilancia e de Defesa do Estado (PVDE; Police for Vigilance and Defense of the State). Combined PIP and PDPS.
10/22/1945	no. 35,046	Policia Internacional e de Defesa do Estado (PIDE; [International Police for the Defense of the State).
11/24/1969	no. 49,401	Direcao Geral de Seguranca (DGS; General Security Directorate). Essentially PIDE with a different name.

Security Council), which had members from PIDE, the GNR, the PSP, the Portuguese Legion, and the Judicial Police. The Council was under the jurisdiction of the minister of the interior, but PIDE was in charge of its daily activities.

Most literature on the Portuguese secret police indicates that the Gestapo and Italian fascists trained the PVDE/PIDE at the beginning and that the latter was "modeled on the Gestapo."[4] I believe the "Gestapo alibi" is false and agree with Wheeler's observation that

The current evidence available strongly suggests that the old well-known claim [the Gestapo alibi] is less than a half-truth and more than a simple lie. . . . Firm evidence of German influence over PVDE [PIDE] is lacking until the Spanish Civil War, 1936–39, when it is probable that at least one or two German intelligence or police agents . . . visited Lisbon and got into contact with PVDE concerning surveillance over Spanish Republicans and communist refugees, agents, etc. (1983, 9–10)

Although good sociohistorical analysis of the Portuguese secret police is still lacking, one is on historically safer ground to postulate that the British MI5 organized and trained the PVDE/PIDE. Wheeler observed, "When one compares the structure of PVDE, using known elements of a table of organization, with the structure of Britain's security service (domestic counterintelligence), MI5, in pre–1965 parlance, one quickly notes a strong resemblance" (1983, 3).

The historical relationship between England and Portugal and the extensive British interests in the Portuguese economy certainly make it highly probable that MI5 assisted the reactionary coalition in the organization and training of PVDE/PIDE. After all, in creating the Estado Novo, the reactionary coalition created a mechanism that protected its own interests and, at the same time, the interests of British investors and other capitalists, who had long exploited the Portuguese economy. The British capitalists, in appreciation, become good friends of the coalition.

In 1938, the president of the Republic, Oscar Carmona, was awarded the Order of the Bath, and in 1941 the University of Oxford awarded Salazar an honorary doctorate in civil law (Fryer and Pinheiro 1961, 130–131). Also 1938 the Anglo-Portuguese Society was formed for "the dissemination of reliable information between the two countries." One of its secretaries was Lieutenant Colonel J. Gross Brown, who had an association with the Spanish and Portuguese copper-mining industries going back to 1905. Brown was a former chairman and managing director of Mason and Barnay, which exploited sulfur and copper mines in Portugal, and had been made a commander of the Portuguese Order of Industrial Merit. Brown became chairman of the Anglo-Portuguese Society in 1960 (Fryer and Pinheiro 1961, 130).

Another British friend of the reactionary coalition was Sir David Kelly, former chairman of the British Council. At an Anglo-Portuguese Society banquet in London in November 1957 (Queen Elizabeth II had visited Portugal shortly before), Kelly observed:

My stay in Portugal coincided with the lowest point of the abyss into which the rotten parasitic republican regime [1910–1926] dragged that pleasant country. . . . Returning to Portugal eighteen years later . . . I was amazed by the transformation effected by Salazar. (Fryer and Pinheiro 1961, 129)

The coalition's British friends had embraced the ideological orthodoxy. Salazar was the savior of the nation. Kelly was not alone in his admiration of Salazar. Every British friend of the reactionary coalition, every member of the Anglo-

Portuguese Society, admired Salazar. Another friend, Society member, and, therefore, admirer of Salazar was Sir Alexander Roger, president of the Anglo-Portuguese Telephone Company, director of Lisbon Electric Tramways, vice president of the Federation of British Industries, former deputy chairman of the Midland Bank, vice president of the Anglo-Portuguese Society, a recipient of the Grand Cross of the Portuguese Order of Industrial Merit, and a Commander of the Military Order of Christ. In May 1958, Sir Alexander stated:

Undoubtedly the present strong and healthy condition of the Portuguese economy is greatly attributable to the wise guidance and counsel of H. E. Dr. António Oliveira Salazar. . . . The qualities of leadership and example which Dr. Salazar has brought, and continues to bring, to the service of his country are recognized and appreciated not only throughout Portugal but also in many other countries. (Fryer and Pinheiro 1961, 129)

In view of such friendly relationships, it is safe to postulate that the PVDE/PIDE was organized and trained by the British MI5.

The coalition's secret police had the power of arrest, which often was done without warrants and late at night. Moreover, the common practice was to hold those arrested for months without their being charged with any specific crime, and without their receiving any assistance from legal counsel. It also was not unusual for those arrested to disappear. Anyone living in Portugal between 1926 and 1974 had a relative, a friend, or a neighbor who had been arrested by the PVDE/PIDE at 3 A.M. and was never seen again.

The Portuguese Communist Party was involved in most of the labor unrest Portugal experienced in the 1930s and early 1940s. It became the principal enemy of the coalition, and thus kept the GNR, the PSP, the Portuguese Legion, and the PVDE/PIDE quite active. In an attempt to crush illegal labor demonstrations, sit-ins, walkouts, and strikes, as well as political dissent, the coalition opened a concentration camp on Tarrafal Island in the Cape Verde Islands, and deportation centers in the Azores and Timor Islands. Labor leaders, Communists, and opponents of the regime were systematically deported or placed in the concentration camp at Tarrafal. On October 29, 1936, 150 opponents of the coalition's regime arrived at Tarrafal (Duarte 1962, 114). The latter became known as the "camp of slow death" because of its inhuman living conditions; and it was there that many of the *desaparecidos* spent the last years of their lives. The camp has been described as follows:

The concentration camp of Tarrafal [was] a rectangle of barbed wire fence, surrounded by a ditch four meters wide and three meters deep. [The camp] was two hundred meters long and one hundred and fifty wide. It was built on a plain with the sea by the west side, and mountains by the north, the south and east side. The camp was also surrounded by a platform three meters high, which [was] the sidewalk of the black guards. Inside the camp, there were four barracks which could not be considered hygienic, a few wooden barracks which housed work-shops, showers and a dirty kitchen. (Duarte 1962, 114)

The living conditions at the camp were exacerbated by the climate and by the abuses, beatings, and punishments to which the prisoners were subjected. Many opponents of the reactionary coalition died at Tarrafal. Among them were Bento Gonçalves, the secretary general of the Portuguese Communist Party, who was deported to Tarrafal in October 1936 and died there in 1942. Francisco Esteves died in January 1938; Alfredo Caldeira, in December 1938; Fernando Alcobia, in December 1939, at the age of twenty-four. Most literature on Portugal mentions that the Tarrafal camp was closed in 1954 (Gallagher, 1979a). But it seems that the camp was still open in August 1969. "So Luandino Vieira [writer] was in the Tarrafal [in August 1969], the concentration camp that brings to mind sad memories, and which we were told had been abolished" (Rego 1974, 85).

The PVDE/PIDE was feared. Although not easily identifiable, the coalition's secret police were ubiquitously and constantly present, and thus were very feared and very effective. The inculcation of fear in the minds of the people was its greatest success. The people knew of arrests without charges, of deportations to the camp of slow death, and of torture and murder of prisoners. It was fear that assured "order in the streets," one of the accomplishments of the reactionary coalition.

Furthermore, PVDE/PIDE was very sophisticated in its methods of torture. It knew how to apply psychological and physical pain. Prisoners were deprived of sleep and were brutally beaten. The horse whip was a favorite instrument of torture. But the PVDE/PIDE technique of torture that became best-known was the *estátua* (statue); the prisoner was kept standing facing a wall where, at eye level, the secret police affixed a list of questions to be answered. The prisoner would remain in standing until he/she answered the questions. Eating and defecating was done standing. Prisoners remained in the *estátua* position for several days and nights. Joaquim Carreira, a Communist worker, remained in the *estátua* position, without sleep, for 148 hours straight. And a young woman, a worker in the cork industry, remained standing for five days (Duarte 1962, 50–54).

A variation of the *estátua* allowed the prisoners to walk from side to side, but not to sit down or to lie down on the floor. And there was another variation: "Oscar Reis and Francisco Pinto were forced to stand on their feet for days on end, and they had their genitals nailed to the wall" (Fryer and Pinheiro 1961, 197).

No one knows exactly how many people PVDE/PIDE murdered on behalf of the reactionary coalition. I say "on behalf of" the coalition because PVDE/PIDE was its most effective instrument of domination and subjugation. It is "beyond doubt that the secret police killed hundreds [if not thousands]" (Marques 1972, 188). It is known that PVDE/PIDE assassinated the following opponents of the reactionary coalition: Manuel Vieira Tomé; Germano Vidigal; Francisco Ferreira Marques; José António Patuleira; José Moreira; Joaquim Lemos de Oliveira; Manuel da Silva Filho (sixty-nine years old when murdered); Raul Alves; Américo Gomes; Aurelio Dias; Alfredo A. Dias; Alfredo Ruas; Armando Ramos; Antonio de Almeida; Antonio Mano Fernandez; Augusto A.

Martins; Elvira Mendonca; Joaquim Correia; Ferreira Soares, M.D.; Joaquim Lopes Martins; Manuel Simoes Filho; Ricardo da Silva; José Dias Coelho; Augusto A. Martinho; Amilcar Cabral; Air Force General Humberto Delgado; Arajaryr Campos; and many others (Luso Soares n.d., 72).

In 1969, Marcello Caetano, the newly appointed prime minister, changed the name of the secret police to Direçao Geral de Segurança (DGS; General Security Directorate). The people, however, kept calling it PIDE/DGS, for they knew nothing had changed. On April 26, 1974, one day after the fall of the reactionary coalition, PIDE/DGS was abolished.

NOTES

1. "Marcello Caetano, respondendo a pergunta de outro jornalista acerca de censura em Portugal, disse que não se encontra projectada qualquer lei de abolição do sistema e explicou que 'apos 43 anos de existência, a população portuguesa e geracões de jornalistas que nasceram durante a sua vigência encontram-se habituados ao regime de censura.' Acrescentou que se ela fosse abolida, o facto so serviria para lancar a confusão, tanto no publico como nos proprios profissionais da imprensa'' (Caetano 1974, 44).

2. António O. Salazar, speech at Second Congress of the Catholic Center (1922), quoted in (Campinos n.d., 38).

3. Bruneau (1984, 19).

4. Many sources could be cited. See Fryer and Pinheiro (1961); Martins (1971); Soares (1975).

4

The Colonial Empire

BACKGROUND INFORMATION

Physical Characteristics

When the reactionary coalition seized power in the early 1920s, the five-hundred-year-old Portuguese empire, twenty-two times the size of continental Portugal, was comprised of the overseas possessions shown in Table 4.1. I have not included in the Portuguese empire the Azores and Madeira Islands in the Atlantic Ocean, 800 miles west and 600 miles southwest of continental Portugal, respectively. This exclusion is based on two reasons. First, these islands have always been "settler colonies," not "capitalist colonies." Crotty (1986) classifies as "settler" colonies those which initially were not inhabited, or the indigenous population and/or culture was "effectively erased." By contrast, "capitalist colonies were established by superimposing individualistic, capitalistic culture on top of non-individualistic and non-capitalistic, indigenous food-producing cultures" (1986, 35). Second, these islands have remained territorial possessions of Portugal.

History

In the latter part of the nineteenth century, Portugal (whose presence in Africa was by then three centuries old) did not have a well-planned, well-executed imperial trade system or concrete economic and political policies for the colonies. In fact, "The survival of Portuguese colonies on both coasts of Africa was more the result of the few white inhabitants' ability to maintain a modest and uncertain *modus vivendi* with the African peoples, than of Lisbon's sporadic efforts to transplant European cultural values" (Duffy 1961, 290).

Table 4.1
Population of the Portuguese Empire, 1961 (estimated)

Africa	Area (Sq. Kms.)	Africans	Creoles	Europeans	Half-Castes
Cape Verde Islands 1	4,033	---------	180,000	3,200	---------
Guinea-Bissau	36,125	600,000	5,000	2,600	---------
Sao Tome Area 2	964	70,000	---------	1,500	---------
Angola	1,246,700	4,500,000	---------	200,000	40,000
Mozam-bique 3	784,961	6,200,000	---------	90,000	20,000

Asia and Oceania		Indians	Chinese	Indonesians	Europeans
India 4	4,194	710,000	---------	---------	1,000
Macau 5	16	---------	250,000	---------	2,500
Timor	14,926	---------	---------	500,000	700

Total	2,091,918		13,187,000		

[1] An archipelago consisting of 14 islands.
[2] Also known as São Tomé e Principe, consisting of the island of Principe and the small territory of Sarame.
[3] Mozambique had an Asian population numbering 12,000 in mid-1961.
[4] India was taken from the Portuguese in 1961 by the Indian armed forces.
[5] Macau, near Hong Kong, is to be returned to the Chinese government.
Source: J. Paxton, ed., *The Statesman's Yearbook, 1973,* 1267; Antonio de Figueiredo, *Portugal and Its Empire: The Truth* (London: Victor Gollancz, 1961), 153–154.

In the nineteenth century the Portuguese population never exceeded three thousand in the "whole of Africa South of the Sahara"; and in Angola, Portugal "controlled less than a tenth of the country's area" (First 1973, 2–7). If we exclude the rather profitable period of slave trade, until the beginning of the twentieth century, Portugal did not develop and implement mechanisms that rendered the colonies a source of national revenue (Newitt 1981, 153). Up to 1974, the holder of a rather vast overseas empire was itself a poor and under-developed country.

At the Berlin Conference of 1885, European colonial powers decreed that legitimate title to colonial possessions was to be determined by "effective oc-cupation." Under this new definition, Portugal lost its claim to the Congo region, and faced the threat of losing other colonies. Hence, the decisions and actions of other European colonial powers forced Portugal to implement expeditions (*campanhas de pacificação*) in order to secure "effective occupation." Specif-ically, Portugal responded to the threats by giving greater priority to an ambitious plan drawn in the 1870s to extend its African empire from the Atlantic Ocean to the Indian Ocean, from Luanda in Angola to Lourenço Marques in Mozambique.

In 1886, Portugal published what came to be known as the *Mapa cor de rosa* (Pink Map), which showed the Portuguese African empire extending from the Indian Ocean to the Atlantic Ocean, south of the Sahara. The territory claimed and the publication of the Pink Map were based on the Portuguese transcontinental expeditions by Serpa Pinto and others. Portugal's expansionist plans were not well received by Great Britain, for they were against British interests in the region. Cecil Rhodes had interests in South Africa that included a Cape-to-Cairo railroad. Second, the British missionaries in the Shire district of Nyasaland wanted ''to strengthen their hold on the Lake Nyassa region'' (Anderson 1962, 99).

In 1887 the British government informed the Portuguese authorities that it rejected the Portuguese transcontinental claims, because the areas indicated in the Pink Map were not ''effectively occupied'' by Portugal. Realizing, belatedly, that expeditions did not constitute effective occupation, Portugal sent additional expeditions to establish control or sovereignty in the regions of Mashonaland and Nyasaland. Great Britain's response to the Portuguese seizure of control of those regions was known as the Ultimatum of 1890. The Portuguese government acquiesced and withdrew most of its claims.

Portuguese colonialism was also undermined by the underdeveloped condition of the Portuguese economy. Portugal lacked the domestic capital, the skilled labor, the technology, and the natural resources necessary for the industrialization of its economy. Moreover, being an underdeveloped, dependent country, it could not undertake economic development in its African colonies. Unable and unwilling to colonize the empire directly, Portugal found a way of doing so indirectly; exploitation would be achieved through intermediaries. In the latter part of the nineteenth century, Portugal followed the then common British and Dutch practices and established chartered companies. These became the new partners and beneficiaries of the system of *prazo*, concessions of land by means of which large estates were settled by owners designated by the monarchy. But there was a difference: The British and the Dutch granted land concessions to national entrepreneurs, while Portugal granted large areas of its colonial empire to foreigners: Belgian, British, French. Portugal created concessionary colonialism.

In 1894 the northern district of Cabo Delgado was granted to the Nyasa Company, and a large area between the Sare and Zambeze rivers was granted to the Mozambique Company (Chilcote 1967, 9). The latter company was granted the right to exploit and to administer, as a sovereign state, more than sixty-two thousand square miles. A third company, Zambesia, was given control of eighty thousand square miles of land (First 1973, 3). The chartered companies had exclusive rights in mineral exploration, commercial activities, land transfers, and tax collection within the *prazo* areas (Marques 1972, 102), which for all practical purposes were semisovereign political states. The companies implemented their own laws and had their own police forces. Through the chartered

Table 4.2
Emigration from Portugal, 1908–1930

Year	Total Emigration	To Brazil	To Africa
1908	40,145	36,262	15
1912	88,298	74,860	90
1916	24,897	10,002	--------
1920	64,783	33,651	1,153
1925	--------	13,280	329
1928	--------	27,705	189
1930	23,196	11,834	372

Source: James Duffy, *Portuguese Africa* (Cambridge, Mass.: Harvard University Press, 1961), 265.

company/*prazo* system, Portugal's colonialism was accomplished indirectly, by means of imperialism; the empire was leased to enterprising foreigners. There was, of course, direct colonization and exploitation, but it is undeniable that during the coalition's regime, Portugal was an imperialistic landlord, not a colonialist in the usual term of the word.

Republican Colonial Policies

The First Portuguese Republic, faced with the old problems of colonialism, implemented new and more liberal policies in its African territories and terminated old, and granted new, concessions. The old problems were a lack of capital and a lack of people willing to emigrate to the colonies. Table 4.2 shows that between 1908 and 1930, emigration to Brazil was much more common than to the African territories.

The Republic's policies on overseas territories showed more concern with the empire, an interest in developing a more profitable colonialism, and, at the same time, a colonial policy based on extensive decentralization under the supervision of the mother country. In the Constitution of 1911, the words "colony" and "province" were used to refer to the overseas territories. But Foreign Minister Bernardino Machado (1910–1911) revealed a "patrimonial" notion of colonialism when he "stated that the new government regarded the Overseas dominions as a patrimony as sacred as the territory of the motherland itself" (Marques 1972, 225).

The policy of decentralization called for granting administrative autonomy in Angola and in Mozambique to local (European) authorities. This autonomy was to be formally extended under an Organic Charter for the Colonies, implementation of which was postponed until after World War I. The best-known spokesman for the Republic's "new look" toward Africa was Norton de Matos, governor-general of Angola from 1912 to 1915 and from 1921 to 1924. Reflecting the views of the Republic, Norton de Matos opposed de facto slavery, forced labor, and corporal punishment, and he believed that every African farmer was entitled to the full ownership of his farming plot. But, on behalf of the Republic, Norton de Matos granted important privileges to the concessionary Diamong (Angola Diamond Company, founded in 1917 with Belgian, French, English, American, and Portuguese capital). Thus, one wonders if de Matos' "liberal" views were genuine or simply in tune with the needs of the more profitable mineral (diamond) concessions. Diamong had "exclusive rights to diamond extraction all over the colony and extensive authority over several thousand square miles. It organized its own police system, built its own road system, and created its own towns" (Marques 1972, 248).

THE EMPIRE AND THE REACTIONARY COALITION

Metaphysical Colonialism

The prevailing characteristic of the Portuguese empire, an "empire without imperialism" (Figueiredo 1961), did not really change with the formation of the reactionary coalition's Estado Novo. The policy of the Estado Novo regarding the overseas territories was to recodify colonial laws, cancel the Republic's policies of colonial autonomy/decentralization, and to establish closer diplomatic relations with South Africa. But the Estado Novo's theorizing on, and explaining of, Portugal's "mission in Africa" was another matter.

With the coalition's seizure of power and the formation of the Estado Novo, the Republic's experiment in decentralization was replaced with a centralized administrative system. A new term, *Império Colonial Português* (Portuguese colonial empire), appeared in the official terminology (Marques 1972, 227). Moreover, the reactionary coalition ideologues began explaining to the nation and to the world Portugal's mission in Africa. Although not capable of engaging in real imperialism, Portugal could be active in "metaphysical imperialism." Salazar stated:

I have in mind now the great old figures of Portuguese colonization. They pass back and forth in my memory, these men of yesterday and those of today, the soldiers and administrators of the public trust in Africa and the East. . . . [the 1930s colonial legislation is] a perfect expression of our national consciousness, and a close affirmation of the colonizing temperament of the Portuguese . . . [it is designed] for the aggrandizement of Portugal . . . and to make clear to the rest of Europe our position as a great colonial power. . . . (quoted in Duffy 1961, 270)

And Armindo Monteiro, minister of colonies in the early 1930s, observed:

It is often said that we Portuguese have the vice of history. Some even say that we take refuge in the past to compensate for the smallness of the present-day, obeying the doleful law of empire corroded by stagnation and decadence. In Portugal, however, we now feel that we are so much the legitimate heirs of a great tradition that the generation of today is entitled to invoke the past not as a remembrance of dead things, but as a source of inspiration for the future. (quoted in Duffy 1961, 269)

The periodical *O Mundo Português* (The Portuguese World) in 1935 carried in an editorial:

We must always keep alive in the Portuguese people the dream of beyond-the-seas and the consciousness and pride of the Empire. Africa is more than a land to be exploited . . . Africa is for us a moral justification and a raison d'être as a power. Without it we would be a small nation; with it we are a great country. (Bender 1978, 6)

The reactionary coalition's imperial ideology accomplished two noncolonialist tasks. First, it presented Portuguese colonialism as the embodiment of "altruism, abnegation, faith and a historic responsibility of civilization," instead of exploitation, oppression, and subjugation of African peoples (Bender 1978, 6). Hence, Portuguese colonialism was a unique type of colonialism, different from, for instance, British colonialism. Second, the coalition succeeded in producing a national pride in the empire, even though the pride was "manufactured not by machines but by the tip of the [ideological] pen." Portuguese "metaphysical imperialism" stood for "the glorification of the past and the importance of Portugal's accomplishments," which included the "Mission in Africa" of bringing civilization to the African peoples (Bender 1978, 6).

The Colonial Act and Other Colonial Legislation

In 1928, the Portuguese colonies were gradually incorporated into the Estado Novo. The neoimperialism of the coalition was stipulated in legislative documents: the Colonial Act of 1930, and the Organic Charter and the Administrative Overseas Reform Act of 1933. In these documents, the coalition affirmed Portugal's imperial destiny, stipulated how the empire was to benefit the mother country, and required a more formal relationship between the colonies and the continental government. The Colonial Act of 1930, considered to be the constitution for the overseas territories, was the brainchild of Salazar, who in 1930 was minister of colonies.

Article 2 of the Colonial Act affirmed that "to the organic essence of the Portuguese Nation [belonged] the historical mission of possessing and colonizing overseas dominions, as well as civilizing the native populations encompassed by them." Article 5 stated that the Portuguese colonial empire was interdependent in its several parts and with the mother country. Article 12 terminated the practice of granting concessions, but allowed the existing ones to continue until the contracts expired. Article 20 extended to the state the right to force natives to labor "in public works of general interest for the community, in occupations the result of which belongs to them, in execution of penal judiciary decision, or the fulfillment of fiscal obligations." Article 22 dealt with "special Status" for the natives, and their stage of civilization (Marques 1972, 227).

The Colonial Act was modified in 1935, 1945, and 1951, when it was incorporated into the Constitution of 1933. The incorporation was motivated by the reactionary coalition's desire to show the world that the mother country and the overseas territories were bound by a common constitutional entity. The coalition's additional colonial legislation was the Organic Charter of 1933 and the Administrative Overseas Reform Act of 1933. The charter was modified in 1935, 1937, and 1946. In 1955 it was replaced by the *Lei Orgânica do Ultramar Português* (Organic Law), which in turn was replaced by the Statute of the Portuguese Natives of the Provinces of Guinea, Angola, and Mozambique.

In the early 1950s anticolonialism began to emerge. The United Nations initiated a program under which members with colonial territories were asked to submit reports regarding their management. To render the Charter of the United Nations inapplicable to its colonies, the reactionary coalition amended the Constitution of 1933. The Colonial Act was incorporated into the constitution as Title 7, under the heading ''On the Portuguese Overseas.'' The words ''colony'' and ''colonial'' were replaced with ''overseas provinces'' and ''overseas.'' Henceforth, Portugal was no longer a de jure colonial power, for it no longer had colonies. Portugal comprised continental and overseas territories.

Article 134 of the constitution stated, ''The overseas territories of Portugal are given the generic name ''provinces'' and have a politico-administrative organization suitable to their geographic situation and their . . . social environment.'' Article 135 read, ''The overseas provinces as an integral part of the Portuguese state are linked to each other and to the metropolis.'' Article 136 noted that ''The solidarity between the overseas provinces and the metropolis includes especially the obligation of making an appropriate contribution to guarantee the integrity and defense of the Nation as a whole (Duffy 1961, 280).

Uneconomic Imperialism

In spite of ideological rhetoric about Portugal's ''mission in Africa,'' in reality the colonialism of the reactionary coalition was no different from the colonialism of the Republic and the monarchy that had preceded it. Portugal's imperialism was always characterized by ''uneconomic imperialism'' (Hammond 1966). That is, as a nation, Portugal and, more important, the majority of its people did not benefit from colonialism. Only a few continentals and foreigners could allocate the gains of colonial exploitation to themselves. This is why Portugal remained Western Europe's poorest country, with a rate of emigration second only to Ireland, until 1974.

Two factors explain Portuguese uneconomic imperialism. First, when the reactionary coalition seized power, Portugal was an underdeveloped nation. Consequently, it lacked the structure and resources to exploit its colonial empire by investing heavily and by building necessary infrastructures. Portugal ''never had the resources to export serious amounts of fixed capital to its colonies,'' and there never was ''a real technological investment of the colonial terrain''

Table 4.3
Distribution of Work Force in Three Small Colonial Powers (percent)

Country		Primary Sector	Secondary Sector	Tertiary Sector
Belgium (1)	(1957)	11	49	37
Holland	(1957)	19	30	41
Portugal	(1950)	50	24	26

(1) With a population almost exactly the same as Portugal's, nine million.

Source: Perry Anderson, "Portugal and the End of Ultra-Colonialism," *New Left Review* (1962), no. 15:84.

(Anderson 1962, pt. 2, 98). The backwardness of Portugal's economic structure is easily discernible if we compare the distribution of the work force in several European colonial powers.

Table 4.3 shows the degree of Portuguese economic backwardness in the 1950s. Portugal was then an agricultural country. In 1950, half of the labor force worked in the primary sector and the level of industrialization was extremely low, with heavy industry virtually nonexistent. Hence, the metropolis of the Portuguese empire could engage only in limited exploitation of its satellites.

The second factor that explains Portugal's uneconomic imperialism was the reactionary coalition's aversion to competitive, liberal economic development and industrialization. The economy of the coalition had its base in agriculture, which required a specific social organization. Therefore the reactionary coalition implemented an economy designed "to freeze the social structure in a way that maintained the hegemony of a backward and neo-feudal ruling class" (Lomax 1983, 110).

In my view, the coalition was, in a way, following Portuguese precedents. While it is true that the coalition rejected a liberal capitalist society, this rejection was more in agreement than in disagreement with historical–structural antecedents. The First Republic had been only a concession, an experiment. To paraphrase Marx, the past was indeed on the backs of the coalition's members.

In the language of positivist sociology, the central explanatory (independent) variables of economic backwardness in the metropolis and of uneconomic imperialism in the satellites (the dependent variables) are as follows. First, at the beginning of the eighteenth century, Portugal entered into commercial agreements with England. The Methuen Treaty, signed by England and Portugal in 1703, established specific trade practices between the two countries. Under the treaty, English textiles had free entry into Portugal, and Portuguese wines had preferential entry into England. Soon, however, the terms and conditions of the treaty became advantageous to English cloth manufacturing industries and disastrous for the Portuguese economy. The development of the Portuguese textile industry was arrested. Land exploitation and land labor were shifted from basic food production to viticulture.

This shift in the use of land was eventually serious enough to cause increases in the importation of food and a deficit in the balance of trade. Portugal, a country with a colonial empire, become a dependent country, a satellite of English economic interests. "In sum, the Methuen Treaty made the final arrangements and gave explicit juridical status to a qualitative gap that had opened up between Great Britain and Portugal and consolidated Portugal's position as a dependent primary [goods] producer" (O'Brien 1974, 21–22).

Second, Portugal's dependence on England had consequences for the Portuguese class structure and class struggle. The rather small and weak capitalist class of the eighteenth century represented a threat first to the monarchy and later to the nonmodern agriculture-based hegemonic sector. To maintain its political hegemony, its existence, and its economic interests, the monarchy and, later, the reactionary coalition were willing to "subordinate [the interests of the nation] to the international interests of the British bourgeoisie" in exchange for "British political support" (O'Brien 1974, 22). And political support they received. Portugal never experienced a truly bourgeois revolution. Instead, Portugal remained underdeveloped, dependent, and the poorest country in Western Europe.

Both before and after the reactionary coalition seized power, the British commercial and industrial interests in Portugal, with the cooperation of the Portuguese *comprador* (ruling) class, blocked autochthonous possibilities for the development of competitive industrial capitalism, for the transformation of Portugal into a modern nation. The economy of continental Portugal and of its colonial empire became subordinated to the interests of British capitalists. Not only did continental Portugal become a market for British manufactured products, but the production of native port wine and cork (two major exports) became, and has remained, controlled by British enterprises. Moreover, transportation and communication systems were installed and run by British companies. The Portuguese colonial empire became de facto an extension of the British empire. British capital was involved in mining, commerce, communications, and transportation. Most of the Portuguese African railway systems were built with British capital (Tanganyika Concessions, Ltd.).

Portugal, due to its economic colonization by Great Britain, never has been able to achieve a significant measure of industrialization, and has therefore never been able to realize the transformation of its imperial enterprise into the type of colonial system which evolved elsewhere in Africa. Without industry, Portugal had no need for large African markets for cheap industrial products, much less outlets for quantities of capital. (O'Brien 1974, 29)

British–Portuguese trade relations were characterized by the asymmetries of core–periphery relations. And such relations rendered Portugal a de facto colony of England (Sideri 1970; Pereira 1971).

Table 4.4
Angolan Population by Race and "Civilized" Status, 1940 and 1950

Race	Total Population	Total "Civilized"	Percent "Civilized"
1940			
African	3,665,829	24,221	0.7
Mestizo	28,035	23,244	82.9
White	44,083	44,083	100.0
1950			
African	4,036,689	30,089	0.7
Mestizo	29,648	26,335	88.8
White	78,826	78,826	100.0

Source: G. F. Bender, *Angola under the Portuguese: The Myth and the Reality* (London: Heinemann, 1978), 151.

Economic Exploitation

Forced Labor

The colonial rhetoric of the reactionary coalition referred to Portugal's historical "mission" of bringing civilization to the African people. In reality, however, civilization was not what Portugal brought to Africa. Portuguese colonialists exploited the native population and considered it to be intrinsically inferior to Europeans. In fact, "Portugal's self-adulation over 'civilizing mission' was dependent upon that inferiority" (Bender 1978, 7).

Vincent Ferreira, a former high commissioner and governor of Angola, stated:

These so-called civilized Africans, all colonial sociologists have recognized, are generally no more than grotesque imitations of white man. With rare exceptions . . . the "civilized African" maintains a primitive mentality, poorly concealed by the speech, gestures and dress copied from Europeans. (quoted in Bender 1978, 7)

The existence of cultural racism and social inequality was reflected in the practice of dividing the population into the categories of *indígena* and *non-indígena* (whites and assimilated Africans or mulattoes). The assimilated African was, according to the Native Code of 1921, the African who could speak Portuguese, had abandoned his or her tribal customs, and worked regularly. Table 4.4 shows the distribution of the Angolan population by race and by "civilized" status, (*assimilado* or *non-indigena*). The distribution of the population in four other colonies in 1959 is presented in Table 4.5.

Instead of carrying out its "historic mission" of bringing civilization to the African people, the Portuguese brought discrimination and exploitation. The African population was treated "as little more than a resource of unpaid labor" (Bender 1978, 149). The historic and systematic practice of forced labor char-

Table 4.5
Population Distribution in Four Colonies by "Civilized" Status, 1959

Colony	Noncivilized	Civilized	Percent
Guinea	502,457	1,478	0.2
Sao Tome	16,747	37,950	70.0
Mozambique	5,646,957	25,149	0.4
Timor	434,907	1,541	0.4

Source: Instituto Nacional de Estatística (1959), quoted in Antonio de Figueiredo, *Portugal and Its Empire: The Truth* (London: Victor Gollancz, 1961), 93.

acterized Portuguese colonial exploitation. "It is this [systematic use of forced labor] which immediately identifies the Portuguese variant of colonialism as against all others" (Anderson 1962, pt. 2, 149). The first decree on forced labor applied to the African colonial population was issued in 1899. It stipulated that all able-bodied adult male *indígenas* were required to work at productive activities. The definition of "productive" was, of course, determined by the colonial authorities. By the early 1960s, there were six categories of African labor (excluding labor for subsistence): (1) correctional labor; (2) obligatory labor; (3) contract (forced) labor; (4) voluntary labor; (5) forced cultivation; (6) emigrant (export) labor (O'Brien 1974, 27).

Correctional labor was prescribed for Africans who violated the criminal law or labor codes. In Mozambique, this type of labor was also imposed as a penalty for failure to pay the native head tax. (In Angola, the penalty for nonpayment of that tax was obligatory labor.)

Obligatory labor was imposed by the government when there were not enough "voluntary" workers for public works projects (port installation, railroads, sanitation works, etc.). Those under the age of fourteen and over sixty, and those who were sick or invalids, were exempt. Also exempt were employed Africans, tribal chiefs, and workers who had been at home for less than six months from the date of their last contract work. Although women and children were excused from this type of labor, their use was common.

Rural roads are invariably built and maintained by the unpaid conscripted labor of the people of the area through which the road passes. These people have to furnish not only their labor, but also their food, and often enough also their own tools. Since many men are absent on forced labor elsewhere, [the] local chief or herdsman, in whose hands responsibility for the road is left, will frequently call up women and quite small children. That is why one sees women with babies on their backs, and pregnant women and quite small girls, scraping at roads with primitive hoes and carrying cupfuls of earth in little bark containers on their heads. (Davidson 1955; quoted in Anderson 1962, pt. 2, 89).

A significant report on forced labor was presented to the National Assembly by Colonial High Commissioner Henrique Galvão: "To cover the deficit [of local colonies] the most shameful outrages are committed, including forced labor of independent self-employed workers, of women, of children, of the sick, of decrepit old men, etc. . . . Only the dead are really exempt from forced labor'' (Galvão 1949; quoted in Bender 1978, 143).

Contract labor was the most economically important form of forced labor in the Portuguese colonies. Any African who could not prove that he had been employed for at least six months of the previous year was liable to contract (compulsory) labor for the state or for a private employer. In Mozambique, an African could prove that he was not "idle" if he was employed permanently by the state, administrative Corps, or industry; had been, within the last six months, working in the Union of South Africa or in Rhodesia under a legal contract; or had completed active military duty and was still within the prescribed twelve months of reserve status. In Angola, every able-bodied *indígena* had to be able to show proof of employment. Moreover, the state could force *indígenas* to work if (a) they owed taxes; (b) if they were deemed to be incapable of satisfying minimal needs of subsistence for themselves and their families; or (c) if they resided in dwellings considered unfit for human habitation.

In view of the ambiguity and vagueness of the official language, the ultimate criterion for being "not idle" was "prior integration in the colonial and administrative system." Such a criterion subjected 95 percent or more of the *indígena* population in both Angola and Mozambique to forced labor.

Voluntary labor called for contracts between workers and employers without interference of, or recruitment by, the government. The main difference between this type of labor and contract labor was that in voluntary labor, *indígenas* worked in the region where they lived.

Under forced cultivation, formerly African-owned land was expropriated, removed from the subsistence economy, and converted into plantations and estates for growing cash crops, such as cotton, to meet the needs of monopolistic concessionaires. The latter gave seed to the Africans and forced them to cultivate cotton on the concessionaire's land. Later, the African picked the cotton and sold it to the concessionaire at "fixed prices quite below free market levels." Within concessionary estates where forced cultivation was practiced, no other form of wage labor was permitted.

Migrant labor was the type of forced labor that gave colonial administrations vast revenues. The Mozambique–Transvaal agreement was signed in 1909 and reviewed in 1928, 1934, and 1940. By the early 1960s, the agreement called for a maximum import of 100,000 *indígenas* from Mozambique to the Transvaal gold mines in exchange for the use of the port of Lourenço Marques, 47.5 percent of all seasonal imports to the Johannesburg area, and 340,000 cases of citrus fruit exported from South Africa. Moreover, the Witwatersrand Native Labor Association paid the Mozambique government about U.S.$5.00 for each contract recruit, and forwarded to that government half of the recruits' wages, to be disbursed to them upon their return at the end of the eighteen-month contract period. For both South Africa and the Mozambique government, migrant labor was a profitable form of a capital accumulation. In Angola, *indígenas* were

Table 4.6
Forced Labor in Angola and Mozambique, 1954

Angola	
Contractual labor	379,000
Voluntary labor	400,000
Total	779,000
Mozambique	
Cotton conscripts	519,000
Contracted agricultural workers	100,000
Migrant contracted workers	400,000
Total	1,019,000

Note: In 1954 the total labor force in Mozambique was 2,094,000 (incuding migrant workers).
Source: Perry Anderson, "Portugal and the End of Ultra-Colonialism," *New Left Review* (1962), no. 16: 96.

recruited for labor in Northern Rhodesia and South-West Africa. The rate of import labor from Angola was between 15,000 and 20,000 per year (Anderson 1962, pt. 2, 93). (See Table 4.6.)

Not interested in social change or in economic, political, or social development, and much interested in capital accumulation and profit maximization, the reactionary coalition expropriated the surplus value from indigenous workers through forced labor. Anderson is absolutely correct in affirming that "Forced labor in the Portuguese colonies [was] the most extreme form of exploitation existent anywhere in Africa. Its human regime [was] a degradation beyond anything that any other colonialism has produced" (1962, pt. 2, 97).

Cotton

Within the limitations of its underdeveloped economic system, Portugal followed the classic British model of colonial exploitation. A raw material, cotton, was produced in its African colonies, exported to the Continent, and shipped back to the colonies as a finished, manufactured product. Until the early 1900s the rather small and weak Portuguese textile industry imported most of its cotton from foreign countries. In 1925, the annual cotton requirement was approximately seventeen thousand tons. Angola and Mozambique supplied only eight hundred tons. In 1926, the Portuguese continental authorities established cotton as a cash crop in both Angola and Mozambique. Areas were designated as cotton producers, and the inhabitants were forced to cultivate cotton.

In Northern Mozambique, the main crop is cotton. Twelve Portuguese companies have monopoly concessions over the whole area within the territory. Africans are given seed by the companies, assigned acreage quotas by the administration, and must cultivate cotton on their land. . . . The land forcibly converted to cotton is subtracted from the subsistence economy. (Anderson 1962, pt. 2, 97)

The African producers sold the cotton to the monopolistic concessions at a very low price. ''In 1958, the crop was bought from the producers at the rate of 2.70 [Portuguese] escudos a kilogram, while on the world market it would fetch a price of 20–25 escudos per kilogram'' (First 1973, 5). At the beginning of World War II, Africa was satisfying 30 percent of Portugal's cotton requirements, and by 1950 it satisfied 95 percent. Africa had by then become the main supplier of extremely low-priced cotton for the Portuguese textile industry. Forced cultivation yielded high rates of profit for the monopolistic companies and severe losses for the African producer, for whom the consequence of growing a cash crop was hunger.

Such a phenomenal rise [in cotton production] . . . had an immediate boomerang effect on reducing almost equally phenomenally the natural native crops. Groundnuts, maize, manioc, kaffir corn, and beans all reached almost famine production figures in the North of the colony. (Harris 1958; quoted in Anderson 1962, pt. 2, 92).

Alcohol

Another example of Portuguese colonial exploitation was the trade in alcohol between Portugal and the colonies. In order to assure the monopoly of the market for alcoholic beverages in Portuguese Africa, Portugal passed a law in 1902 that prohibited the manufacture and sale of rum by Europeans, and the making of native beverages (Bender 1978, 145; Figueiredo 1961, 62). Until 1960, wine was Angola's number one import. In 1947, Angola imported wine from continental Portugal valued at 98,249,000 Portuguese escudos. Between 1934 and 1969 more than two-thirds of Portuguese wine exports went to Angola and Mozambique. In 1969, these two colonies imported 86.6 million and 37 million liters of wine, respectively. Portuguese exports of wine to foreign markets, in the same year, was about 70 million liters (United Nations 1971; quoted in Bender 1978, 147). In fact, because wine was available and cheap, alcoholism ''became one of Angola's principal social problems'' (Bender 1978, 147).

Monopolies and Foreign Capital

The economic activities and power of the forty-four Portuguese families who controlled the economic cartels or groups included the Portuguese empire. They were very active in the direct and indirect exploitation of the empire in general and of Africa in particular. These families were the beneficiaries of Portuguese colonialism, for while Portugal and the majority of the hardworking people profited little from the resources of the empire, the reactionary coalition, and some segments of the petite bourgeoisie, gained immensely from the ''uneconomic imperialism.'' For example, Guinea-Bissau was for all practical purposes an economic fiefdom of Companhia União Fabril (CUF).

Monopolistic groups involved in Portuguese African economic activities were the following:

Companhia União Fabril (CUF)—Banco Totta-Standard de Angola; A. Silvia (agribusiness, Angola); Companhia Textil do Pungue (Mozambique); Cicomo (agribusiness, Mozambique); Companhia Nacional de Navegação (shipping line)

Espírito Santo—Sociedade Agrícola do Cassaquel (sugar production, Angola); Sociedade Agrícola do Incomati (sugar production, Mozambique); Companhia Angolana de Agricultura (coffee production, Angola); Companhia de Algodão de Mozambique (cotton); Petrangol (oil exploration, Angola); Purfina (oil exploration, Angola); Nocal (beer, Mozambique); Sonap (oil exploration, Mozambique); Sonarep (oil exploration); Companhia de Seguros Tranquilidade de Mozambique (insurance); Banco Interunido (Angola)

A. de Champalimaud—Companhia de Cimentos de Mozambique; Companhia de Cimentos de Angola; Siderurgia de Angola (steel production); Banco Pinto & Sotto-Mayor (Mozambique, twenty-six branches); Banco Pinto & Sotto-Mayor (Angola, fifty-one branches); Companhia de Seguros Mundial (insurance, Angola and Mozambique); Companhia de Seguros Confiança (insurance, Angola and Mozambique)

Banco Nacional Ultramarino—Banco Nacional Ultramarino (the issuing bank for the colonies); Companhia de Cimentos Secil do Ultramar (Angola); Companhia Geral de Algodões (cotton, Angola); Companhia de Seguros Náuticos (maritime insurance, Angola); Companhia de Seguros Lusitana (insurance, Angola); Companhia Fidelidade Atlántica (insurance, Angola)

Banco Português do Atlântico—Banco Commercial de Angola; Sociedade Hidroelétrica do Reve (Angola); Petrangol (oil exploration, Angola); Sociedade Algodeira de Fomento Colonial (cotton, Mozambique)

Banco Borges & Irmão—banking branches in Angola and Mozambique, tire production in association with Mabor

Foreign ownership of businesses in Portuguese Africa was as follows:

Caminho de Ferro de Benguela (railway)—90 percent owned by Tanganyika Concessions, Ltd.

Diamong (mining, Angola)—de Beers Consolidated Mines, (South Africa), Anglo-American Corporation of South Africa (capital is British, Belgian, U.S., South African)

Companhia Carbonífera de Mozambique (mining)—60 percent owned by Société de Recherches Minières de Sud-Katanga (Belgian)

Lobito Fuel Oil Co.—70 percent owned by Compagnie Financière Belge des Pétroles

Sacor and Sonap—associated with Compagnie Française des Pétroles

Petrangol and Purifina—branches of Petrofina (Belgian and Dutch capital)

Companhia Agrícola de Angola—80 percent owned by the French group Rallet & Cie

Companhia Geral dos Algodões—majority ownership by the Belgian group Lanuvit

Table 4.7
Continental Portugal's Net Balance of Payments with the Colonies, 1964–1971
(millions of escudos)

	1964	1965	1966	1967	1971
Current transactions	3221	3224	2102	3923	553
Merchandise	1460	2165	1519	2512	448
Foreign travel	354	449	332	483	789
Transportation	134	188	132	174	186
Insurance	25	30	25	36	22
Investment income	689	826	476	660	723
Government	-1482	-2072	-1655	-1763	-2619
Other services	331	401	88	61	149
Private transfers	1710	1237	1185	1760	837
Capital movements	-1328	-250	-83	-1501	-561
Short-term	109	62	-91	-565	12
Long-term	-1437	-312	8	-936	-573
Private	-38	39	-92	-645	-123
Official	-1399	-351	100	-261	-450
Errors and omissions	-32	-29	-17	-5	-174
Total	1861	2945	2002	2417	-200

Source: Bank of Portugal, Report of the Board of Directors for 1964, 1967 and 1971 (Lisbon, 1965, 1968, 1972), quoted in Eric N. Baklanoff, *The Economic Transformation of Portugal and Spain* (New York: Praeger, 1978), 109.

Banco Standard-Totta de Mozambique and Banco Standard-Totta de Angola—associated with the Standard Bank of South Africa

Banco Commercial de Angola—associated with Barclays Bank International (England)

Banco Interunido—45 percent owned by First National City Bank (United States)

Matola Oil Refinery (Mozambique)—Procon (British and U.S. capital)

Gulf Oil Co. (Angola)—Chase Manhattan National Bank and First National City Bank of New York

According to data for selected years, the economic relationship between continental Portugal and the colonies was profitable to the monopolistic groups and segments of the petite bourgeoisie, despite "uneconomic imperialism."

The data in Tables 4.7 and 4.8 clearly indicate that continental Portugal's balance of payments with the colonies yielded surpluses in the current account (with positive merchandise balances) and deficits in the government expenditures (amounting to 4.1 billion escudos in 1972) and long-term capital accounts. But, perhaps more revealing of the importance of the colonies for the hegemonic class fractions and some segments of the petite bourgeoisie were (a) income from accumulated direct investments, (b) private remittances by Portuguese colonialists, and (c) receipts from transportation and other services. All of these were

Table 4.8
Continental Portugal's Net Balance of Payments with the Colonies, 1972–1976
(millions of escudos)

	1972	1973	1974	1975	1976
Current transactions	3667	83	-3247	2423	1993
Merchandise	2110	172	-4444	-302	-350
Foreign travel	653	1031	1781	1893	284
Transportation	142	186	378	99	-150
Insurance	59	55	78	27	-6
Investment income	901	1242	1262	14	-12
Government	-2436	-4090	-4979	-3017	973
Other services	301	-------	487	-69	201
Private transfers	1947	1487	2190	3778	1053
Capital movements	-4555	1846	5498	3162	1777
Short-term	-196	4011	6664	2647	1590
Long-term	-4359	-2165	-1166	515	187
Private	-244	-90	233	1005	191
Official	-4115	-2075	-1399	-34	-4
Errors and omissions	237	-43	37	11	-47
Total	-641	1886	2288	5596	3723

Note: The former Portuguese colonies were returned to African nationals in 1974 and 1975.
Source: Bank of Portugal, Report of the Board of Directors, for 1972–1976 Lisbon, 1973–1977,
quoted in Eric N. Baklanoff, *The Economic Transformation of Portugal and Spain* (New
York: Praeger, 1978), 109.

consistently high. Income from investment totaled 689 million escudos in 1964 and 1.262 billion in 1974. Private transfers (remittances) totaled 1.710 billion escudos in 1964, 2.190 billion in 1974, and 3.778 billion in 1975, shortly before the independence of the colonies. The latter were also a good source of income for non-Portuguese enterprises.

Since the eighteenth century, Portugal had been a satellite of Great Britain. The relationship of satellite-metropolis, of unequal exchange, was extended to the Portuguese colonial empire. The latter was Portuguese de jure, but British de facto in terms of industrial exploitation. Concessionary monopolies were granted to British concerns in both Angola and Mozambique. In the latter colony, British capital owned two of the three largest concessions, including the Sena Estates. In Angola, the diamond company Diamong was the best example of British ownership and exploitation in the Portuguese colonial empire. Founded in 1917, its concession contract was extended in 1955 by the reactionary coalition for an indefinite period of time. Diamong occupied an area of 1,025,700 square miles and was itself an empire within an empire. It had exclusive property rights and paid no taxes, no import duties on machinery, and no export duties on diamonds. Diamong was also the largest private employer of African labor in Angola. In 1955, Diamong agreed to give the Portuguese government 11 percent of its capital stock (Duffy 1961, 339). During the period 1953–1957, the reactionary coalition received U.S.$16,870,000 in dividends and bonuses.

Although Diamong was mainly British and Belgian, other international concerns also owned stock in the company: Anglo-American Corporation (South Africa), Oppenheimer Group, Morgan Bank, de Beers (South Africa), Guggenheim, T. F. Ryan, Forainière, Union Minière de Haut-Katanga, Guaranty Trust Bank, and the Société Générale de Belgique (Anderson 1962, pt.2, 170).

For a very long time, Portugal had a rich and vast empire. But the beneficiaries of that empire, the ones who took the lion's share, were, with the exception of a few Portuguese nationals, foreigners. "The massive role of foreign capital in the exploitation of the Portuguese colonial resources [was] unmistakable . . . [the reactionary coalition] ensure[d] the bureaucratic and military conditions of profitability, and [was] paid in return" (Anderson 1962, pt. 2, 70).

THE BEGINNING OF THE FALL

U.N. Decolonization

Three events shook the Portuguese empire in the mid–1950s. First, European colonial powers gave independence to their colonies. The British, the French, and the Belgians began the decolonization of their African colonies. New African states were emerging, and they made possible the creation of anticolonial liberation movements. Second, the Indian government began pressuring Portugal for a solution on the Portuguese Indian possessions of Gôa, Damão, and Díu. Finally, in the United States, anticolonial views were developing. In 1956 and 1957 the legal status of the Portuguese colonies was discussed at sessions of the United Nations. Several Arab and Asian nations, with the support of the Soviet Union, began suggesting that the Portuguese overseas possessions were not self-governed territories. Consequently, under Chapter XI of the U.N. Charter, Portugal was obligated to provide the United Nations with periodic technical reports on its overseas territories.

The reactionary coalition then initiated a position/policy that was to last until the fall of the empire, including thirteen years of colonial war in three colonies. According to the coalition, Chapter XI of the U.N. Charter did not apply to Portugal because its overseas territories were provinces, not colonies, and as such were political extensions of continental Portugal, governed under and subject to the same constitution. The privileges of the continental and overseas provinces were similar. Hence, Portugal should not be required to supply periodic reports on its provinces. Many people rejected the coalition's self-serving argument, and one of the first to seek negotiations for decolonization was Nehru.

India (Gôa, Damão, Díu, Dadra, and Nagar-Haveli)

The Portuguese possession of Indian territories dated back to 1510. Until the departure of the British from India in 1947, Portugal had a good relationship with the Indian authorities. But after decolonization of India, nationalists began demanding the incorporation of the Portuguese enclaves into the nation of India. In 1954, Indian President Nehru submitted to the reactionary coalition proposals for a negotiated decolonization of the enclaves. The coalition refused the proposals, and made it known that the status of its Indian provinces was unchangeable, and thus not negotiable. To the coalition, Gôa, Damão, Díu, Dadra, and Nagar-Haveli were Portuguese, not Indian.

At 4:00 A.M. on December 18, 1961, Indian armed forces invaded Gôa by land, sea, and air. The small and poorly armed Portuguese garrisons were no match for the thirty thousand Indian troops. Less than forty hours later, Gôa, Damão, Díu, Dadra, and Nagar-Haveli were no longer Portuguese enclaves. Four centuries of occupation came to an end. Salazar held the military responsible for the loss of the Indian enclaves, and initiated a court-martial for the military commander in India, General Vassalo e Silva. Although the court-martial was later dropped because of pressure from the military, Salazar's reaction was not forgotten. The loss of the Indian enclaves was the beginning of the fall of the Portuguese empire.

Africa

The fall of the Portuguese empire in Africa began with the independence of other European colonies, for anticolonial movements of liberation could find sanctuaries in the newly independent African nations. Liberation movements erupted in the Portuguese African colonies of Guinea-Bissau, Angola, and Mozambique in the early 1960s. The first revolt erupted in Luanda, the capital of Angola, in February 1961. The following months witnessed massive and violent rural uprisings. Armed Africans killed hundreds of white settlers. In 1963, uprisings began in Guinea-Bissau, and in Mozambique in the following year. By 1964, Portugal was facing various anticolonial and nationalist groups: in Guinea-Bissau, Partido Africano da Independência de Guiné e Cabo-Verde; in Angola, Frente Nacional de Libertação de Angola and Movimento Popular de Libertação de Angola; in Mozambique, Frente de Libertação de Moçambique.

Initially, the Portuguese response to the uprisings was counterinsurgency measures, with particular emphasis on increased repression. The colonial army of three thousand men in early 1961 was increased to more than fifty thousand troops by the end of the year. Thousands of Africans were killed by the troops or detained in camps by the PIDE.[1] The latter became quite active in Africa, running networks of informers. From 1964 to 1974, Portugal was engaged in war on three fronts against native movements demanding the liberation and independence of their lands. To wage war in its African colonies, Portugal increased its colonial army from 3,000 men in 1961 to almost 220,000 by 1972. The cost of the war was extremely high, but the reactionary coalition was willing to defend and to keep the empire at all costs. Portugal would not follow in the steps of Belgium, France, and England.

In conjunction with counterinsurgency measures, Portugal responded to the uprisings with major social changes designed to win the loyalty of the African population. Six months after the outbreak of the violent demonstrations against Portuguese rule, Portugal enacted several laws, five of which were designed to (1) repeal the status of *indigenato*, thereby abolishing the distinction between *indígenas* ("noncivilized," noncitizens, a category that represented more than 90 percent of the African population) and "civilized" citizens, which in 1950 included all whites, 89 percent of the *mestiços*, and 0.7 percent of the Africans; (2) increase the regulation of land concessions and occupation; (3) organize local African administrative bodies; (4) coordinate "general" and customary laws; (5) create the Provincial Settlement Board of Angola and Mozambique. The decrees also abolished forced labor (Bender 1978, 109).

Within a few months after the outbreak of the wars of liberation, Portugal implemented more social reforms than it had done in a hundred years. But the social reforms arrived too late, for the wars were to last more than ten years, and the empire was to fall.

THE AFRICAN WARS

The Cost

For analytical purposes, one must divide the cost of the wars into the tangible material cost and the cost in terms of changes the wars brought to the society built and maintained by the reactionary coalition from 1928 to 1961. Between 1961 and 1974 the wars against the African nationalists consumed almost half of the annual budget. By 1973, the cost of maintaining an operational army of more than two hundred thousand (including seventy thousand in Angola, sixty thousand in Mozambique, and forty thousand in Guinea-Bissau) amounted to 48 percent of total public expenditures. Portugal, the poorest country in Western Europe, was spending U.S.$425 million per year on the military. In contrast, South Africa, "with a gross national product three times that of Portugal," in the same year spent "about the same amount (U.S. $448 million)" (Maxwell 1982, 342). With a per capita income of just over U.S.$1,000, Portugal in 1973 was spending a "minimum per capita amount of 63.27 U.S. dollars on military expenditures" (Harsgor 1976, 13).

In continental Portugal there were two phases in the development of the capitalist mode of production: the phase that lasted until World War II, and the phase that commenced during the war years. In the Portuguese colonial empire, particularly its African colonies, there also were two specific phases. One phase existed until the liberation and nationalist uprisings of 1961. The second began in 1961 and lasted until the fall of the empire in 1974.

Until 1960, Portuguese exploitation of Africa followed, within the limitations imposed by the economy, the classical model of colonialism: extraction of raw materials in the colonies, transformation of raw materials into finished goods on

Table 4.9
Metropolitan Portugal's Exports and Imports, 1968–1972 (percentages)

Exports to	1968	1969	1970	1971	1972
All foreign markets	75.02	75.21	75.50	78.55	85.30
All overseas territories	24.98	24.79	24.50	21.45	14.70
Angola	13.31	13.00	12.51	11.29	6.50
Mozambique	9.05	8.94	9.06	7.41	5.40
Imports from					
All foreign markets	84.22	84.97	85.24	86.76	88.40
All overseas territories	15.78	15.03	14.76	13.24	11.60
Angola	9.35	9.43	9.72	9.08	7.80
Mozambique	5.62	4.72	4.20	3.42	3.20

Source: Banco Nacional Ultramarino, Boletim trimestral, no. 95 (July–September), 1973, 78.
Quoted in Lawrence S. Graham, *Portugal: The Decline and Collapse of an Authoritarian Order* (Beverly Hills, Calif: Sage, 1975), 22–25.

the Continent, and selling of the goods in the colonies. In the Portuguese case this model was utilized in a limited way because of the backwardness and underdeveloped conditions of the continental Portuguese economy. The Portuguese colonial empire was mostly exploited by foreigners.

In 1961, however, the relationship between Portugal and its colonies began to change. The wars in Guinea-Bissau, Angola, and Mozambique began producing structural changes both in Africa and on the Continent. In continental Portugal, the wars caused increases in public spending, money supply, purchasing power, demand for goods and services, and inflation. The effect of the latter was considerable, since one of the pillars of the economic strength of the reactionary coalition had been the strong escudo, a currency whose value, prior to the early 1960s, had never gone up or down during the coalition's rule. The relationship between continental Portugal and the African colonies was also changed by the effect of the wars on the economic condition and position of the colonies themselves, and that in turn altered the trading practices between the Continent and the colonies. Trade between the Continent and the colonies (the so-called escudo zone) declined while foreign trade "for metropolitan Portugal, Angola and Mozambique, as self-contained economic entities" increased (Graham 1975, 17).

This reduction in the economic importance of the colonies, combined with the high cost of the wars, increased, at a more rapid pace than before, the drain on metropolitan budgetary resources and for the first time made the colonies less and less profitable. Tables 4.9–4.11 clearly show the decline in trade between continental Portugal and its colonies, and the increase in foreign trade outside the escudo zone.

With the continuation of the colonial wars, Portugal's trade increasingly occurred outside the empire. Moreover, the colonies began trading directly and to

Table 4.10
Angola's Exports and Imports, 1968–1972 (percentages)

Exports to	1968	1969	1970	1971	1972
All foreign markets	60.25	57.45	61.24	64.12	70.07
Metro. Portugal	34.38	37.25	34.28	30.45	26.11
Other overseas territories	2.92	3.41	2.66	3.18	2.50
Unaccounted	2.45	1.89	1.82	2.25	1.32
Imports from					
All foreign markets	60.75	60.39	61.85	64.69	74.55
Metro. Portugal	36.45	36.95	35.19	31.60	23.25
Other overseas territories	2.78	2.66	2.86	3.70	2.12
Unaccounted	0.02	0.00	0.10	0.01	0.08

Source: Banco Nacional Ultramarino, *Boletim trimestral*, no. 95 (July–September 1973), 78. Quoted in Lawrence S. Graham, *Portugal: The Decline and Collapse of an Authoritarian Order* (Beverly Hills, Calif.: Sage, 1975), 22–25.

Table 4.11
Mozambique's Exports and Imports, 1968–1972 (percentages)

Exports to	1968	1969	1970	1971	1972
All foreign markets	56.09	50.81	53.56	53.40	55.20
Metro. Portugal	36.71	41.14	38.23	37.40	38.30
Other overseas territories	4.79	5.27	5.42	5.40	3.70
Unaccounted	2.41	2.78	2.79	3.80	2.80
Imports from					
All foreign markets	63.57	65.67	68.83	70.30	72.90
Metro. Portugal	32.95	31.13	27.59	26.50	23.90
Other overseas territories	3.44	3.16	3.55	3.20	3.10
Unaccounted	0.04	0.04	0.03	0.00	0.10

Source: Banco Nacional Ultramarino, *Boletim trimestral*, no. 95 (July–September 1973), 78. Quoted in Lawrence S. Graham, *Portugal: The Decline and Collapse of an Authoritarian Order* (Beverly Hills, Calif.: Sage, 1975), 22–25

a greater extent with foreign markets than with continental Portugal. "By 1972 almost three-quarters of Angola's and Mozambique's trade was going to and coming from markets outside Portuguese territory" (Graham 1975, 23). The decline in trade between the Continent and the colonies changed the nature of Portuguese colonialism and reduced the economic importance of the empire. Gradually, the reactionary coalition faced the cruel reality that the cost of maintaining the empire was greater than the gains from exploitation. But the colonies were still a source of revenue for the coalition.

As late as 1973 . . . the wages of the Mozambique miners working in South Africa were converted into gold shipments to Lisbon—in effect a hidden subsidy to the Portuguese war effort, since the bullion was valued at the official rate of US$42.20 an ounce instead of the world market price that rose to nearly $200 an ounce in 1974. During the three years before the coup, the official value of the gold amounted to at least $180 million. (Maxwell 1982, 358)

Thirteen years of fighting in Africa, combined with structural changes both on the Continent and in the colonies, gave birth to various class fractions with specific solutions for the problem of "imperial inversion."

The term "imperial inversion" was used to explain the distinctive set of relationships which developed between Brazil and Portugal prior to Brazilian independence and the devastating economic blows suffered by Portugal in the aftermath. . . . Political independence for Portuguese Africa meant also economic independence and the loss of important revenues for the Portuguese state. Once again the specter of Brazilian independence. (Graham 1975, 20, 23)

Solutions to Avoid/Reduce the Impact of "Imperial Inversion"

During the 1960s and early 1970s, Portugal had experienced much social change triggered first—albeit in an embryonic stage—by World War II and, second, by membership in EFTA and by the liberation movements in its African colonies. The economy of the reactionary coalition was collapsing, and its political regime was near its end. Different sectors of the Portuguese capitalist bourgeoisie had different ideas about solving or reducing the problem of "imperial inversion." The rationale for the solutions submitted by each group was based on its position in the Portuguese capitalist mode of production, and on the interests it had in the colonies. Hence, both CUF and Champalimaud, the two monopolistic groups involved in secondary economic activities in both Angola and Mozambique, favored political independence of the colonies and economic neocolonialism. But the banking sector—Banco Espírito Santo, Banco Borges & Irmao, Banco Fonsecas & Burnay, and others—opposed both independence and neocolonialism. Inasmuch as their profits came from forced labor, unequal exchange, and import/export, they wanted to maintain the status quo. Portugal was to keep the empire.

Segments of the petite bourgeoisie, also favored the maintenance of the status quo. They did not want to lose the colonial markets for their textiles, wines, and shoes. They favored strong colonialist positions. The *roceiros*, continental Portuguese who had become colonial planters and farmers, also favored the continuation of the empire. They actually became the shock troops of the ultra-reactionary forces in the colonies (Costa 1975, 153–154). The interests of Western European, North American, and South African capital were protected "as long as the Portuguese government showed no willingness whatsoever to negotiate a settlement with the African nationalists" (Maxwell 1982, 342).

THE FALL OF THE EMPIRE

In 1974, the Portuguese armed forces, acting on behalf of the modernizing sector of the new hegemonic class fraction (which was composed of "developmentalists" or "Europeanists"), seized power. The Europeanists favored integration into Europe and termination of the colonial empire through a negotiated settlement. They also rejected neocolonialism, perhaps because of their awareness of the underdeveloped state of the Portuguese economy. A member of the Movimento das Forças Armadas (Armed Forces Movement) told the *Nouvellé observateur*, "We have no desire to construct a neocolonial community" (Maxwell 1982, 358). A bulletin made public by the Armed Forces Movement shortly after the coup stated:

Those who benefited from the war were the same financial groups that exploited the people in the metropolis, and, comfortably installed in Lisbon and Oporto or abroad, by means of a venal government obliged the Portuguese people to fight in Africa in defense of their immense profits. (quoted in Maxwell 1982, 359)

The table below shows when Portuguese colonies were returned to African and Indian nationals.

Colony	Date Returned
Guinea-Bissau	September 10, 1974
Cape Verde Islands	July 5, 1975
Mozambique	June 25, 1975
São Tomé and Principe	July 12, 1975
Angola	November 11, 1975
Indian enclaves	December 31, 1974
	(retroactive to 1961)

NOTE

1. Amilcar Cabral, the organizer of PAIGC, was assassinated by the PIDE on January 20, 1973.

Opposition to the Reactionary Coalition

THE NATURE AND TYPES OF OPPOSITION

Real opposition in Portugal from 1926 to 1974 was both limited and ineffective. Except for the first years following the implementation of the New State, mass-based organized opposition to the regime of the reactionary coalition did not exist. Opposition in Portugal was from above and was characterized by elitism, with the opponents of the regime having more in common with the coalition's members and upper-level civil servants than with the masses. Moreover, the reactionary coalition's long rule was facilitated by the nature of the elitist opposition. In this chapter I argue that to understand the nature of the opposition (the *explanandum*), responsible in part for the lengthy existence of the coalition, we must consider the wider economic and social context (the *explanans*).

According to Martins, there were four types of opposition in Portugal, "the two cross-cutting criteria being legality and time-perspective (short-term and long-term)":

1. "Opposition in a narrow sense," anti-regime behavior oriented to the legal or semi-legal opportunities for political conflict [traditional opposition]; 2. "Conspiracy" hallowed by the Portuguese praetorian tradition, illegal and short-term by definition; 3. "Resistance," underground opposition with a long-term strategic perspective. "Resistance is the most costly of all opposition strategies in authoritarian regimes. The repression against this opposition mode is so severe and inescapable, the rewards so uncertain and remote, that few organizational types dare to adopt it"; 4. "Paideia," manifest long-term action such as the "metapolitical" strategy for modernizing the thought-forms and culture mentality of the Portuguese intelligentsia "adopted by . . . Seara Nova [intellectual] group." (1969, 253)

The most prevalent type of opposition was in the narrow sense, followed by conspiracy and limited resistance. Paideia, while it might have modernized the Portuguese intelligentsia or cultural elite, did nothing to modernize the thought forms and culture mentality of the working class. Except for a very short period of time between the late 1920s and early 1930s, opposition in Portugal was from above.

In my view, the resistance type of opposition was not only long-term and covert, but also short-term and overt. The latter form of opposition to the re-actionary coalition was the prevalent type in the first years of its rule. And it was short-term simply because the coalition's forces of control and oppression succeeded in crushing overt class struggle and demonstrations. The four types of opposition can be juxtaposed with opposition activities that have been divided into three time periods: up to 1937; 1945–1958; and the decades after 1958, principally after 1968 (Robinson 1979).

RESISTANCE TO THE NEW STATE

Mass-Based Political Movements

Class Struggle: The Anarcho-Syndicalist Workers' Movement

During the first years of its existence, the reactionary coalition faced a mass-based workers' opposition organized by the strong anarcho-syndicalist workers' movement. During the late 1920s and early 1930s, the movement overtly fought for its class interests and opposed the New State and the coalition's rule. The reactionary coalition soon realized that its existence required the total destruction of revolutionary syndicalism. In February 1927, during the military dictatorship, Portugal witnessed violent organized demonstrations by workers against the coalition. The uprising was a failure, for the workers met stronger counterre-volutionary forces. In 1933 and 1934 workers organized large general strikes. And in 1935 the syndicalists were involved in a coup. But all revolutionary attempts failed.

Military Rebellion: Attempts to Restore Parliamentary Rule

Republican military officers and sergeants became the second locus of overt, and sometimes violent, short-term resistance against the coalition's rule (some officers engaged in long-term opposition in the narrow sense as well). The Republican officers and sergeants fought for the restoration of parliamentary rule and for the reinstallation of the Republic. The Oporto Revolution of 1927 was also a military revolution. In 1928, Republican officers founded the Paris League and organized a plot to overthrow the military dictatorship. In 1931 Republican officers who had been exiled to Madeira assumed control of a working-class rebellion and proclaimed the existence of the Republic on the island (Bandeira 1976). The British navy assisted the reactionary coalition's suppression of the

"Atlantic Republic" (which lasted only twenty-eight days) under the pretense of "safeguarding the interests of British citizens" on the island, which was a haven for British retirees (Fonseca 1963, 251; Bandeira 1976, 8). (Madeira has been, and is, Portuguese de jure, but British de facto.)

On September 9, 1936, shortly after the Spanish Civil War broke out, the crews of three warships anchored in the Tagus River near Lisbon mutinied and planned to join the Spanish Republican navy. The mutiny failed. Facing heavy fire from land, the crews surrendered. The rebel Republican sailors were arrested and sent to the concentration camp of Tarrafal.

THE PORTUGUESE COMMUNIST PARTY

The Portuguese Communist Party (PCP) was organized in 1921 and reorganized in 1929 by its general secretary, Bento de Gonçalves. It became the underground party of the working class in 1934. For the next forty years, the PCP was the only opposition group involved in long-term, illegal covert resistance against the reactionary coalition, and the major troublemaker for the New State. Its mere existence was proof that the corporatist idea of a class-transcending harmony was a farce. And the clandestine activities of the PCP, such as the penetration of the coalition's controlled labor syndicates, were a threat to the existence of the coalition itself. The latter developed and implemented coercive apparatuses of self-defense such as the PVDE-PIDE, which considered its primary task to be the hunt for, and the surveillance, arrest, and torture of PCP members and sympathizers. Communists were at the top of the list of the coalition's enemies.

In 1935 and 1936, Bento Gonçalves, the PCP's general secretary, and José de Sousa, Júlio Fogaça, Militão Ribeiro, and Sergio Vilarigues, all party functionaries, were arrested and deported to Tarrafal, where Gonçalves died in 1942. The party was almost wiped out after the mid–1930s, when the reactionary coalition eliminated overt mass-based movements, but began to recover and to reorganize by 1941, under the leadership of the lawyer Álvaro Barreirinhas Cunhal. After the fall of the coalition's regime in April 1974, "the then [legal] twenty-two strong PCP central committee had served a total of 308 years in the [coalition's] gaols" (Gallagher 1979a, 390). They had outlived the regime of torturors.

A MORATORIUM ON RESISTANCE

The Disappearance of Anarcho-Syndicalism

The reactionary coalition developed and implemented repressive mechanisms that successfully eroded overt and violent opposition to the regime. The anarcho-syndicalists were arrested, exiled to Tarrafal, and co-opted. Mass-based overt movements of resistance were short-term because of the lack of organizational skills and unification of the workers and, more important, because of the violent measures the coalition used to eradicate such movements. The coalition forbade strikes, abolished labor unions, and replaced the unions with controlled labor syndicates. Revolutionary syndicalism disappeared from the arena of political opposition to the coalition.

From 1937 to 1945 there was a moratorium on opposition attempts to restore parliamentary rule, but the suspension was not total. There were illegal strikes in Lisbon organized by the PCP in the fall of 1942 and in the summer of 1943. The first strike involved twenty thousand, and the second fifty thousand, workers. In May 1944 there were strikes that included rural workers. But by then the working-class movements were less violent, less threatening, and easily suppressed by the coalition's forces of social control. In the 1944 strike, a military officer "arrested several hundred strikers and kept them in the bull-ring at Vila Franca de Xira for a time" (Robinson 1979, 66).

The Demise of Military Rebellion

Military opposition also was suspended by the mid-1930s. The Madeira Revolt was actually the beginning of the end. Republican officers were dead, in jail, or in exile, or had become demoralized with the failure of overt armed opposition. A minority in the armed forces, they disappeared from the scene of overt short-term resistance. A few of them later engaged in activities of opposition in the narrow sense.

The Bourgeoisification of the Portuguese Communist Party

The PCP represented organizational long-term resistance. In Portugal only the PCP took the opposition underground and continuously engaged in covert activities against the coalition. Party functionaries were arrested and exiled. Portuguese Communists engaged in the most dangerous and costly form of opposition. They were tortured by the coalition's forces of repression, and some died in exile or at the hands of PVDE-PIDE.

Yet the PCP was not the oppositional force that it could have been or, more important, that Portugal needed. Although it controlled the covert working-class movement after 1934, the PCP actually replaced radical syndicalism with, at best, reformist activities and long-term plans and strategies. Its membership showed very little working-class representation. Instead, the PCP was composed of "doctors, lawyers, small businessmen in the countryside and intellectuals, students, members of the professions and shop and office workers in the towns" (Lomax 1983, 108). In 1939, the International terminated relations with the PCP because of the latter's bourgeoisification. In 1943 the party, under the directorship of Álvaro Cunhal, allied itself with bourgeois oppositionists and sponsored the creation of the National Anti-Fascist Unity Movement, which was to be directed by a former Republican war and colonial minister, General Norton de Matos.

According to the "memories of a former clandestine party functionary" in the 1960s, the PCP was "a party of the city" and "never attained any real implantation among the peasantry." Moreover, "the direction of the proletarian and communist political struggle in the country was always in the hands of a certain radical petite-bourgeoisie" (Silva 1977; quoted in Lomax 1983, 108).

By the mid-1960s the PCP was "fundamentally a party of cadres" in favor of a "national and democratic revolution," which was first advocated by Álvaro Cunhal in 1943. The PCP "seemed more interested in establishing itself as an organized and entrenched force that would have to be reckoned with in any postfascist state, than in articulating, let alone practicing, any actual strategy for the overthrow of the regime" (Lomax 1983, 108).

More interested in being a power broker in its own right than in radical social change that was necessary to better the living conditions of the working classes, the PCP, under Cunhal's leadership, was able and willing

to collude to a considerable degree with the existing regime, in order to be able to build up its apparatus and widen its base, by working through quasi-legal front organizations like the Democratic Electoral Commissions established in 1969 and the General Trade Union Confederation, Intersindical [legalized] in 1970. (Lomax 1983, 108)

Overt short-term resistance to the reactionary coalition and efforts to restore parliamentary rule ended in 1937. The overt and violent opposition "came to an end" on July 4 of that year, the day Salazar survived a bomb attack by a small group of anarchists. Regarding the attack, Salazar stated, "There can be no doubt about it, we are indestructible because providence has willed it so" (Robinson 1979, 66).

The faith in Providence was only for public consumption. Shortly after the bomb incident, the coalition created a new paramilitary force of repression and surveillance, the Portuguese Legion. Henceforth, the masses of urban and rural workers would be totally depoliticized. For under the coalition's rules, political activity, interaction, and limited opposition were to be allowed only among the governing reactionary coalition, its principal supporters (the Roman Catholic Church, the civil bureaucracy, the military and paramilitary forces), and, paradoxically, the "traditional" opposition.

THE "LIBERALIZATION" OF THE NEW STATE

Both the influence of World War II and the postwar international climate (and the defeat of fascism) forced the reactionary coalition to open up (or, rather, to give the illusion that it was opening) its political system and make it more liberal, more democratic, more pluralistic. The coalition was willing to introduce some liberalization measures because it had secured foreign backing for its existence. It had friends in the Western democratic nations. In exchange for the guarantee of their interests in Portugal (the air force base in the strategically located Azores

Islands) and their interests in Portuguese African colonies, the victorious allies extended their support to the coalition's authoritarian New State. Thus, the coalition was confident that it could loosen (not eliminate) its reins on censorship and on opposition, and that it could give the New State the image of a liberal and progressive political regime. That way, the coalition could tell the world that Portugal had free elections, "as free as they are in the free land of England," Salazar said in 1945 (quoted in Robinson 1979, 67).

"Traditional" Opposition

"Free" Elections

Starting in 1945, when Portugal and Spain were the only bureaucratic–authoritarian regimes left in Europe, the coalition allowed individual opposition, oppositional groups, and the candidacy of opposition candidates in free elections. Civilian opposition and even military dissidents could now organize, adopt electoral strategies, pick a candidate, and run in the parliamentary and presidential elections. The bureaucratic–authoritarian regime was going to allow political pluralism. Knowingly or otherwise, the coalition was admitting either that corporatism had never existed in Portugal or that it had failed, since the existence of the now semilegal opposition stood as clear evidence that class-transcending harmony had not been achieved.

In November 1945 the traditional opposition was born. The National Anti-Fascist Unity Movement was reorganized so that it would cease to be an illegal, underground movement, and could assume a semilegal existence. The movement changed its name to Movement of Democratic Unity and included democrats, antifascists, and Communists.

"Freed" Time

Under the coalition's policy of free elections, the opposition had one month prior to elections of "freed" time (Martins 1969, 253). During that period, there was a relaxation of censorship, and of coercive and repressive measures, and amnesty for political prisoners. During the four or five weeks of "sufficient liberty," the opposition could engage in attacks against the New State and in activities of political mobilization (Robinson 1979, 67). However, once the period was over, and the elections had been held, overt and organized opposition to the regime was prohibited, and censorship and repressive measures were reapplied in full force. The traditional opposition would then wait for the next period of freed time. Nevertheless, in part through the policy of free elections, the coalition did secure a degree of international acceptability and admission to the community of nations constituting the free world.

Opposition and Regime Candidates

Prior to the new policy of free elections, the president and the deputies to the National Assembly were elected under a plebiscitary system in which all candidates were nominated by the National Union (UN), the coalition's party. In the 1948 presidential elections, under the new policy of free elections, General Norton de Matos was a candidate nominated by the opposition. Matos was a member of the old guard, a liberal Republican, and a former war and colonial minister. But, just before Election Day, Norton de Matos did what most opposition candidates for the presidency were to do in future elections: He withdrew his candidacy "for lack of guarantees" (Fonseca 1963, 42; quoted in Bandeira 1976, 13). General Oscar Carmona, the UN candidate, was reelected once more (he had been "elected" in 1928, 1935, and 1942).

Upon Carmona's death, the coalition's General Craveiro Lopes became president and elections were scheduled for 1951. The opposition had two candidates, Admiral Quintão Meireles and a civilian, Rui Luís Gomes. Meireles withdrew before the elections, and Gomes was ruled ineligible. It has been observed that

When the opposition candidates withdrew, they were protesting an undemocratic system, in which a combination of coercion, corruption and eligibility restrictions on both the electorate and candidates all ensured that the [coalition's] candidates would invariably win. (Bandeira 1976, 13)

Craveiro Lopes won the presidential election of 1951. During the period of free elections (1945–1958), opposition candidates were never elected to political office. The president was always a UN man and, until 1974, a high military officer as well.

The Elitist Nature of Traditional Opposition

Portugal had a very low level of literacy—approximately 50 percent in 1940—and the educational gap between the elite and the working class was even greater. Portuguese elites had very little in common with the poorly educated or illiterate masses of urban and rural workers. Hence, in a country where social status was still ascribed, the traditional opposition to the reactionary coalition was "overwhelmingly an urban, educated middle-class movement dominated by lawyers, doctors, engineers and cafe intellectuals" (Raby 1983, 63).

In view of its class background, the elitist traditional opposition, although opposed to what it perceived to be the excesses of the coalition's rule, never demonstrated any interest in the political organization of workers and peasants and, more important, felt quite comfortable with the rather feudal social arrangements and relations maintained by the reactionary coalition's social formation. For example, the traditional opposition never showed sensitivity to the degrading and exploitative nature of domestic service.

A young man who had been in jail for his activities in the MUD-Juvenil, a left-wing youth movement, astonished us when we visited him by punctuating the conversation with peremptory summonses to the maid. She was obviously busy in the kitchen preparing dinner, but he called her for the most trivial things: to pick up a newspaper he had dropped on the floor and would not permit us to stoop for: to answer the telephone which was at his elbow (the calls were invariably for him): to bring his cigarettes from the room he had left them in. And this boy was no *fidalgo*, or aristocrat, nor heir to wealth. . . . Nor was he the arrogant young prick one might expect from this kind of behaviour. On the contrary, he was gentle, unassuming and humorous, and not at all lacking in intelligence. It had clearly never occurred to him to treat servants otherwise. (Fryer and Pinheiro 1961, 207)

And the *dona de casa* (wife) of a middle-class cultured liberal complained, "Servants are not what they used to be. Just imagine, I caught one of my girls taking my cast-off nylons. She wanted to go out in nylon stockings. Really, the next thing we shall see the servants wearing hats, just like us!" (Fryer and Pinheiro 1961, 207).

The traditional opposition was as elitist as the reactionary coalition. It "always [spoke] with the emotion of the 'people', but with few exceptions they [were] totally uninterested in the political organization of the workers and the peasants" (Fryer and Pinheiro 1961, 208).

Opposition in a Narrow Sense

Traditional opposition as defined above was opposition in a narrow sense. The opposition's active participation in the coalition's free elections did not produce meaningful and real resistance to the regime.

The pre-electoral four weeks of "freed time" granted conditionally to the opposition was not long enough to carry through the tasks of political mobilization required for successful upsurge that would ultimately elude the elite opponents of the regime in forty years of dedicated but ineffectual opposition. (Gallagher 1979a, 391)

Thus, instead of winning state power, the traditional opposition's active participation in the elections had the effect of "giving the regime a spurious degree of legitimacy" (Gallagher 1979a, 391). Moreover, by taking part in the elections, the traditional opposition enabled the coalition to identify the opponents of the regime. In 1947, the coalition removed twenty-two politically active professors from the universities, and replaced them with academics loyal to the coalition. In March 1948, the coalition outlawed the Movement of Democratic Unity (Ferreira and Marshall 1984, 26).

The coalition's process of "democratization" and "liberalization" (freed time and free elections) were essentially "para inglês ver"![1]

THE 1958 PRESIDENTIAL ELECTION

The Rebirth of Resistance

Humberto Delgado and the 1958 Presidential Election

The opposition candidate in the presidential election of 1958 was General Humberto Delgado. Unlike former opposition candidates, Delgado was not a liberal Republican attempting to restore parliamentary rule. He was a former high official of the reactionary coalition. Delgado's coalition credentials were extensive and impressive. He had been an enthusiastic participant in the coalition's seizure of power in 1926; a military adviser to the Portuguese Legion; author of a radio play dedicated to Salazar; a key negotiator with the Allies during World War II; director general of civil aviation in 1944–1946 and again in 1957; military and air attaché in the United States and Canada; and Portugal's representative on the Military Committee of NATO (Robinson 1979, 73). But by 1958, Delgado was totally dissatisfied with and alienated from the coalition.

The coalition's candidate was not President Craveiro Lopes, but the minister for the navy, Admiral Américo Tomás. Craveiro Lopes was being dropped because the coalition had lost confidence in him. He had wanted to be a president according to the Constitution of 1933, not a mere figurehead under de facto control of the president of the Council of Ministers, Salazar. Craveiro Lopes had become unreliable, and thus had to be replaced with someone willing to be the coalition's yes-man. In Américo Tomás the coalition found the ideal man for that job.

Initially the opposition, including the PCP, rejected Delgado's candidacy. In view of his past, Delgado was considered a reactionary and a fascist. Equally, if not more, important was the opposition's perception of him as the candidate of "the United States and United Kingdom embassies—in fact a 'Coca-Cola' General" (Robinson 1979, 73). Consequently, the opposition first had its own candidates, Cunha Leal and Arlindo Vicente. The former withdrew in favor of Delgado on May 20, 1958. Nine days later, Arlindo Vicente, the candidate of the PCP, also withdrew in favor of Delgado, who by then was arousing much popular enthusiasm and interest in the election. Delgado become the candidate of the opposition.

The air force general had opened his campaign by stating that, once elected, he would fire Salazar and would dismantle the reactionary coalition's repressive state apparatus. Because he said publicly what no opposition candidate had dared to say, Delgado become immediately known as *O general sem medo* (the fearless general).

Despite a tremendous popular following, Delgado lost the election. Officially he received 236,528 votes; 758,998 were cast for the coalition's candidate (Bradford 1973, 86). The coalition offered Delgado the position of air force attaché in Canada in exchange for ending his political activities, but he declined the offer. Instead, having anticipated the victory of the coalition's candidate, Delgado organized the Independent Military Movement, and with General Botelho Moniz began negotiations with key military figures, including former President Craveiro Lopes, for a coup d'état that was scheduled for March 11–12, 1959. But the coup did not take place because none of the key actors initiated it.

Progressive Populism

A characteristic of progressive populism is ''a strong tendency to radicalize the left in the course of the political process, polarizing popular sentiment against the dominant bloc and/or against external domination'' (Raby 1983, 63).

Delgado was definitely a progressive populist. He was very popular even in the most backward and isolated parts of Portugal. These northern regions, home of peasants and holders of small plots, of strong conservative views, and of popular support for the reactionary coalition, had been impenetrable to the views of the traditional opposition and the Communist resistance. The latter were identified with educated and urban middle-class and professional groups, not with the rural working class. Nevertheless, Delgado's candidacy and views had an impact in such regions. Throughout the country, working people were touched when Delgado said, *''Que o país deixe de ter medo* (Let the country cease to be afraid).

Reasons for Delgado's Popularity

Delgado was indeed a charismatic individual with a very magnetic personality. But the personal characteristics of the ''fearless general'' are not sufficient to explain his impact on the political and social apparatus of the reactionary coalition. One must instead look at the wider social-structural context of Portuguese society in order to find the real reasons for the popularity of Delgado. A friend and collaborator of the general observed:

It is clear . . . that [personal characteristics] would have been insufficient to allow Humberto Delgado to play the role he did in Portuguese society. They had to be inserted, as was in fact the case, in a highly favorable set of circumstances, which included the real convergence under fascism of different class interests, the weakness of the Portuguese proletariat as a social class *for itself*, the virtual non-existence of political parties, the *ideology* of anti-fascism (which concealed the antagonistic contradictions, even under the fascist regime, of class interests at stake), and the extreme weakness of proletarian theory in our country. (Sertorio 1970, 53–54; quoted in Raby 1983, 73)

The presidential elections of 1958 reflected the changes that had occurred in the system of political economy of the reactionary coalition. The Law of Industrial License of 1945 had become a mechanism that favored the monopolistic groups and the financing capital, and hindered the interests of the petite and medium bourgeoisie. It also facilitated and accelerated the concentration of ownership in the monopolistic groups, which in turn accelerated the proletarianization of many small landowners and business people. In 1950 there were 136,000 small landowners. In 1960, the number had been reduced to 76,000 (Costa 1975, 70).

The conflict of interests between an octopus-like, large monopolistic bourgeoisie and a static petite and medium bourgeoisie was exacerbated by Portugal's entry into the European Free Trade Association at the beginning of the 1960s, which increased the gap between these groups. Finally, in absorbing small businesses, many of which were run by families, monopolistic capitalism increased the subordination of the working classes to the large bourgeoisie, which by then was the main beneficiary of the coalition's social formation.

Delgado became the hope and the spokesman (indirectly) of the petite and middle bourgeoisie, which since 1945 had been abandoned by the New State, had been losing ground, and was being absorbed by the monopolistic groups. Delgado's success, therefore, was much determined by the prevalent economic, not political and ideological, structural configurations.

Resistance Beyond Freed Time

Delgado was the first opposition candidate really to challenge the coalition during and after the elections. Instead of following the traditional opposition's willingness to consider the election campaigns and legal opposition to be a one-month, one-shot affair, Delgado brought his cause out in the open, beyond the allowed month of freed time. He took his opposition seriously and made it a full-time occupation. Delgado was doing in the late 1950s and early 1960s what the civilian and military Republicans—the people he had fought against—had done in the late 1920s and early 1930s. He was involved in overt resistance against the reactionary coalition.

The End of "Liberalization"

On August 9, 1958, Admiral Américo Tomás was sworn in as president of the Republic, but for the coalition the election of 1958 had been unsatisfactory (Martins 1969, 250). The intensity of dissent shown in both the urban and the rural areas of the country shook the regime. The popularity of Delgado was seen as a tremendous challenge to Salazar and to the regime. After all, Delgado was not a supporter of pre–1926 Republican Portugal; he was a distinguished former high-level member of the coalition. And this former servant, who had stated that, if elected, he would fire Salazar and dismantle the coalition's regime, had nearly toppled the regime. Such a dangerous challenge could not be allowed, and thus retaliatory measures followed.

Five days after the inauguration of Tomás, Minister of Defense Santos Costa and Minister of the Presidency Marcelo Caetano were forced to retire. General Botelho Moniz was appointed defense minister. Officers involved in the opposition's political campaigns were transferred to different units. Humberto Delgado was forced to leave the country and go into exile; in 1965, he was assassinated by the PIDE (Delgado's Brazilian bodyguard also was murdered). The killing of Delgado is proof of the challenge and the threat he was to the coalition, and the latter's preparedness to eliminate its enemies.

After the election of 1958, the reactionary coalition changed the Constitution of 1933 and abolished direct presidential elections. Future presidents were to be elected by members of the National Assembly and the Corporate Chamber. The coalition put an end to the liberalization of the postwar period.

PUTSCHIST STRATEGIES FOR THE SEIZURE OF POWER

The masses of urban and rural workers were never organized into an effective force for the overthrow of the coalition. Even Delgado, with his popularity and populist candidacy, had not been interested in organizing the workers and peasants into a homogeneous and effective political force. The elitist nature of the Portuguese opposition explains this lack of interest and the predilection, instead, for putschist strategies used in the several attempts to seize power. Hence, although these strategies "occasionally resulted in spectacular and dramatic action," they "rarely, if ever, resulted in mobilizing large-scale mass opposition to the dictatorship" (Lomax 1983, 107). And for almost fifty years, the putschist strategies never succeeded in toppling the coalition.

The Constitutional Coup d'Etat of 1961

The possibility of war in Africa and its consequences for the Portuguese economy intensified, for a time, the military's discontent with António Salazar. Some high-ranking officers favored a negotiated settlement in the emerging Angola conflict. A few weeks after the outbreak of the liberation uprisings in Angola in 1961, the air force chief of staff, General Albuquerque de Freitas, convinced the defense minister, General Botelho Moniz, that the time had come for a constitutional coup d'état; they must persuade the president of the Republic to exercise his constitutional power and dismiss Salazar as prime minister. Botelho Moniz and other generals of the High Command decided that to persuade the president to exercise his power, they would pass a motion of no confidence in Salazar at the forthcoming Defense Council meeting of April 8. Salazar learned of the attempted coup and did not attend the meeting. Three days later, Botelho Moniz and other generals visited the president of the Republic, Américo Tomás, and asked him to remove Salazar from office. Tomás replied that "he would not dismiss the greatest statesman of the century since Churchill" (Robinson 1979, 77).

Meanwhile, Salazar had secured the support of most of his ministers and of the military and paramilitary units in the Lisbon area (the loyal GNR, the Portuguese Legion, and the PIDE). On April 13, Botelho Moniz and other dissident generals met and "agreed to move on government positions at 16:00 hours that day." But, once again, no dissident military unit moved. The putschist attempted coup was a failure. The generals involved in the plot were dismissed and put under surveillance. Salazar, with the backing of the *ultra* wing of the reactionary coalition, placed in motion the measures necessary to begin the colonial wars.

Seizure of the *Santa Maria*

Captain Henrique Galvão and some fellow officers hijacked the Portuguese passenger liner *Santa Maria* in 1961. Galvão, a former high colonial official of the coalition, had become one of its most severe critics. He listed the coalition's "inoperative institutions" as follows:

The Constitution, undermined by the dictator's decree-laws; a National Assembly, with Deputies appointed by the only political party, whose President is Salazar; a Corporative Chamber with members chosen by the government; a council of state with councilors appointed at will. In short, all the scenery, actors and extras of a farce put on to deceive world opinion. (Galvão 1961, 19)

Although worldwide denunciation of the political situation in Portugal was achieved, primarily because of the international press coverage of the hijacking, the seizure of the *Santa Maria* (renamed *Santa Liberdade*) was another putschist failure. Galvão had planned to sail the liner to Angola and, once there, to set in motion a movement to overthrow Salazar and install his old friend General Delgado. But the overthrow did not occur, and after thirteen days at sea with little water and fuel, and under the close watch of the U.S. Navy, Galvão surrendered the *Santa Liberdade* to Brazilian authorities in exchange for political asylum.

The Skyjacking

In November 1961 Herminio da Palma Inacio (future head of the Liga de União e Acão Revolucionária, United League for Revolutionary Action, formed in Paris in 1967) hijacked a Portuguese airliner and used it to drop leaflets on the cities of Lisbon, Beja, and Faro. It was a spectacular demonstration with very little effect.

The Beja Uprising

At 2:00 A.M. on January 1, 1962, about thirty men, some civilian but most military, under the command of Captain Varela Gomes and Manuel Serra, an officer in the merchant marine, took over the tank regiment in Beja. The commander of the regiment wounded Varela Gomes, fled the area, and alerted the Guarda Nacional Republicana and the Lisbon authorities. Two civilian members of the PCP were shot. The under secretary for war was accidentally shot by his own troops shortly after his arrival from Lisbon. The Beja uprising was another failure. Sixty-five persons, including Varela Gomes and Manuel Serra, were arrested and given prison sentences. During his trial for high treason, Gomes accused the government of

selling for nothing the military bases, privileges and other portions of the collective patrimony, which is exactly what happened in Beja with the German base; secret treaties are signed agreeing to the invasion of foreign troops, like those existing with Spain and South Africa. (quoted in Bandeira 1976, 16)

The failure of the Beja uprising demoralized the military traditional opposition. No other military putschist attempt to seize state power occurred until 1974. In 1966, the reactionary coalition celebrated the fortieth anniversary of the "National Revolution," the seizure of power from the Republican government on May 28, 1926. The coalition seemed to be quite secure, with no broad-based and homogeneous opposition threatening its existence. A factor contributing to this state of affairs was the colonial war in Africa.

THE AFRICAN WARS: A TEMPORARY MORATORIUM ON OPPOSITION

Appeals to Nationalism

The outbreak of the wars of liberation in Africa neutralized the traditional opposition and dissident military officers, and, consequently, strengthened the regime of the reactionary coalition. Even Republicans supported the coalition's colonial policies. Some also believed that without the colonies, Portugal could not survive as an independent nation, and some had economic interests in the colonies. The wars, the measures of liberalization designed and implemented in Africa in the first years of the wars, and the radical changes in the economy exposed Portugal to a novel situation. This had the effect of giving a certain stability to the regime, even though the stability was actually the calm before the storm that was to come in 1974.

Since the maintenance of the colonial order was regarded as the overriding priority, the regime was able to compensate for its moral atrophy by appealing to reactionary nationalism, and to subordinate economic growth to such "higher" political goals—once more *politique d'abord*. (Martins 1971, 303)

The internalization of the colonial wars also stabilized the regime. The coalition was forced to open the country to foreign capital investment and to seek greater foreign penetration of the colonial empire.

Economic and Social Change

With the expansion of the colonial wars and the economic and social change that occurred after 1961, two new opposing fractions emerged within the hegemonic class. One, known as "the economic medievalists of Europe," consisted of (1) latifundists, the old core and main beneficiaries of the coalition's regime; (2) the small and medium industrialists who were dependent on the extraction of raw materials (cotton) from Africa at one-fourth the price on the world market; (3) segments of the petite bourgeoisie who did not want to lose the colonial markets; (4) the Portuguese and foreign interests in Africa who depended on the forced labor of the native workers; (5) the state bureaucratic apparatus, characterized as "politico-bureaucratic parasitism," which ran the administration of a political regime that derived 60 percent of its revenue from indirect taxation (Martins 1971, 63–64; Bandeira 1976, 32).

The economic medievalists were the major supporters of the reactionary coalition, and were against changes in the status quo. They also wanted to maintain the empire, and thus supported the war effort. Inasmuch as the medievalists were dependent on the colonies, they were, as Avelino Cardoso put it, "incapable of thinking in neo-capitalist terms . . . signing fascism's death warrant" (Cardoso 1974; quoted in Bandeira 1976, 32). A medievalist observed:

An unbridled industrialization, led by these technocrats out there who are ready to sacrifice us to international capitalism, is not in accord with the traditions of our people whom geography and history have turned towards the Atlantic, conferring them with a mission which possibly the Occident may not recognize. (Mercante 1975, 44; quoted in Bandeira 1976, 32)

The medievalists had been losing control in the economic structure of the country since World War II but, paradoxically, they were still ideologically hegemonic and in control of the activities and decision-making process of the New State.

The second group comprised the monopolistic groups associated with international finance and multinational firms. The monopolistic groups (CUF, Champalimaud, and others) had made investments in Europe, Brazil, and the United States. They had joined the world of international capitalism. They were "Europeanists," turned not to the Atlantic but to Europe. To them, the empire was no longer important, and the colonial wars were increasingly becoming barriers to their economic interests. To them the wars were a drain on the national budget, and military expenditures were using the capital necessary for investment and economic growth. They were aware that the political regime of the reactionary coalition was becoming an obstacle to the development of a more rational and dynamic capitalism. The Europeanists favored political change from above through the organization of urban and rural workers.

THE PREMIERSHIP OF MARCELLO CAETANO

The Appointment of Caetano

On September 6, 1968, António Salazar—the "organic intellectual," the "thinking and organizing" element of the reactionary coalition—fell from a deck chair and suffered a cerebral hemorrhage. During recovery from surgery, he had a stroke that left him incapacitated and unable to work. For the first time during its thirty-six-years existence, the coalition faced the novel circumstance of having to appoint a new prime minister. Several loyalists were mentioned as possible successors to Salazar. Foreign Minister Franco Nogueira and Adriano Moreira were at the top of the list. The former, a shepherd's son, was a wealthy lawyer and adviser to the Espírito Santo family who had vast interests in the colonies. The latter, the son of a policeman, had been overseas minister in the early 1960s. Generals Deslands and Kaúlza de Arriaga, an *ultra*, were also mentioned. The *ultra* wing of the coalition chose Santos Costa, the former defense minister and the most reactionary member of the coalition. Also considered was Marcello Caetano, a loyal intellectual.

On September 25, 1968, Américo Tomás appointed Marcello das Neves Caetano president of the Council of Ministers, prime minister. Caetano, the son of a primary school teacher, was a strong loyalist. An ambitious lawyer, he married into a wealthy family and at the age of twenty-three became a legal adviser to Salazar when the latter was finance minister. Caetano was also one of the key drafters of the coalition's political organization, especially the administrative code of 1936. From 1940 to 1944 Caetano was commander of Mocidade Portuguesa (Portuguese Youth). He was also a leading member of the União Nacional, the coalition's party, and from 1944 to 1947 he was minister of the colonies. His last official position had been minister of the presidency (vice prime minister), a post in which he was responsible for economic planning. In 1958 he was forced to retire because of disagreements with Salazar and became rector of Lisbon University, where he taught administrative law. Caetano had resigned from the university in 1962 (Robinson 1979). When appointed prime minister in 1968, Caetano had, officially, been away from politics for six years.

When Caetano became prime minister, Portuguese society was changing rather rapidly. The prevailing conjuncture and the coalition's political regime were separated by a wall of enormous and unsolvable contradictions. Caetano, a more cosmopolitan ideologue of the coalition, was aware that time was running out for the New State. Hence, his first serious policy issue was the replacement of the New State with the more liberal and less introverted Social State. The *imobilismo* of the former would be replaced with progressive change in the latter. But the change would, of course, be slow. Caetano's administrative slogans were "renewal in continuity" and "evolution without revolution."

Caetano's reformist measures soon were perceived, even by the traditional opposition, as measures of needed liberalization. The political regime of the coalition was being opened up. These were the days of hope. Limitations were placed on censorship of the press. Restraints were placed on the oppressive activities of the PIDE, whose name was changed to General Directorate of Security. Oppositionists in exile were allowed to return to Portugal.

Parliamentary Elections

The real indication of Caetano's willingness and plans to transform the political regime of the coalition, albeit with limitations, was the approval of free elections for the National Assembly in November 1969. The traditional opposition submitted a list of candidates from the Democratic Electoral Committee (CED) and from the Electoral Committee of Democratic Union (CEUD). The existence of more than one list of opposition candidates indicated divisions in the opposition at a time when such divisions were counterproductive. And, more important, both sides of the opposition failed to involve and organize the workers in the electoral process. The reason, in the words of the oppositionist Mario Soares (1975), was that the country "was politically asleep."

The coalition had not given Caetano the power it had been forced to give to Salazar. For six years Caetano was to fight constantly with Américo Tomás (who for the first time in his presidency had become aware of his constitutional powers) and with the *ultra* wing of the coalition, which held the bureaucratic strings of the regime and of key positions in the armed forces. The coalition rigged the parliamentary elections, and all newly elected deputies were from the coalition's party, Acção Nacional Popular (ANP; Popular National Action). "Official figures recorded that some 88 per cent of voters had endorsed the UN list, compared with 11.8 per cent the CED/CEUD lists . . . the opposition had had its campaign, but the government its election" (Robinson 1979, 169).

Some of the new deputies, however, formed a liberal wing that would be independent of the ANP, and attempted to liberalize the regime from above and within. After the elections, Caetano formed a government made up of young technocrats interested in modernizing the nation and in turning it away from the Atlantic and toward Europe. Some of the young liberal deputies and technocrats had been members of the opposition group SEDES.

The Society for the Study of Economic and Social Development (SEDES)

Formally founded in 1970, SEDES was an interest group. The product of systemic changes that Portugal had been experiencing since the early 1960s, it represented not the Portuguese workers but the "modern," emerging segment of the economic hegemonic class (the class of the society's founders and the majority of its members). SEDES "included leading representatives of the liberal (monopolistic) bourgeoisie, above all intellectuals who were striving for a reform of the political system from within" (Kohler 1982, 182). When the founders requested the legal incorporation of SEDES, six deputies of the National Assembly, two ministers of the government, and the son of Prime Minister Caetano signed the petition (Blume 1977). SEDES was a traditional opposition group made up of professionals and urbanites:

Of the 147 signatories 104 classified themselves as professionals . . . [the] largest representation [was] engineers 22, economists 14, and lawyers 14 . . . [and] of 408 members
in 1971, 320 were from Lisbon . . . of 588 members in 1972 450 were from Lisbon and
109 from Porto. (Blume 1977, 355)

SEDES was the first traditional opposition group to be legalized in Portugal
during the forty years of the reactionary coalition's regime. Caetano, even in
the period of "evolution without revolution," was "reluctant to accept the
petitioners' request for incorporation." SEDES waited ten months "for the
personal approval of both the Prime Minister and the Minister of Interior" (Blume
1977, 355). Claiming not to be a political group, SEDES sought social change
that would permit the incorporation of Portugal into the industrial and democratic
world of modern Europe. Its members wrote articles for daily newspapers and
held public meetings on a variety of economic, political, and social topics. Its
major "white paper" was "*O país que somos, e o país que queremos ser*" (The
Country We Are, and the Country We Want to Be). SEDES was critical of the
reactionary coalition's social formation:

the poor and unproductive state of Portuguese agriculture and fishing, the deterioration
of public administration, the lack of planning in housing, transportation and environment,
the insufficiency and inadequacy of health services, investment banking and aid to small
and medium sized business and university education. (quoted in Blume 1977, 355)

SEDES was an ardent supporter of political pluralism, and it embraced the
ideology of equal social and economic opportunities for all members of the
population. Portugal needed to move from the status-based society that it had
been for so long to a new and more dynamic achieved-based society. In its white
paper on constitutional reform, SEDES

supported one of its members [the late] Sá Carneiro, and his positions in the National
Assembly which it specifically endorsed. Among them were the direct election of the
President of the Republic by the people, a return to parliamentary democracy, freedom
of religion, press and assembly, equal opportunity for all, and restraint placed on the
government's use of preventive imprisonment. (Blume 1977, 360)

But SEDES did not speak for the Portuguese workers. A traditional opposition
group, it was actually the main voice of the liberal monopolistic business community and technological intelligentsia that aspired to a more modern and efficient
capitalist society. The reactionary coalition had favored accumulation in a feudal
and mercantilist society, which reduced the risks and kept the worker on a leash;
the modern segment wanted both capitalism and a capitalist society. The modern
segment of the hegemonic class wanted a historical break, albeit not a radical
one, with the past. In Gramscian terms, it wanted its own historical bloc.
    Hence, SEDES was also an elitist group. As such, it was uninterested in
mobilizing mass opposition to the reactionary coalition, in waking the country,

from the North to the South, from the East to West, from its very long political sleep.

Intersindical

The social changes and contradictions that Portugal began experiencing in 1961 brought oppositional forces among the workers. The condition of the country may not have been that of deep sleep, as some elitist oppositionists mistakenly believed it had been. In 1970, opposition workers were elected to the executive bodies of eighteen of the reactionary coalition's *sindicatos*. In the same year, radicalized union members revived an umbrella union organization named Intersindical (originally an underground trade union founded by the PS in 1933), "a body which was to have a growing significance in the Portuguese political and industrial life both before and after the April coup" (Insight Team of the Sunday Times 1975, 64).

Intersindical wanted to free workers from the coalition's *sindicatos* and to operate like a truly free labor union. Caetano, perhaps concerned with the repercussions that would follow a denial, approved Intersindical's legal existence. The new organization became very active in public debates regarding "normal trade union rights, such as freedom of association, free choice of union leaders and the right to strike" (*The Sunday Times* 1975, 104). Strikes were still illegal in 1970, and the coalition would not allow them. In June 1971, Intersindical requested

formal recognition by the International Labour Organization, the Geneva-based United Nations Agency. . . . Intersindical wanted to occupy the seat reserved for the representative of Portugal's workers. Caetano refused to answer a letter which made the request; whereupon Intersindical protested directly to the ILO. At this point Caetano . . . banned Intersindical. (*The Sunday Times* 1975, 65)

The workers' umbrella organization went underground and again became an arm of the PCP, engaged in covert resistance to the coalition's regime. As such, it was very active in covert organization of illegal strikes, workers' demands for increases in wages, and in working-class struggle and militancy.

The End of the New State

Marcello Caetano was appointed prime minister with the support not of Américo Tomás and the *ultras* but of the modernizing, Europeanist segment of the hegemonic ruling class. From 1968 to late 1971, his "political spring," and the concomitant governmental policies (the liberalization of the coalition's regime), had been implemented in order to open the country, to reduce, albeit slowly, the coalition's imposed obstacles to the development of a more extroverted and dynamic capitalism. By early 1972, however, Caetano's liberalization policies had been terminated. The end of "renewal in continuity" and "evolution without revolution" came with the reelection of Américo Tomás to a third term as president of the Republic in July of 1972 (Tomás was seventy-eight years old). His election was a clear indication that Caetano's reformist experiment was over. And, more important, the election indicated that although they were no longer economically and ideologically hegemonic, the *ultras* had retained power. The military and paramilitary forces and the church were still the major pillars of support for the coalition. Even between 1968 and 1974, "there were no oppositional forces on the left that appeared to be potential mobilizers of a movement capable of overthrowing the fascist regime" (Lomax 1983, 110). In view of the nature of the Portuguese opposition, particularly its elitist element, only a military coup could end the forty-eight-year regime of the reactionary coalition.

NOTE

1. *Para inglês ver*, literally "for English to see," used to be a very popular idiomatic expression and means giving the appearance that something *is*, when in reality it *is not*.

6

The Military and the Coup of April 25, 1974

THE MILITARY'S ROLE IN THE REACTIONARY COALITION'S REGIME

The Ubiquitous Presence: Co-optation

On behalf of the reactionary coalition, the armed forces seized power from the Republican government in 1926 and established a military dictatorship. Seven years later, with António de Oliveira Salazar at the helm of the new civilian government, the reactionary coalition established its own political system, the Estado Novo. Although the military dictatorship was replaced with a civilian government, and the president of the Council of Ministers, the prime minister, was also a civilian, the military never lost its key positions in the coalition's power structure. Supreme power was held by the military during the life of the coalition both symbolically and constitutionally. Until the fall of the reactionary coalition in 1974, the president of the Republic was always a high-ranking military officer, and he had the constitutional authority to dismiss the prime minister.

Furthermore, high-ranking military officers, colonels and up, were involved in almost every aspect of the economic, political, and social organizations of Portuguese society. Their presence was ubiquitous. They served in the Corporative Chamber as *procuradores*, and in the Legislative Assembly as deputies. And, since these legislative groups were not the real centers of policy-making, the military were also present, as an important constituent, in the real center of the coalition's policy-making apparatus, the União Nacional (National Union).

Until 1974, the top echelons of the military were greatly intertwined with the civil society. Their presence was everywhere, and their co-optation almost total. "The co-optation of the higher-level officers was complemented by their participation in directorships of the great monopolies. This 'directorship craze' was a phenomenon which came to be accentuated in recent years'' (Martins 1971, 71).

For example, Air Force General Kaúlza de Arriaga was a board member of Petrangol, an Angolan oil concession that was a subsidiary of the Belgian Petrofina Corporation and the Espírito Santo monopolistic group. Admiral Sarmento Rodrigues was president of the Torralta monopolistic group. Admiral Henrique Tenreiro owned one of Portugal's largest fishing fleets. Army General António de Spínola, at the outset of the African wars, was on leave from the army and a full-time director of the steel monopoly Metalúrgica Nacional, owned by the Champalimaud group. ''The percentage of military in the government and on the administrative boards of the big companies [was] usually high compared with any other dictatorship'' (Fonseca 1963, 41).

During the reactionary coalition's regime, the military was the first and most loyal pillar of support. (The second pillar was the Catholic Church.) The high-level military officers were, for almost half a century, in the service of the latifundists and their commercial and industrial allies, and later in the service of monopolistic big business. That is what the armed forces of a country are supposed to do. But, in the case of Portugal, there was a ''close association of the Generals with political and economic power'' (Bandeira 1976, 20). During the military dictatorship and the reactionary coalition regime, the role of the Portuguese military and paramilitary forces was that of semicovert guardian of the state. According to Luckham, when the military assumes the posture of guardian,

Its political role is to uphold and extend support to ''The State'' internally as well as externally. Ideologically, therefore, it is disposed to regard itself as the Platonic custodian of a vaguely defined ''national interest''. On those occasions that it does put coercion to political use, this occurs because of dispute with other elites as to the definition or methods of pursuit of the national will, rather than because it acts as the agent of particular interests or power agents. (1971, 8).

During the coalition's regime, however, the military assumed the role of guardian of the national interest neither in an overt-direct nor in a covert-indirect way, but in what I consider a semicovert-overt way. In the overt-direct case, Luckham says, the military ''takes direct responsibility for the affairs of the state by ruling for long periods itself.'' Hence, in Portugal, overt-direct guardianship is applicable only to the military dictatorship of 1926–1933. In covert-indirect guardianship, ''the military may act in such a way as to support over the long run a political order that it considers capable of following the national interest and providing it with adequate support in the pursuit of national security'' (Luckham 1971, 9). While the Portuguese military and paramilitary forces did indeed support a political order, the Estado Novo, in the long run, it did not remain in the barracks but participated directly in political affairs.

The active military collaboration with the support of the coalition's regime was present in the sectors indicated below, which included military and non-military, full-time and part-time, paying positions.

1. Commanding the key paramilitary organizations of the New State, training, and serving as auxiliary consultants for the following: (a) State correctional prison services (guards, jailers); (b) Portuguese Legion (1936–1974); (c) Mocidade Portuguesa (1936–1974); (d) GNR (Guarda Nacional Republicana), a "second army"; (e) Civil Police (PSP); (f) Secret Police (PIDE/DGS); (g) Guarda Fiscal (customs, frontiers, immigration)
2. Volunteering for the Portuguese Legion campaign (*viriatos*) in the Spanish Civil War (1936–1939); an estimated twenty thousand "volunteers" were sent, of whom six thousand to eight thousand died
3. Serving in state censorship service (usually as a second job)
4. Holding office as cabinet ministers or in central, district, and local administration in Portugal and the Atlantic islands
5. Fulfilling assignments in colonial service in African or Asian colonies, at all levels from governor-general or high commissioner down to local *chefes de posto* (Wheeler 1979, 201)

In the service of the reactionary coalition, the high echelons of the military establishment were indeed everywhere. Until the colonial wars, the sole function of the armed forces was to protect and support the coalition's regime, to be the guardian of its interests.

The Influence of Foreign Military Aid

Foreign military aid to the reactionary coalition was instrumental in the co-optation of the Portuguese armed forces. Aid extended to Portugal by West Germany averaged three to four million U.S. dollars a year. Shortly after World War II, the close collaboration between the two countries, which developed out of mutual colonial interests, brought a one-hundred-person German military mission, the Zentral Deutsch Verbindungstelle, to Portugal. England also granted military aid to Portugal, and before World War II the British navy established modern naval schools in Portugal. After the war many Portuguese officers were trained by the Royal Navy (Bosgra and van Krimpen 1972, 76; quoted in Bandeira 1976, 24). Portuguese air force pilots were trained by the Royal Air Force and proudly displayed the R.A.F. wings on their uniforms. Military training abroad enhanced their careers.

In 1949, Portugal became a member of NATO. The membership brought modernization to the armed forces, in terms of new equipment and better training of personnel. NATO made available training for higher-level officers at its defense college in Paris, at the Vilseck School in West Germany, and at the Command Staff College in Fort Leavenworth, Kansas. In 1951 the United States began military assistance to the reactionary coalition. A military assistance ad-

Table 6.1
Portuguese Military Personnel Trained in the United States, 1951–1970

Year	Number
1951-1963	2,288
1964-1968	205
1969-1970	130

Source: William Minter, *Portuguese Africa and the West* (London: Pelican Books, 1972), 104.

Table 6.2
U.S. Assistance to Portugal, 1951–1968 (millions of dollars)

Year	Military Assistance Program	Total Military	Economic
1951-52	10.6	10.6	51.2
1953-61	270.1	301.4	27.2
1962	4.4	1.8	69.1
1963	8.7	9.3	7.4
1964	5.6	6.1	16.5
1965	7.5	7.6	7.0
1966	1.5	1.7	5.8
1967	2.2	4.6	10.9
1968	3.2	3.7	7.2

Source: M. Hanlon, "Beyond Colonialism: The United States, Portugal and Portuguese Africa,"
        The Human Factor (1974), 91, quoted in Antonio Rangel Bandeira, "The Portuguese Armed
        Forces Movement: Historical Antecedents, Professional Demands, and Class Conflicts,"
        Politics and Society 6 (1976): 23.

visory group was stationed in continental Portugal. The group had a staff of forty-five in 1958, and of twenty-five in 1969. The United States trained Portuguese officers and noncommissioned officers at its bases in both Europe and the United States. Table 6.1 shows the number of military men trained in the United States. The United States also influenced the Portuguese military establishment through direct military and economic assistance. Table 6.2 shows U.S. assistance to Portugal, according to official figures, from 1951 to 1968.

These official figures of military aid to Portugal may not, however, give the real picture. "Revelations in the U.S. Congress showed that in 1971 foreign military aid was twelve times larger than the amount officially declared by the Pentagon" (Bosgra and van Krimpen 1972, 63; quoted in Bandeira 1976, 24). Foreign military influence also was exercised through foreign military bases installed on Portuguese soil. The United States had a major air base in the strategic Azores Islands, with five thousand military personnel, and West Germany had a major base in continental Portugal (Bandeira 1976; Winter 1972).

The Portuguese armed forces served and protected the reactionary coalition's regime. The great majority of the officers above the rank of colonel were either members of the hegemonic coalition or were co-opted by it. Their loyalty and service were rewarded with sinecures in the military and paramilitary forces, and in the civil society. They were granted profitable contracts and prestigious positions, and were given advanced military training with European and U.S. armed forces.

Minority Dissent Putschist Strategies

It has been observed that "There is a long tradition of direct intervention in civilian political power structures by Portuguese armed forces" and that such interventions have been "motivated by politico-ideological considerations" (Bandeira 1976, 20). It also has been argued that in the 1926 and 1974 coups, "the active intervention of the armed forces in the government and politics" was "apolitical, professional in nature . . . [and] based upon the belief that the 'honor of the army', or of the armed forces, as an institution, had been severely compromised by its role as a defender of the now-discredited regime" (Wheeler 1979, 207).

I take issue with both arguments. In my view, the prevalence of Portuguese military intervention in politics must be qualified, and the real cause of the coups of 1926 and 1974 was neither political ideology nor professional grievances. The argument regarding direct military intervention in politics is, I believe, based on the fact that twenty-one military coup d'état attempts took place in Portugal between February 1927 and March 1974 (Wheeler 1979, 210). Emphasis on their number, however, leads one to ignore the nature of the coups. For example, during what I call the first wave, thirteen coups were attempted by Republican military officers who had never accepted the legitimacy of the reactionary coalition, and who wanted a return to democratic parliamentary rule. These coup attempts occurred between 1927 and 1947. From 1947 to 1958, there was no military intervention in the politics of the coalition.

The second wave of coup attempts occurred between 1958 (after the presidential election) and February 1965. A closer analysis reveals that during this period only eight coups were attempted, this time by discontented former supporters of the regime, both civilian and military. During this period Portugal experienced tremendous economic, political, and social change: higher concentration and centralization of economic power, a very popular presidential candidate, changes in the presidential election procedures, the African wars, penetration of the introverted economy by foreign capital. No attempts were made between February 1965 and March 1974.

The intervention of the military in the political process has been exaggerated and poorly understood. During the regime of the reactionary coalition, the majority of the officer corps defended, supported, and protected the coalition's social formation. Only a few military officers opposed the regime, and most of their opposition occurred after the presidential election of 1958. Until 1974,

"The reactionary coalition controlled the state through the army whose highest echelons were amply rewarded" (Ginner 1982).

THE COUP OF APRIL 25, 1974

On April 25, 1974, a putschist coup d'état terminated the regime of the reactionary coalition, "the longest established fascistoid regime in the history of the world" (Hammond 1982). Shortly after midnight, a radio disc jockey put on a banned song, "Grandola," giving the signal for the coup to begin. Twenty-four hours later, the longest bureaucratic–authoritarian, fascist regime ceased to exist. Almost immediately, masses of working-class people—for so long silenced by the coalition—took to the streets and enthusiastically demonstrated their joy.

The coup was planned and executed by a group of 240 military officers. They had first organized into the "Captains' Movement," but at the time of the coup, they called themselves the Movimento das Forcas Armadas (MFA, Armed Forces Movement). In the following sections of this chapter, I present the causal factors that explain the organization of the "Captains' Movement" and then of the MFA, and the execution of the coup of 1974. I have emphasized factors because in analyzing the origins of the MFA, one must avoid mechanistic and reductionist explanations. For example, to explain the origin of the MFA solely on the basis of a Marxist class analysis would not yield an accurate and complete understanding, for it would neglect the causal significance of several equally important factors responsible for the emergence of the "Captains' Movement" and the MFA. A nonmechanistic and nonreductionist class analysis broadly circumscribes "the field of investigation, and [then] makes possible an assessment of the importance and relative autonomy of outside factors inhibiting or determining the behavior of a group" (Nun 1967, 73; quoted in Bandeira 1976, 24). That is, in addition to the social background of the military conspirators, other variables codetermined the appearance of the MFA and the coup.

ORIGINS OF THE MFA AND REASONS FOR THE COUP

Changes in the Class Origin of the Military Officers

Until the 1940s, the Portuguese officer corps was composed of the sons of aristocratic, latifundist, and haute bourgeois families. Traditionally, these families directed one of their sons into a military career. In the Portuguese navy, aristocratic officers were overrepresented well into the 1950s. "Crested family rings were worn by 91 per cent of the cadets who entered in the so-called 'marquis promotion of 1944,' and although this was a particular vintage year, blue blood continued conspicuously into the early 1950s" (Porch 1977, 70).

The aristocratic army officer candidate attended the elitist Colégio Militar in preparation for admission to the Escola do Exército (later called Academia Militar). Until the 1940s in the army, and until the 1950s in the navy, a career as

Table 6.3
Social Origins of Naval Academy Cadets, 1944–1958

Year	Cadets	Aristocrats No.	Aristocrats Percent
1944	11	10	91
1945	9	6	66
1946	11	2	18
1947	10	3	30
1948	10	4	40
1949	11	5	45
1950	13	4	31
1951	10	2	20
1952	22	3	13
1953	32	4	12
1954	24	2	8
1955	14	1	7
1956	9	0	0
1957	7	1	14
1958	30	2	6

Source: Douglas Porch, *The Portuguese Armed Forces and the Revolution* (London: Croom Helm, 1977), 88.

an officer was not possible for the sons of middle-class families. The military academies were not accessible to these youths. Instead, they attended private and public lyceums or, more likely, technical schools.

After World War II, a military career began to be less attractive to the aristocratic and upper-class families. Instead of going to the Escola do Exército, the sons of the wealthy families more often began attending the universities to prepare them for the liberal professions. In view of this, middle-class youths began to be admitted to the Escola do Exército (Bandeira 1976, 25). (See Table 6.3)

Gradually, middle-class young men began replacing officers from the aristocracy, the rural oligarchy and the haute bourgeoisie. But, while the access of the middle class to the military academies began the process of differentiation between junior and senior officers, the democratization of admission to military institutions of higher learning was very limited. The new class of officers came from the better-off middle-class families, and "tended to ape the ways of the old aristocratic officer corps" (Opello 1985, 67; Wiarda 1975). This they did with the assistance of the reactionary coalition, which, in an "effort to dissociate the officers from the lower classes, decreed that a Portuguese officer could only wed a woman with secondary education, who could prove her economic situation with a dowry of at least 2,000 dollars which had to be deposited in a bank" (Fonseca 1963, 35; quoted in Bandeira 1976, 26).

Table 6.4
Rural–Urban Origins of Portuguese Officers (percent)

Date of Admission to Service Academy		Army	Navy	Total Civilian Population
1910--19	U	51.9	-----	15
	R	48.1	-----	85
1920--29	U	51	57.1	16
	R	49	42.9	84
1930--39	U	47.1	54.1	17
	R	52.9	45.9	83
1940--49	U	45	48.1	17
	R	55	51.9	83
1950--59	U	35.3	60.1	17
	R	64.7	39.9	83
1960--69	U	31.4	56.7	18
	R	68.6	43.3	82
1970--79 (1976)	U	36.4	47	18
	R	63.6	53	82

Note: U=urban; R=rural.

Source: Maria Carrilho, "Origems socias do corpo de oficiais das forcas armadas portuguesas ao longo do século XX," *Analise Social* 18 (1982): 1155–1164.

Rural-Urban Origins of the Portuguese Officers

In many countries of Europe, and in the United States, the officer corps is commonly rural in origin (Janowitz 1960; Korvetaris and Dobrats 1973). Portugal was an exception. Between 1910 and 1959, the majority of the officers in both the army and the navy were from urban areas (eighteen cities with populations between fifteen thousand and fifty thousand, except Lisbon, with a population of seven hundred thousand, and Pôrto, with three hundred thousand, in the 1950s; see Table 6.4.)

The overrepresentation of cadets from the urban areas was indicative of the underdevelopment of the rural sectors of Portugal. The increase in admissions of cadets from rural areas after 1959 reflects the changes in the recruitment patterns of the armed forces.

Recruitment Patterns of the Service Academies

The expansion and success of the monopolistic groups not only increased the number of professional job opportunities, it made them more attractive than a military career. Aristocratic and upper-class youths were the first to make the switch, but by the 1950s the sons of the better-off middle-class families also began entering the universities to prepare for a liberal profession and/or a high-level position within the monopolistic cartels. The university student population

Table 6.5
Naval Cadets from Nobility, 1950–1958

Year	Percent
1950	31
1952	13
1953	12
1954	8
1955-1958	7

Source: Douglas Porch, *The Portuguese Armed Forces and the Revolution* (London: Croom Helm, 1977), 70.

increased as follows: 1926, six thousand; 1940, nine thousand; 1950, fourteen thousand; 1960, twenty thousand; and 1965, thirty-five thousand. The consequence of the switch from military to civilian careers was a substantial decline in the number of applications to the Escola Náutica (Naval Academy) and the Escola do Exército.

Faced with a potential shortage in the junior officer corps, the reactionary coalition abolished tuition at the service academies. This policy changed the recruitment patterns of the service academies, since it opened them to the sons of less-well-off middle-class families. The recruitment pattern was thus democratized. After 1958 there was a change in the class background of cadets for the permanent officer corps (Quadro Permanente, or QP). And, as De Toqueville (and more recently, Janowitz) observed, ''democratization equals politicization'' (Janowitz 1960, 10). Thus, ''The Portuguese army after 1958 eased down the slippery slope to 'democratization' and eventual 'politicization' (Porch 1977, 69). At the Naval Academy, the aristocratic profile was reduced substantially, as Table 6.5 shows.

The democratizing changes in the patterns of recruitment to the service academies produced a marked cleavage within the QP: the different class backgrounds of the ''old'' members (officers above the rank of lieutenant colonel) and of the ''new'' members (officers with a rank of major or below). This cleavage caused a clear and bitter division in the armed forces. ''This situation partially explains why the MFA junior officers, in spite of their efforts, gained the support of only 2 colonels and 4 lieutenant colonels during the conspiratorial phase, and 9 generals and 30 colonels by the April 25 coup.''[1]

The Effects of the African Wars

The Colonial Wars

The wars against colonial liberation movements caused profound change in the military institutions. A rather obvious change was the substantial increase of military personnel. The growth in the size of the armed forces is shown in Table 6.6.

Table 6.6
Portuguese Armed Forces Personnel, 1962–1972

	Year	Personnel
	1962	58,000
Army	1970	150,000
	1972	179,000
	1962	12,500
Air Force	1970	17,500
	1972	21,000
	1962	9,300
Navy	1970s	18,000

Source: United Nations, ''Report of the Special Committee on the Independence of Colonial Countries and Peoples,'' A/9023/ADD3 and A/9023 pt. IV (New York: September-October
1973), quoted in António Rangel Bandeira, ''The Portuguese Armed Forces Movement:
Historical Antecedents, Professional Demands, and Class Conflicts,'' *Politics and Society*
6 (1976) 21.

By 1972, the total strength of the Portuguese armed forces was approximately
220,000 men, which was extremely high in proportion to the total continental
population of just over 8 million. Eventually, Portugal was to have the ''second
highest percentage of men of military age in the armed forces in the world''
(Porch 1977, 23). Military service was compulsory and extended to five years,
and the maximum age for the draft was raised to forty-five years. Not every
man, of course, was drafted. In a country with so much ascribed status,

The well-connected like socialist party chief Mario Soares, could get a medical certificate,
a student deferment, or if pushed, could travel abroad until the heat was off. Many
potentially good fighting men took trains north to France, leaving for the most part those
who lacked the money or the energy to emigrate, to man the trenches. (Porch 1977, 23)

Further Democratization in Recruitment to the Service Academies

After the outbreak of the colonial wars, applications to the service academies
declined rapidly. The likelihood of serving a tour of duty in Africa combined
with the very high possibility of dying or being seriously wounded, made a
military career something to be avoided at all costs. ''In the 1950s a place in
the air force academy was so coveted that some three hundred applications would
be received for 30 places. By the mid-sixties those figures had been reversed''
(The Insight Team 1975, 16). Table 6.7 shows the rapid decline in the number
of applications to the Military Academy, particularly after the 1967–1968, the
period when the fighting reached its peak.

The democratization of recruitment to the Military Academy implemented in
1958 did not stop the decline in the number of applications. In 1969, for instance,

Table 6.7
Military Academy Applications and Admissions, 1960–1973

Year	Applicants	Admissions
1960	381	174
1961	559	257
1962	444	266
1963	392	180
1964	307	137
1965	283	129
1966	199	90
1967	175	90
1968	149	58
1969	112	33
1970	151	62
1971	169	103
1972	154	72
1973	155	88

Source: Douglas Porch, *The Portuguese Armed Forces and the Revolution* (London: Croom Helm, 1977), 72.

applications were down 80 percent from 1961 (Porch 1977, 72). Although the colonial wars partially explain this decline, there is another, equally important reason for the failure of the 1958 democratization policy. Free tuition at the academies did not make the academies "free" to the sons of less-well-off middle-class and petite bourgeois families because those classes could not afford a nonemployed son. The reactionary coalition realized this situation in 1969 when it began offering military cadets a stipend of three thousand escudos per month. This decision opened the academies to lower-class youths and caused the second, much more marked cleavage within the QP. It had a greater democratizing effect on the recruitment patterns to the academies than the 1958 policy of free tuition.

A military career was now accessible to the sons of the petite bourgeoisie and of working-class families. The 1969 decision also increased recruitment to the military community, specifically the paramilitary forces of social control, such as the Security Police, the National Guard, and the Border/Harbor Patrol. Lower-class youths replaced the aristocratic, upper-middle and middle-class junior officers. Thus, cleavages within the armed forces based on class background became much more pronounced after 1969. Tables 6.8 and 6.9 show the changes of class origins for both the army and the navy academies.

In the army, recruitment from within increased for the post-1930 classes of cadets. Both the army and the navy experienced an increase in the number of cadets whose fathers were government bureaucrats and members of the forces of social control. More than 24 percent of the army officers born in the 1940s (those who entered the army academy in the 1960s) were sons of lower-level civil servants.

Table 6.8
Class Origins of the Portuguese Army Officer Corps (percent)

| | Date of Birth | | |
Father's Occupation	1930--1939	1940--1949	1950--1959
Armed forces	15.2	16.3	24.6
Civil servant, police	20.9	24.3	22.0
Liberal profession	5.7	4.6	5.2
Proprietor	16.3	11.2	7.8
Commercial businessman	8.9	8.6	8.9
White-collar worker	9.4	7.6	5.4
Skilled white-collar worker	7.6	10.9	11.9
Farmer, nonowner	3.3	4.2	2.6
Skilled blue-collar worker	12.7	12.3	11.6

Source: Maria Carrilho, "Origems sociais do corpo de oficiais das forças armadas portuguesas ao longo do século XX," *Analise Social* 18 (1982): 1160.

Table 6.9
Class Origins of the Portuguese Navy Officer Corps (percent)

| | Date of Birth | | |
Father's Occupation	1930--1939	1940--1949	1950--1959
Armed forces	26.8	18.4	20.6
Civil servant, police	16.3	21.2	20.3
Liberal profession	11.6	13.6	6.3
Proprietor	6.8	3.5	4.2
Commercial businessman	6.7	9.2	4.2
White-collar worker	10.1	10.0	9.8
Skilled white-collar worker	12.3	11.6	18.9
Farmer, nonowner	0.3	1.5	1.3
Skilled blue-collar worker	6.1	11.0	14.7

Source: Maria Carrilho, "Origems sociais do corpo de oficiais das forças armadas portuguesas ao longo do século XX," *Analise Social* 18 (1982): 1160.

Changes in the Educational Background of Young QP Officers

The educational requirements of the young QP officers were first altered in 1958, when the reactionary coalition made the military academies tuition free. At the same time, the requirement that military cadets had to meet the educational standards of university students was dropped. In 1969, when the monthly stipend policy was passed, the educational standard of the cadets was further lowered as a consequence of the lower social background of the cadet corps. Entrance exams and test scores declined, and the cadets' education was limited to military subjects with "no training in non-military topics, such as political science, economics, public administration, modern management, etc." (Wiarda 1975, 54).

The reactionary coalition was not interested in an enlightened officer corps. In the 1950s, the passing mark in the final academy examinations was 80 percent. A decade later, cadets were becoming professional military junior officers with a passing mark of 50 or 55 percent. Thus, the democratization of recruitment to the service academies produced an additional division between the permanent upper-middle-rank officers and the permanent junior officers: educational cleavage. A middle-ranking naval officer remarked, "You could sense the difference between the middle and the junior officers . . . the younger ones were less educated, they had less *culture générale*" (Porch 1977, 68).

The colonial wars caused clear divisions within the QP of the Portuguese armed forces, divisions based on differences in age, class origins, and educational background. As the wars progressed, an additional division within the QP emerged that was to play an important role in the formation of the MFA. It was the junior officer corps, sons of petite bourgeois and working-class families, who in many cases had been proletarianized by monopolistic capitalism and other economic/social changes. They fought in the African wars, as company-grade officers, "to defend the property of an oligarchy to which they did not belong," while field-grade senior officers, largely from upper- and upper-middle-class origins, remained in continental Portugal, holding staff positions and profitable sinecures (Oppelo 1985, 67; Hammond 1982, 78). It was the "regular" junior officers "who had to take command of [even lower social class] men in the swamps, jungles and savannahs of Africa, and it was they who came into contact with the guerrillas" (The Insight Team 1975, 17).

Divisions between the Regulars (QP) and the Conscripts (QC)

The outbreak of the wars of liberation in Africa widened an old division within the Portuguese armed forces, and introduced a new element in their composition. In addition to the QP, the armed forces included the *milicianos*. The latter constituted the Quadro de Complemento (QC), which was made up of conscripted civilians serving the compulsory tour of military duty. The *miliciano* officers were better educated, with a high school or a university education. We must, however, keep in mind that during the rule of the reactionary coalition both the secondary and tertiary institutions of education were notoriously elitist and conservative. It would be an error to see the university students/graduates of the 1960s and 1970s as political radicals. The MFA was originally formed by members of the QP, not of the QC. "Political indifference and even more, political ignorance, are the characteristic traits of most Portuguese students today, more than a year after the fall of fascism" (Alves 1975, 14; quoted in Porch 1977, 31).

As the colonial wars progressed, the social class origins of the QC became higher than those of the QP. Most *milicianos* resented having to fight in Africa. A conscript junior officer said:

In Guinea, the anti-war feeling was strong among the *milicianos*. Bissau was a beastly place. We had a very common saying: "I'm fed up with this place! I'm fed up with

them—meaning the regular officers! Get me out of here!'' . . . The *milicianos* felt that
they were being used to do the dirty work. (Porch 1977, 64)

In reality, however, *milicianos* commanded garrison troops that carried out
civic action programs, patrols, and intelligence gathering. The QP did most of
the fighting.

Elite, often black units of commandos, paratroops or marines shifted about the country
doing most of the fighting. Those men were led by regular officers or keen *miliciano*
volunteers and contrasted sharply with the often timid stationary units captained by
milicianos. (Porch 1977, 64)

But the colonial wars were to cause still greater divisions between the permanent
officer corps and the *milicianos*.

The Rebelo Decree-Laws

Despite the democratization in the patterns of recruitment to the service academies, in the early 1970s the reactionary coalition faced dangerous shortages
of manpower in the junior and middle ranks of QP officers. The colonial wars
had caused a tremendous increase in troop strength and, at the same time, had
made a military career rather unattractive. In 1972 there were only 72 admissions
to the Military Academy, compared with 266 in 1962. The pool available to
increase the number of junior QP officers was found in the conscripted *milicianos*.
In the past it had been common practice for conscripted QC officers to enter the
service academies under normal entrance procedures and to be admitted to the
QP after graduation. But with the spread of the wars, *milicianos* did not relish
the idea of entering the academies as cadets after having served a tour of duty
in the wars. Besides, a professional military career had lost its attractiveness
and prestige.

In July 1973, the minister of defense, General Sá Viana Rebelo, instituted a
new procedure to eliminate or reduce the shortage of manpower in the officer
corps. Decree-Law 353 (known as the Rebelo Decree) implemented an accelerated procedure for *milicianos* to join the QP and to expedite their promotion
to higher ranks. After their obligatory military service, the *milicianos* could now
become part of the QP after just one year (two semesters) of officer training at
the academies, instead of the four years required for regular entrants. In addition,
the decree stipulated that when entering the academies—and a future military
career—the *milicianos* could count their former military service toward promotion within the QP corps. In other words, the *milicianos* could now become
members of the QP officer corps in a rather short period of time and, more
important, upon graduation from the academy they could be promoted more
quickly than regular academy graduates and QP officers.

During the reactionary coalition's rule, promotion in the Portuguese armed forces was based not on seniority plus ability but exclusively on seniority plus loyalty. The Rebelo Decree, however, based the seniority of the former *milicianos* not on the year they graduated from the academy but on the year they were drafted.

It was not many days later that my military adjunct informed me that the Decree-Law had not been well received in the army. . . . There are captains, he told me, who have jumped lieutenant colonels [in seniority]. And he reminded me of the enormous importance a soldier attaches to his seniority on the ladder: "seniority is a job." (Caetano 1974, 185; quoted in Porch 1977, 65)

It did not take long for the "regulars" to react to the Rebelo decree. The service academy graduates found the decree unfair. After years of fighting in Africa, their long-overdue promotions would be delayed still further. They believed that the decree devalued the professional education and training of the service academies, and felt that their careers were threatened. They made their views known to the Caetano government, and after much protest, a second decree was implemented. But the new Decree-Law 409/73 amended the Rebelo decree only with regard to protecting the seniority of QP officers above the rank of captain. Consequently, it only gave the junior QP officers additional reasons to be dissatisfied and to continue their protests. Junior QP officers in both continental Portugal and the colonies began expressing their discontent publicly. They circulated letters and petitions of protest. Thirty-eight officers from all branches of the armed forces signed an open letter of protest addressed to the government. They pressured the Supreme Army Council to reconsider the decrees, but Defense Minister Rebelo did not change his position and reaffirmed that his reforms were vital to the existence of the armed forces.

The former *milicianos* also aired their views on the decrees in the summer of 1973. In the circular "Stagnation or Progress," they declared:

Since the French Revolution . . . countries have always looked to place the most clever, the most capable, those who offer guarantees of progress and evolution in important positions. There have always been—and there will continue to be in the eternal march of humanity struggling for protection—conservatives and reactions of a minority or a silent majority. Our country is no exception. . . . After fighting overseas, after enduring the bitterness of the war and the bitterness of following orders, these conscripts, many of whom have studied one, two, three, four or more years at a university, and who have chosen a military career, joined the regular cadres, now find themselves thanks to decree law 353–73 placed in the military hierarchy at the point warranted by their diplomas and determined by the country's evolution. Despite the opinions of a few reactionaries, no one can cast aspersions upon our military qualifications, our medals and laurel colored with bitterness. Few can doubt our professional competence without calling into question the universities, the Military Academy, the courses for *miliciano* officers and sergeants, our military chiefs and the theaters of operations where we learned our profession. Since 1961, this country, where military service is obligatory, has fought a war largely with its conscripts—officers, sergeants, and soldiers—who are our technicians, engineers, doctors, lawyers, economists, architects, etc. This is a country of conscripts of whom some for various reasons have chosen to enter the professional officer corps and follow the career of arms: WE WILL NOT PERMIT STAGNATION, THE OLIGARCHY OF AN EXTREME RIGHTWING MINORITY. (Rodrigues et al. 1974; quoted in Porch 1977, 66)

The open letter to the government signed by thirty-eight QP officers, some of whom were to rise to positions of leadership within the MFA, stated:

These officers, who believe that they are speaking for all their comrades, ex-cadets of the old Army School and the present Military Academy, feel wounded in their prestige, in their dignity, in their professional honour and intellectual standing by the thought that a two-semester course can in any way substitute for the four-year course which they completed at the Military Academy. Faced with the growing demands of international life, with technical progress which has influenced certain aspects of military life and with educational improvements which all countries are striving for, they feel that the Military Academy course must be intensified, expanded and made tougher, accessible only to the most interested and adept, to create an elite which will guarantee that the missions confided to the armed forces can be carried out. They feel that with this decree, the best qualified Portuguese will not be attracted to a badly paid career requiring great sacrifices and lacking intellectual prestige comparable to that of the professional schools. . . . They feel that as their major mission is to lead men and that as their own lives are at stake more intense preparation will be necessary to guarantee a high position recognized by a country which wants always to count on capable and prestigious armed forces whose preparation will be compatible with the authentic values of the dignity of man. . . . These officers, therefore, cannot remain silent before this flagrant inversion of values. (quoted in Porch 1977, 67)

Further Reaction to the Decrees

The Congress of Overseas Combatants

In June 1973, in the city of Pôrto, the reactionary coalition organized a Congress of Overseas Combatants to enhance the prestige of the armed forces and to increase public support for the colonial wars. The planners of the congress had decided that high-ranking military officers were publicly to display loyalty to the coalition's regime, and to call for increased support for the war effort. Earlier, news about the forthcoming congress had not been well received by the junior officers fighting in Angola, Guinea-Bissau, and Mozambique. The officers in Guinea-Bissau opposed the motions of support for the war. They contacted other officers in continental Portugal and created an opposition group. They then informed the coalition's government of their desire to speak at the congress. The request was denied. The junior officers' next step was the collection of approximately five hundred signatures in support of an opposition document which argued that motions passed at the congress were invalid because opposing views had not been permitted.

The Congress of Overseas Combatants had two main consequences. First, it widened the divisions that already existed between high-ranking military officers and junior officers. The former, many of them generals, members of "the Rheumatic Brigade," had been co-opted by the coalition, promoted to their ranks on the basis of seniority/loyalty to the regime, and appointed to profitable sinecures. They were, of course, staunch supporters of the African wars. Second, the congress ignited the discontent and opposition that had been taking shape in the armed forces. A small number of discontented officers saw an opportunity to organize military opposition into a concrete and united form. Junior officers of different political persuasions and class backgrounds were to be united within a very short period of time and to associate themselves into what they called first the "Captains' Movement," and later the Armed Forces Movement.

The Evora Meeting

In September 1973, approximately 140 junior officers, none above the rank of captain, and almost all with service in the colonial wars, met at a farmhouse near the town of Evora, in southeastern Portugal. The main purpose of the meeting was to discuss and to decide which course of action to take regarding the Rebelo decrees. In addition to the main grievance, the loss of prestige and professional standing of the QP, other issues were discussed: the low level of military pay; the African wars and the condition of the country; the long tours of duty, which caused long separation from their families; poorly equipped combat units and antiquated equipment; the incompetence of the "Rheumatic Brigade"; and the rapid increase in the cost of living caused by inflationary pressures. One of the original members of the MFA, Captain Dinis de Almeida, later said:

We said to the officers present that it was not a political meeting but a professional one. We met only to discuss professional problems. But of course we had a political intention. In the meeting we observed the other officers, what they said, what they thought and the general discussion. We took notes particularly about what was said by any officer we didn't know well. (quoted in The Insight Team 1975, 35)

At the conclusion of the meeting, which was considered a success, the junior officers prepared a document of collective protest about the Rebelo decrees. It called for the government to find "a just solution for ex-*miliciano* officers who become regulars, without, however, compromising the interests of professional officers or the prestige of the army which serves faithfully" (Rodrigues et al. 1974, 78). A week later 190 junior officers signed the document (97 additional signatures were placed on it in less than a month), which was then taken to the office of the prime minister. A delegation of junior officers had a meeting with the chief of staff, General Costa Gomes, who was sympathetic to their situation. Costa Gomes later went to see the prime minister and told him that he was speaking on behalf of the captains "since they had no generals in the army who could speak for their aspirations.'' Caetano later wrote about the reply that he gave to Costa Gomes:

I told him that the armed forces cannot exist without respect for discipline and the attitude of the captains, shown in the organization of their movement and the presentation of their demands, is clearly undisciplined. This attitude would irremediably undermine the military hierarchy: after the captains, who can deny the legitimacy of a movement of sergeants? or a soviet of soldiers? A government conscious of its responsibilities cannot recognize any movements. Much less talk with them . . . if the armed forces want to force their will there is only one thing to do—take over the government. (Caetano 1974, 187; quoted in Porch 1977, 78)

Later, however, General Rebelo was replaced with General Silva Cunha, the decrees were rewritten, and, in January 1974, a pay increase was given to the armed forces. But by that time, as Caetano was to observe later, "the Captains' Movement progressed, politicized each time more under the influence of left-wing officers, set firmly on the road to a conspiracy" (Caetano 1974, 188; quoted in Porch 1977, 79).

The October 6 Meeting

A second meeting took place on October 6, 1973, in Lisbon. At this meeting delegates from the colonies and metropolitan units, and observers from the air force and the navy, were united into one formally organized Movimento dos Capitães (Captains' Movement). They discussed the wars, inflation, and the incompetent military leadership, and threatened the reactionary coalition with collective resignation if their claims were ignored. But for the majority of the junior officers, a coup was not yet on the agenda. As Vitor Alves, one of the left-wing captains, observed: "Our attitude and motivations were above all professional and concern for the prestige of the armed forces. . . . We wanted to redirect this professional motivation until we were able to create a group sufficiently strong to make political demands."[2]

The War in Guinea-Bissau and António Spínola

The War and Its Effects

Portugal waged wars against liberation movements in three African colonies for thirteen years. In the colony of Guinea-Bissau, Portugal was defeated by the Partido Africano para a Independência da Guiné e de Cabo Verde PAIGC. Under the leadership of the charismatic and intelligent Marxist thinker Amilcar Cabral (assassinated by PIDE/DGS agents on January 20, 1973), PAIGC was well organized and well equipped thanks to the sympathetic leaders of Senegal and of the Guineans. It was in control of most of the territory of Guinea.

By the late 1960s the war in Guinea was going very badly for the Portuguese troops, which had been forced back to the towns that lodged Guinea's white

population, numbering two thousand, the majority of whom were colonial administrators. Military strategies used in Vietnam by American soldiers were
adopted in Guinea with no success. Brigadier António Spínola reported to the
reactionary coalition in 1968, after a fact-finding tour of Guinea, that the war
there was lost. He criticized the governor-general, Arnaldo Schultz, for the
adaptation and implementation of military strategies exclusively, and recom-
mended instead civic actions and programs designed to win the hearts and minds
of the colonial population. This was necessary, he explained, not to win the
war—which was unwinnable—but to give Portugal some leverage with which
to negotiate an honorable settlement with PAIGC (Porch 1977, 53).

Spínola returned to Guinea with the coalition's approval to put his "hearts
and minds" plans into practice. And so he did. "For a better Guinea" was
Spínola's motto.

Ninety million escudos were spent to construct over 15,000 houses, 164 schools, 40
infirmaries, 163 fire stations and 86 fountains. Twenty per cent of teachers and 95 per
cent of doctors in Guinea were furnished by the army. Soldiers also advised the Africans
on agriculture and improved roads and air fields. (Porch 1977, 54)

The strategy of "hearts and minds" had an important effect on the minds of
the junior officers, many of whom were from petit bourgeois and working-class
backgrounds. Moreover, most of the "hearts and minds" techniques used by
the Portuguese military were copied from those of PAIGC. In his writings,
Amilcar Cabral argued that his country's lower middle class was the real leader
of the revolutionary struggle. In the absence of a self-aware proletariat, the lower
middle class had to be the revolutionary class. In reading Cabral, the junior
officers became more politically aware and began to realize that they were fighting
the Guinean people to defend the economic interests of the monopolistic groups,
such as the CUF, that in the past had owned the Guinea colony almost entirely.
And the more politically aware they became, the more they respected and admired
the natives of Guinea. By the late 1960s, when Spínola assumed command in
the colony, most officers disapproved of the war and favored a negotiated political
settlement. Several organizing officers of the Captains Movement, MFA, and
the coup of 1974 were veterans of the war in Guinea. Otelo de Carvalho, the
coup's military strategist, was a native of Mozambique and a veteran of the
"hearts and minds" strategies in Guinea.

Spínola and His Book

António Spínola was born into an upper-class family on April 11, 1910. His
father had friends in the reactionary coalition, and was an intimate friend and
adviser of António Salazar. The younger Spínola entered the Military Academy,
as a cavalry cadet, at the age of twenty. He married into one of the richest
families in Portugal, the Melos, who were the main stockholders of CUF. In
the 1950s, Spínola was deputy commander of the Guarda Nacional Republicana,

the elite paramilitary corps that protected the reactionary coalition. He supported Francisco Franco (as did all members of the coalition) and fought for him in the Spanish Civil War. And during World War II, he fought with Nazi troops that invaded the Soviet Union and encircled Stalingrad.

Spínola had been a member of the board of directors of the Champalimaud monopolistic group while on a leave of absence from the army. In the 1960s, he served in Angola in counterguerrilla operations. From 1968 to 1973, Spínola was commander in chief of the forces fighting PAIGC. In a 1969 interview he

berated NATO for not helping the Portuguese war effort in Africa more, sharply scolded the West for not understanding that the Lisbon government had already spent more than two billion U.S. dollars for military expenditures in a cause expressing more than narrow national interests, and complained of the heavy economic yoke under which the Portuguese people had to labor to back the war effort. (Harsgor 1976, 18)

Spínola was relieved of his duties in Guinea and returned to Portugal in 1973. He was given a hero's welcome, and the reactionary coalition awarded him Portugal's highest decoration, the Torre e Espada (Tower and Sword) with palms. The coalition also promoted him to the newly created position of deputy chief of staff of the armed forces. Spínola had been working for some time on a book about Portugal, the colonies, and the wars. In November 1973, he informed Caetano that he intended to publish his book, in which he called for a political solution to the colonies' situation and for the creation of a Portuguese Commonwealth of Nations. Caetano, concerned about the possible consequences of the book, consulted with General Costa Gomes, who observed that Spínola's book was "a brilliant service rendered to the country" (Harsgor 1976, 18).

Spínola's book, *Portugal e o Futuro* (Portugal and the Future), published in early 1974, had an effect that cannot be ignored. Caetano correctly concluded, after reading the book, that "a military coup was by now unavoidable" (Harsgor 1976, 18). With the publication of Spínola's book, the Captains' Movement was given a well-known and well-respected figurehead who would legitimate the coup. In spite of its neocolonialist ideas (naively conceived, since Portugal's economic structure made neocolonialism impossible), Spínola's book was to be used to convince the apolitical and more conservative military officers that the colonial wars were causing insurmountable economic and political problems. Portugal was spending almost half of its annual budget fighting unwinnable wars, and that had to stop. Spínola wrote:

The future of Portugal depends on [an] appropriate solution to the problems raised by the war which, by consuming lives, resources and talent, increasingly compromises the rhythm of development which we must have to catch up with other nations. (Spínola 1974, 12; quoted in Porch 1977, 85)

The book, published by a firm owned by the CUF cartel, was a success. Widely read, it was a catalyst, an "accelerator of events." An officer involved in the military operations of the coup remembered, "When Spínola's book appeared, backed by all its prestige, we were certain that with this man our revolution would not come from the street" (Rodrigues et al. 1974, 253; quoted in Porch 1977, 84).

The Seizure of Power

The Obidos Meeting

The seizure of power by means of a military coup was first discussed by the Captains in a meeting that took place at Óbidos on December 10, 1973. On that date, the Captains' resolution on the possibility of the coup was sufficiently strong to justify the creation of a coordinating committee. This committee was made up of nineteen representatives of the air force, artillery, cavalry, infantry, navy, and logistic services. Heading it were the left-wing officers Otelo de Carvalho, Vasco Lourenço, and Vítor Alves, who were also given the task of drawing up the movement's political program. "The left-wing officers had now formally seized control of the Movement" (Porch 1978, 81). "It was in Óbidos that the Movement took a clear political direction, for only there, meeting with the representatives of all the branches of the armed forces did one feel that a true political consciousness existed."[3]

The Cascais Meeting

The political program of the Captain's Movement was discussed at a meeting held in Cascais on March 5, 1974. Two hundred officers from the three branches of the armed forces attended the meeting. Approximately ninety officers signed the drafted program. But because the air force and the more pro-Spínola representatives considered the draft too left-wing, and the navy representatives considered it too right-wing, it was decided to rewrite the program. The Captains also decided to seek the collaboration of Spínola (they needed him as a figurehead of the movement, and needed the support of the officers loyal to him) and of Costa Gomes.

A month after the Cascais meeting, the reactionary coalition dismissed both Spínola and Costa Gomes because they refused to support the coalition's regime and war efforts. The effect of the dismissal was a putschist attempted coup by some officers of the MFA. Assuming that support from other military units would be forthcoming, an infantry regiment from the town of Caldas da Rainha marched toward Lisbon. But, once again, no support came from other units, and about two hundred junior officers were arrested by military and paramilitary forces loyal to the reactionary coalition. Among the arrested officers was Captain Vasco Lourenço, one of the founders of the MFA. He was exiled to the Azores.

The Coup of April 25, 1974

The military plans and strategies for the coup were masterminded by Mozambique-born Major Otelo Saraiva de Carvalho, with the assistance of Major

Hugo dos Santos and Lieutenant Colonel Garcia dos Santos. One of the reasons that April 25 was chosen was that it coincided with NATO exercises, and the latter would free the Tagus estuary of NATO warships. By 11:00 P.M. of April 24, the leaders of the MFA had put together a small army comprised of tanks and other armored vehicles at condition alert, ready to move to Lisbon and seize the state. Shortly after midnight, a banned song by José Afonso was broadcast by a Lisbon radio station:

> Grandola, brunette town, land of brothers,
> Town, it's the people who give you power.
> A friend in every corner,
> Equality on every face.
> In the shadow of the ageless oak tree,
> I swear to choose your power as my companion.
>
> (Ferreira and Marshall 1984, 30)

The song was the signal for the troops to move. Less than four hours later, the MFA had secured the center of Lisbon. The coup was on, and this time it would not fail. The last loyal servant of the reactionary coalition, Marcello das Alves Caetano, went to the GNR headquarters at Carmo, in the fashionable downtown section of Lisbon. He refused to surrender the government to a young army captain. He said he did not want "the power of the state to fall into the street," and asked for General Spínola, to whom he surrendered. In so doing, Caetano gave the impression that what took place at Carmo was a transfer of state power to a legitimate new holder, and not to rebel military officers or to mobs in the street. Either this was how the Spanish armed forces interpreted the actions at Carmo, or contacts between them and the MFA had taken place before. Otherwise, under the Iberian Pact of 1939, the Spanish would be obligated to march into Portugal to assist the reactionary coalition against the rebel military forces. But that they did not do.

The coup was virtually bloodless. The only casualties were three civilians killed by PIDE/DGS agents.

THE GENESIS OF THE MFA

The genesis of the MFA cannot be explained in monocausal terms. The actions of the junior officers and the creation of the MFA had several causes. To argue, in a rather Marxist way, that the class origins of the junior officers were the determining, independent variable, is incorrect and an exercise in mechanistic economic determinism. In fact, not all members of the Revolutionary Council of the MFA graduated from the Military Academy after 1958. Only about half of the council's twenty-four members in July 1975 had done so. And some of the left-wing and most politicized members of the Revolutionary Council, such as Vítor Alves, Melo Antunes, and Pezarat Correia, had left the Military Academy well before the democratization of recruitment initiated in 1958. Admiral Rosa Coutinho had left the Naval Academy in 1944, and left-wing naval officers Vítor Crespo and Jorge Jesuino had left in 1952. Other active founding members of the MFA—Vasco Gonçalves, Luís Banazol, Franco Charrais, F. Lopes Pires, Costa Bras, Firmino Miguel, and Hugo dos Santos—had left the Military Academies in the 1950s or the late 1940s.

The coup appears not so much one of the younger generation against the older, but of the middle generation of officers in their thirties and early forties together with a few of their younger intellectual peers who regarded themselves as culturally and educationally superior to most of the newcomers. (Porch 1977, 73)

The older MFA activists had a better understanding of the situation of their country and of the economic, political, and social changes that Portugal had experienced since the late 1950s. They had opposed the reactionary coalition's regime for many years, and some, such as Lieutenant Colonel Carlos Fabião (forty-four years old on April 25, 1974) and Major Melo Antunes (forty-one years old), had engaged in antiregime political activity prior to 1974.

The military establishment soon realized that it was fighting unwinnable wars on three fronts. But to many people in Portugal, the wars were being lost because of the incompetence of the armed forces. Even domestic problems on the Continent were blamed on the military. The military became the scapegoat for Portugal's problems, an additional factor that explains the MFA and the coup. An MFA officer later observed, "Since Gôa, the armed forces had been the scapegoat for all that was wrong in Portugal, including the impossible military solution in Africa and the lowering of living standards at home because of the failure in Africa."[4]

In Guinea, the military strategies, first of "search and destroy," and then of "hearts and minds," combined with fact that as early as 1967, the colonial war was considered unwinnable, contributed to the development of political awareness and of leftist political ideas among the junior officers. The colonial violence that they were seeing firsthand transformed in their ideological worldviews. Soon after the outbreak of the colonial wars, they began asking

Who profited from the war they had been pushed into in the name of the country? Could their . . . wages be compared with the profits of the colonial farmers, not to mention the profits of the monopolistic groups, whom they were protecting with their lives? And what was the monthly income of the whites in Luanda and the Beira, and of the Generals and the Ministers that sent them, young men, to war? And, above all, how could the government prove that the country was being defended in Africa, at the expense of the natives who had only revolted against colonial exploitation? (Rodrigues et al. 1977, 349; my translation)

The Captain's Movement and the MFA were born not because of class or military issues exclusively, but because of a multiplicity of interacting factors.

Although in September 1973 a military coup was unthinkable to the majority of the junior officers, in the early 1970s the structure of Portuguese society had become a mass of unsolvable systemic contradictions. Specialists on Portugal have argued that in the early 1970s there were no conditions that helped one to predict a coup or that made a coup inevitable. I take issue with this position. In 1961, immediately after the first guerrilla attacks in the colonies, some generals in the Portuguese military high command, under the leadership of General Botelho Moniz, tried to remove Salazar from power but were unsuccessful. And in the years between 1961 and 1973, systemic change caused unobservable contradictions (such as the entire social formation created by the reactionary coalition, which the *ultras* were still holding on to in early 1974, vis-à-vis the position of Portugal in Europe, in Africa, and in the world capitalist system), which made the end of the reactionary coalition, via a military coup, inevitable.

One cannot, therefore, explain the genesis of the MFA without including the economic and social changes Portugal began experiencing in the early 1960s. The rapid quantitative and qualitative systemic changes that ensued had deleterious consequences. The social formation of the coalition was economically, politically, and socially introverted. From 1926 to the early 1960s, Portugal was not a participating member of the European community.

The mode of production in Portugal was a sort of capitalism characterized by private ownership of the means of production and by extensive state control of the economy (and was precapitalist in the more isolated parts of the country). Throughout its existence, the reactionary coalition favored accumulation/exploitation in a feudalist and mercantilist society that assured high surplus value and reduced risks by controlling competition and by keeping the workers on a leash.

The cost of maintaining the colonial empire, of fighting wars of liberation, forced the regime to open the country to foreign investment, which became quite extensive by the second half of the 1960s. Extensive penetration of foreign capital into Portugal brought about a novel and rapid extroversion of the social formation. The irreversible consequence of this was the emerging contradictions between the formal, de jure, corporatist foundations of the Estado Novo and the radical economic and social realities facing the country and the people. From then on, systemic contradictions made the need for a new superstructure inevitable. Unknown to the junior officers, the economic and social conditions of Portugal in the early 1970s had already facilitated the role of the armed forces as the only structural mechanism capable of seizing power and destroying the reactionary coalition.

In a very dialectical way, the mechanisms used to preserve the empire and the reactionary coalition's regime (foreign investment, foreign loans, foreign influence) expedited the fall of the coalition. Specifically, the penetration of foreign investment increased economic concentration in monopolistic cartels and caused the extinction of many small family enterprises (proleterianization of the petite bourgeoisie). It caused increases in inflation and in the migration of workers to foreign countries. By mid-April 1974, inflation was running at the rate of more than 30 percent a year, the highest in Europe. Emigration caused the working population in metropolitan Portugal to shrink from 3.126 million in 1960 to only 2.925 million in 1973.

Unemployment was rising, and the balance of trade had never been worse. The African wars devoured 40–50 percent of Portugal's annual $1.3 billion budget. The country was maintaining two hundred thousand men in the armed forces, 80 percent of them fighting in three colonies. Military expenditures were limiting economic growth and retarding social mobility. The country was investing/spending little in economic development/diversification, and in health, housing, and education. Finally, the penetration of foreign investment exacerbated the conflicts that had been emerging between the "traditional" segment of the hegemonic class, "the coalition of rural landowners, small businessmen, rentiers and entrepreneurs," which still held power because of the rigidity of the social formation, the lack of a well-organized and mass-based opposition, and much repression, and the "modern" monopolistic "commercial and industrial capitalists" (Hammond 1982; Logan 1985; Arrighi 1985).

Because the Estado Novo had allowed no genuine opposition—definitely not broad, mass-based opposition—and the forces of social control (GNR, PSP, and PIDE/DGS) were still loyal to the *ultras'* regime, the armed forces were called upon to do what no other group could do: seize power on behalf of the modernizing sector of the hegemonic class. This new historical bloc had to seize power in order to transform the economic, political, and social structure of an anachronistic bureaucratic–authoritarian regime into a modernizing and democratic one. The superstructure (read: the state, the relations of production, the ideological and educational apparatuses) of the reactionary coalition had run out of time. A new superstructure, more in tune with the interests and needs of the Europeanist, liberal, middle-bourgeois hegemonic class fraction had to be created and installed from above.

This new superstructure began on April 25, 1974, when the MFA seized power.

NOTES

1. *Expresso* (Lisbon), July 27, 1974; Jane Kramer, "Letter from Lisbon," *The New Yorker*, September 23, 1974, 116, in Bandeira (1976, 26).

2. Vítor Alves, *Expresso* (Lisbon), September 20, 1975, quoted in Porch (1977, 80).

3. Vítor Alves, interview in *Expresso* (Lisbon), September 20, 1975, quoted in Porch (1977, 81).

4. B. Wellfred, "Is Portugal Marching Backward?" *The Guardian* (Manchester), June 2, 1974, quoted in Bandeira (1976, 18).

7

The Revolution of 1974: Democracy from Above

The Portuguese Revolution of 1974 lasted approximately nineteen months, from April 1974 to November 1975. This period coincides with the rise of the Armed Forces Movement (MFA) as a politico military opposition group, and with its fall and the rise of a pluralistic constitutional regime. During this time there was overt upheaval and even left-wing revolt, but there were no truly revolutionary changes. The purpose of this chapter is to show that the "revolution" of April 25, 1974, in reality was not a revolution—it was never meant to be one—and that what took nineteen months to be implemented was bourgeois democratization of Portuguese society from above.

The period of nineteen months is characterized by distinct phases that correspond to specific situations which emerged, had a short existence, and then succumbed to new situations. At the same time, however, and alongside the distinct phases, there was, at a deeper level, much continuity. Superficially, the phases and their respective situations appeared to be radical and taking Portugal into truly revolutionary systemic change. But, at a deeper structural level, radical and revolutionary changes never occurred. The inability to distinguish between appearance and reality has contributed to a misunderstanding of what actually occurred in Portugal between April 1974 and November 1975.

THE MFA AS A POLITICOMILITARY OPPOSITION

The Junta of National Salvation

Upon seizing state power, the MFA established the Junta of National Salvation (JNS), led by the popular and outspoken General António de Spínola. In choosing Spínola, the MFA sent a signal to the old members of the reactionary coalition that continuity, not dramatic and revolutionary change, would shape the future of Portugal. After all, Spínola, while favoring much-needed liberalization of the regime that had rewarded his family and himself so handsomely, was not a friend of the left and definitely not of socialism. It has been observed that his political ambitions "can be summed by the term 'Gaulism' " (Pimlott 1978, 16). Moreover, the Junta, created to give the MFA a formal and legal existence both in Portugal and abroad, was made up of army generals and navy admirals long associated with the reactionary coalition. The MFA also created a Coordinating Committee, made up of founding members of the former Captains' Movement, and a Council of the State.

The Junta abolished by decree the institutions of the reactionary coalition's regime, promised general elections within a year, and assured Portugal's NATO allies that the MFA would respect and satisfy Portugal's international commitments. Censorship was abolished, freedom of assembly and of speech was reinstated, political prisoners were released, and former PIDE/DGS agents were imprisoned. Forty-nine-year-old Mario Soares, secretary of the Portuguese Socialist Party (PSP), and sixty-year-old Alvaro Cunhal, leader of the Communist Party (PCP), were permitted to return from exile, and almost immediately became politically active. While Soares had to start almost from scratch to set up a political base, Cunhal could now use an established and strong political party structure. Sá Carneiro and Magalhães Motta emerged from internal exile and began organizing their conservative-center bourgeois party, the Popular Democratic Party. The Junta stated that the colonies would be given the right of self-determination.

The First Provisional Government

The first provisional government was established on May 15, 1974. The Junta chose António de Spínola as president of the Republic and, at Spínola's request, Adelino da Palma Carlos, a sixty-nine-year-old, formerly apolitical wealthy corporate lawyer and former dean of the Lisbon University Law Faculty, as prime minister. Most members of the first provisional government were civilians, but seven members were senior military officers. Four political parties were represented in the new government: the Popular Democratic Party, (which was to have ministers in every provisional government except the fifth); the Portuguese Democratic Party; the Communist Party; and the Socialist Party.

The first provisional government was dominated by the charismatic Spínola and by the civilian members, most of whom favored a Spinolist solution to the existing situation, including sending the military back to the barracks and leaving the running of the state to the civilians. Many of the MFA members also believed that the military job had been accomplished, that the military should return to the barracks and let the civilians establish a democratic regime.

António de Spínola had known since he began writing his book, *Portugal e o futuro*, that his country faced a serious crisis and must move into the future politically, socially, and economically. Having received control of the state apparatus from Marcello Caetano, and having been chosen by the MFA to be the president of the Republic after the coup, Spínola found himself in a position of power with the support of many followers in the military and in the business community. He had the support of most, if not all, monopolistic groups that had representatives in the civilian body of the first provisional government. Moreover, Spínola's conservative background made him the favorite politician of the right.

Spínola's plan was to send the military back to the barracks and prevent the decolonization of the African colonies, instead creating a "pluricontinental Portuguese Federation" that would extend limited autonomy to each federal member. His neocolonialist ideas would protect the interests and property of white settlers in the colonies, as well as those of the monopolistic groups still much involved in the exploitation of the colonies, such as the Espírito Santo group. As he had stated in his book, it was necessary "to protect the position of the European settlers, who have property there and who built their lives and their dreams there." Spínola's neocolonialist plans would also protect the vast economic interests of Western capitalism.

Realizing that he could not on his own remove the MFA from the political/ state arena, Spínola—perhaps remembering De Gaulle—went beyond the MFA and appealed for a presidential referendum. As elected president, he believed, his position would become more permanent, and that would give him the power he needed to guide Portugal into the future. In July 1974, Spínola convinced Prime Minister Palma Carlos to call for an immediate plebiscite on Spínola's presidency, and on a two-year postponement of election for a Constituent Assembly (Hammond 1982). But Spínola's plan backfired. Portugal was not prepared to vote for president in July 1974. And the MFA (its left wing) rejected Spínola's proposals, specifically the military's return to the barracks and the neocolonialist pluricontinental federation. For the MFA the independence of the colonies was necessary.

The MFA imposed an alternative solution to what became known as the "Palma Carlos crisis": Spínola would remain as provisional president of the Republic; Palma Carlos would resign; and the MFA, not Spínola, would appoint the new prime minister.

The Second Provisional Government

The second provisional government was installed on July 18, 1974. Vasco Gonçalves, one of the original leaders of the Captains' Movement and the head of the Coordinating Committee, was appointed prime minister. Spínola's efforts to monopolize power had backfired, and the MFA was now stronger than before. During the first provisional government the prime minister was a civilian, and only one portfolio had been held by a MFA officer. Now, with Gonçalves as prime minister, the number of MFA officers with portfolios numbered seven.

Moreover, the MFA began institutionalizing itself into a permanent hegemonic role.

On instructions from the MFA, Spínola announced on July 27 that the colonies had the right of self-determination, thus shattering his dreams of a pluricontinental federation. The MFA also recognized that its control of the armed forces was weak. To change this situation, it created two operational units. One was the Fifth Division, a propaganda machine controlled by the MFA left wing, which was to become very effective in creating the illusion that revolutionary systemic change was taking place in Portugal. The other unit was the Comando Operacional do Continente (COPCON; Continental Operations Command), under the command of Otelo Saraiva de Carvalho, who was promoted to commander of the Lisbon military region.

The colonial issue, neocolonialism or decolonization, was the primary reason for a shift to the left that began with the second provisional government. The MFA in general, and its left wing in particular, was quite aware that in the past the colonies had been beneficial mainly to the monopolistic groups and to some segments of the petite bourgeoisie, and not to the nation as a whole. The MFA also knew that the future of Portugal was in Europe, not in Africa. The shift to the left, therefore, was a qualified one. It was not born out of a real concern with the economic and social conditions of the people.

The observation that the shift to the left was a qualified one will be further demonstrated below, but for now, I will submit two examples I find to be relevant. First, while COPCON was initially "a domestic military intervention force . . . composed of units led by officers of the MFA . . . and circumvented the military chain of command," in the beginning it was also employed as "an anti-strike force," and as such "was seen by many on the left as little more than an attempt to resurrect the PIDE/DGS" (Hammond 1982, 81; Lomax 1983, 116). Second, on August 27, 1974, the Gonçalves government passed Decree-Law 392/74, which, for the first time in almost fifty years, recognized workers' right to strike. But, at the same time, it imposed several restrictions on that right and, consequently, was in reality an antistrike law (Lomax 1983, 116).

Counterrevolution: Spínola Appeals to the Silent Majority

Spínola (and his followers) had not given up the desire to seize power from the military and become the Portuguese De Gaulle. His second attempt to do so took the form of an appeal to what he considered to be the silent majority of the Portuguese people who, like himself, he believed, were against what he considered "totalitarian extremism," by which he meant the growing influence of the radicalized MFA officers within the second provisional government. Spínola asked the silent majority to march on to Lisbon to make its will known. A mass public demonstration was set for Saturday, September 28, 1974.

On learning of Spínola's plan, groups of working people in Lisbon set up barricades across key highways, established checkpoints and controls at all roads,

and succeeded in physically preventing entrance to Lisbon. Spínola, in his capacity of provisional president and commander in chief of the armed forces,
ordered the COPCON units to remove the barricades and to open the city to
incoming demonstrators. He also called out the sections of the paratroopers he
thought were still loyal to him. He received negative responses from both military
units. COPCON, on orders from General Otelo de Carvalho, not only did not
remove the barricades, it reinforced the workers.

Spínola soon realized that there was no silent majority, and that the MFA
considered him to be the spokesman of the right and therefore no longer trusted
him. He resigned as provisional president of the Republic. General Costa Gomes
was named president in the third provisional government. Many Spínolist involved in the attempted countercoup were arrested, and those in the government
who held cabinet portfolios resigned and were replaced with MFA officers.

POPULAR POWER: REVOLUTION FROM BELOW?

Spontaneous Activity from Below

"The People Are with the MFA"

With the collapse of the reactionary coalition's regime on April 25, 1974,
there was tremendous support for the MFA and spontaneous activities from
below. The slogan *"O povo está com o MFA"* (The People Are with the MFA)
indicated the popular support for the MFA officers. On April 25, in a show of
appreciation, the people of Lisbon gave carnations to the soldiers, and thus the
revolution became known as the "revolution of carnations." The coup released
tensions and pressures that had existed in Portugal for almost fifty years. Humberto Delgado would have been very happy on April 25, 1974, for on that day
the Portuguese people *deixou de ter medo* (stopped being afraid). For the first
time in almost half a century they could speak their minds and demand social
justice.

The demands for social justice and the revolutionary movements that followed,
however, were exclusively from below, from the masses; they were without any
inspiration or guidance from the MFA or any other left oppositional movement.
Portuguese society during the regime of the reactionary coalition was extremely
stratified, with an enormous social distance between the upper and lower social
classes; there had never been a mass-based opposition. Thus we should not be
surprised that after the coup of April 25, the spontaneous activities from below
lacked support and guidance from the MFA or from left oppositional movements.
Moreover, the MFA, from the beginning, was not interested in radical social
change, in revolution from below. In section B–5 of its program, the MFA
stated, "Major reforms can be adopted only within the framework of the future
National Constitutional Assembly."

Saneamentos and Strikes

Immediately after April 25, 1974, the Portuguese workers began exercising their newly acquired freedom. They made public their long-held grievances, demanded *saneamentos* (purges) of all administrators, managers, and supervisors associated with the previous regime, and demanded higher wages, better working conditions, shorter hours, better medical care, and paid holidays. And to show the seriousness of their position, they used the oldest and most effective labor weapon: strikes. In the first week after April 25 there were seventeen strikes. In the second week there were thirty-one, in the third week eighty-seven, and in the fourth week ninety-seven. By the end of May 1974, two hundred thousand workers had gone on strike, according to one source (Neves 1978, 193–196; quoted in Lomax 1983, 114–115). On May 25, the first provisional government agreed to set a national minimum wage of 3,300 escudos per month, but that figure was considered insufficient by the workers and the wave of strikes continued.

Factory and Business Takeovers

Spontaneous activities from below also took the form of factory and business takeovers, followed by the establishment of worker-managed firms. These activities occurred when workers' demands were not being met, or when employers or managers began laying off workers or cutting production. Because of what they perceived to be economic instability and because of the 30 percent increase in wages, some owners were unwilling to maintain their businesses at the higher costs. Their solution was either to reduce the number of workers or to go out of business. The termination of the business was usually followed by "flight abroad with all of the firm's liquid assets" (Logan 1983, 142). When factories or businesses were occupied and worker-management was established, the primary concern of the workers was to prevent the termination of the business and to assure employment.

Urban Residents' Commissions and Land Occupations

During the reactionary coalition's regime very little, if any, attention was given to housing scarcity and cost. Immediately after the coup, *commissões de moradores* (residents' commissions) were created in working-class neighborhoods, and vacant dwellings were occupied. In the two weeks following April 25, some two thousand properties were occupied, often on the spontaneous initiative of general assemblies in working-class districts. The commissions were also involved in other local problems. Because of their success, the commissions were the models for the *commissões de trabalhadores* (workers' commissions) that were responsible for the wave of strikes.

Rural workers also aired their grievances. Initially, in 1974, their demands were limited to higher wages, the right to form unions, and better working conditions—"largely directed toward the state and the landowners themselves"

(Lomax 1983, 120). Occupation of land did not occur until January 1975, and was limited to the seizure of land the legal owners had not shown interest in cultivating. It was only after March 1975, when many latifundists had fled the country, that landless farm workers in southern Portugal occupied large estates and turned them into cooperatives. In July 1975, however, the provisional government of Vasco Gonçalves (and of the radical wing of the MFA) passed Decree-Law 406A/75 which, although legalizing the cooperatives, stipulated the size and productive potential of land that could be seized and organized into a cooperative.

The Workers Were Not a Class-for-Themselves

The activity from below that occurred immediately after the fall of the reactionary coalition's regime was never organized or nationwide. Most of the working-class activity was concentrated in the industrial areas of Lisbon, Setúbal, Pôrto, Braga and Aveiro. For almost fifty years Portuguese workers had been dominated and oppressed by a specific bourgeois ideology that made the development of class consciousness impossible. It would have been naive to expect Portuguese workers to be anticapitalist and to form a class-for-itself, and thus engage in revolutionary activities with the conscious purpose of transforming Portuguese social and economic relationships. That was never the case, for the Portuguese working class was wholly ruled by a bourgeois mode of thought.

The residents' commissions, workers' commissions and strikes, and dwelling and land occupations were primarily a negative response to a long-term absence of social institutions, of unions that truly defended their interests. The workers' interests were higher wages, better working conditions, paid vacations, health care, and decent housing. Once their demands were met, the revolutionary activity from below was reduced substantially. "Many of the [workers'] commissions turned into union-style bureaucracies or fell into the hands of unrepresentative political activists—either event only reducing popular support and participation even more" (Lomax 1983, 119).

Control from Above

In its communiqué of June 21, 1975, Section 1.1, the MFA stated that it was a movement of national liberation responsible for national independence, and that independence could be attained only through the construction of a socialist society. Section 1.2 of the communiqué defined a socialist society:

A society without classes, obtained by the collectivization of the means of production, eliminating all forms of exploitation of man by man, and in which there will be granted to all individuals equal opportunity for education, work, and advancement, without distinction of birth, sex, religious belief, or ideology.

The communiqué also stated:

The road of transition from peasant society to a socialist society necessarily passes through various phases, the first of which is marked by the transition period fixed in the platform of constitutional agreement and the steps of which will be determined by the political and socioeconomic evolution of the Portuguese people.

The communiqué also informed the Portuguese people that "the MFA has already determined that this path [to socialism] will be made by the pluralist route," and in Section 1.3 it defined pluralism:

Pluralism means free expression and discussion of opinions, as well as experience in the construction of the new society, in open and permanent dialogue with all Portuguese people. Socialist pluralism comprehends the coexistence in theory and in practice of various forms and conceptions of construction of socialist society. At the same time, the MFA rejects the implantation of socialism by violent and dictatorial methods. Party pluralism, as it is stated in the platform of constitutional agreement, implies the recognition of the existence of various political parties and currents of opinion, even if they do not necessarily defend socialist options. At the same time, it admits an opposition whose criticism can be beneficial and constructive provided its actions do not oppose the construction of socialist society by democratic means.[1]

The MFA communiqué of June 1975 clearly indicates a contradiction between the definition of socialism and the determination that it would be reached via the bourgeois pluralist route. This reveals the MFA's petite bourgeois notion of socialism. Second, and more important, the transition to socialism proposed by the MFA was to begin with the platform of constitutional agreement, from above, and not with the "accession of the working class to political power," from below (Sweezy 1975, 15). In fact, not only was the Portuguese working class prevented from obtaining political power, but it was always, even during the highest points of leftist politicizing, greatly controlled from above by the MFA.

The fact is that the radical Gonçalvists and the Communist Party imposed repressive and authoritarian control on the working class and its spontaneous activities. Logan observed:

The main feature of this first year of the revolution from the perspective of the working class was the relative ease with which repression by a corporatist state, in which the workers were not represented, was replaced by the subordination of workers' perceived needs to the requirements of the organizations that purported to represent them. (1983, 143)

Control of workers' most common form of spontaneous activity, the strike, was enforced via Decree-Law 392/74. This law, while it gave the Portuguese worker the legal right to strike, actually took more than it gave, for it "placed draconian limitations on the right to strike" (Poulantzas [1975] 1976, 109). The law was definitely an attempt to harness the working classes, and it reflected the MFA's concern with preventing anarchy and with possible foreign intervention.

The law gave employers the legal right to use the lockout whenever strikes exceeded the limits set by the law. The law prohibited strikes motivated by political or religious goals, solidarity strikes, and strikes aimed at changing the terms of existing union contracts before their expiration. It also prohibited work stoppages by isolated groups of workers in strategic sectors of a firm, as well as factory occupations. The law was not clear on the right of public employees to strike. Article 14 guaranteed access to work by employees who chose not to join a strike. The law required a conciliation period of thirty days after the presentation of written demands before the commencement of a strike, and a minimum seven to ten days' advance notice of the calling of a strike.

Under articles 27 and 28, the government was authorized to suspend a strike, to determine whether a strike conformed to legal requirements, and to impose fines on the parties held in violation of the law. The government also used COPCON, under the direction of Saraiva de Carvalho, to stop strikes and/or occupations in the *Jornal do Comércio*, Sogantal, and TAP (the national airline).

Between April 25, 1974, and November 1975, there was never a revolution from below, and popular power, although revolutionary at times, always remained spontaneous and bourgeois. Popular power was never transformed into the concrete political power necessary to begin the transition to a classless society. In view of its historical experience, "The Portuguese working class had neither the tradition of militancy, the factory-level organization, nor the independent leadership to enable it to resist domination from above" (Logan 1983, 146). The Portuguese workers were not, and could not have been, a class-for-themselves. And even if they could have been, the MFA or Western capitalism would have prevented their access to political power.

THE MFA AS "ACTIVE RULERS"

Counterrevolution: March 11, 1975

Counterrevolutionary forces under the leadership of Spínolists attempted to overthrow the provisional government and seize power on March 11, 1975. Having been told that they were to "put down a left-wing revolt," a company of paratroopers was sent to capture the antiaircraft artillery headquarters that protected the Lisbon air force base and that had to be secured in order to control the international airport. On their arrival, the paratroopers were met by a large number of civilians who formed a human wall around the antiaircraft unit. Within less than three hours, the people and the military loyal to the MFA quashed the attempted coup. Spínola and some of his closest associates were forced to flee Portugal, first to Spain and later to Brazil. Every military officer found to be a Spínolist was expelled from the MFA and removed from a position of power within the armed forces and the government. This event was the beginning of the breakdown of the MFA, in terms of deepening the differences between the members of the various political factions.

The unsuccessful counterrevolutionary coup ended the third provisional government and commenced the fourth, with General Costa Gomes still provisional president and Vasco Gonçalves prime minister. The attempted coup also marked the beginning of the radicalization of the MFA, and the shift of Vasco Gonçalves further left. However, it must be pointed out that between April 1974 and November 1975, appearance/essence, illusion/reality was a permanent fixture. On the level of appearance/illusion there was much leftist politicizing, and even some leftist policies; on the level of essence/reality, revolutionary changes in the Portuguese society never took place.

It was not the spontaneous workers' activities from below nor the position and influence of the Communist Party and other leftist groups that brought about the post–March 1975 radicalization of the MFA. What took the MFA further to the left was the exit of the Spínolists from the government and the "realignment of different military personalities and factions within the various MFA institutions" (Oppelo 1975, 72).

The MFA Defines Itself as a Movement of National Liberation

After March 11, 1975, the radical faction of the MFA began to define the MFA as a national liberation movement and to reorganize the structure of the military movement. The Junta of National Salvation, the MFA's Coordinating Committee, and the Council of the Twenty were merged to form a single governmental body called the Conselho da Revolução (CR, Council of the Revolution). The CR was made up of thirty members recruited from the ruling radical faction of the MFA. Moreover, the Council of the 200, the military general assembly, was expanded to 240 members (120 from the army, and 60 each from the navy and the air force); for the first time it included noncommissioned officers and enlisted men.

The CR legitimized workers' and citizens' groups such as workers' and neighborhood commissions, but at the same time, and rather significantly, it stressed the pluralistic responsibilities and roles of political activities and political parties. Moreover, despite the radicalization of the MFA and the leftist orientation of the Gonçalvists, limitations were imposed on democratization from below and from above. The two pillars of support of the former reactionary coalition's regime, the ten-thousand-member Guarda Nacional Republicana and the four-teen-thousand-member antiriot Polícia de Segurança Pública were not abolished or restructured. In fact, these reactionary forces of social control regularly assisted COPCON in antistrike activities.

The radical Gonçalvists did not alter Portugal's NATO activities and relationships with the U.S. government. The Gonçalvists, so often incorrectly called Communist sympathizers, never "suggested that Washington give up its facilities in the [strategic] Azores bases," and "as late as August [1975] the Premier [Gonçalves] made a point of attending a ceremonial IBERLANT [Portugal-based

NATO regional command] lunch in Sintra to the surprise of NATO ambassadors''
(Szulc 1975–1976, 61).

Nationalizations

The Communist Party and its military allies held key economic and planning
positions in the fourth provisional government, which was formed on April 25,
1975, under Vasco Gonçalves. Although the Communist Party had long favored
the nationalization of most of the Portuguese-owned banking and large-scale,
monopolistic commercial and industrial enterprises, the nationalizations were
actually carried out in an attempt to resolve an existing crisis. It is thus a mistake
to consider them as ''the work of radical-pushing (or communist inspired) MFA,''
for in reality they ''were a response to immediate events, not the culmination
of a plan'' (Pimlott 1978, 18). In fact, some more moderate members of the
MFA were against nationalizations and land reform, because they would alienate
conservative senior military officers and the bourgeoisie. They submitted an
alternative plan whereby the government would take 51 percent ownership instead
of full ownership via nationalization (Hammond 1982). The nationalization issue
showed internal differences in the MFA.

Major industries that were nationalized entirely included electricity, cement,
oil, petrochemicals, steel, railroads, and long-distance bus lines. The number
of firms nationalized totaled 117, but since these firms had a majority ownership
(more than 50 percent) in 219 firms, the government actually assumed control
of 336 firms (Hammond 1982). Although the ruling military became the manager
of a large share of the economy, it stated many times that it was not interested
in seizing small or foreign-owned property. This shows the true economic and
political colors of its members.

The nationalization of major monopolistic firms and the land reform of the
latifundia were not undertaken because such actions and policies were warranted
under a grand revolutionary plan to change the structure of Portuguese society
and to make Portugal socialist. The real reasons were economic-political crises
such as the flight of capital, popular demands from below, and, equally important,
the petite bourgeois views of MFA members regarding monopolistic capitalism.

Elections for the Constituent Assembly

In order to proceed in accordance with the schedule decided in 1974, the
ruling military allowed elections for the Constituent Assembly. The military
became aware, however, that the elections would introduce two problems. First,
they would open the political arena to new power structures in which political
parties would play major roles. Second, the activities of the new political actors
could very well marginalize the military as power holders.

Unwilling to risk losing power, the military, through the Council of the Revolution, developed a ''platform of constitutional agreement'' with the political

Table 7.1
Results of Constituent Assembly Elections, April 25, 1975

Political Party	Percent of Vote
Portuguese Socialist Party	38
Popular Democratic Party	26
Portuguese Communist Party	12.5
Portuguese Democratic Movement	5.0
Five small left groupings	2.0
Social and Democratic Center	7.0
Blank ballots	7.0

Source: Portuguese daily press.

parties. Any political party that wanted to participate in the elections for the Constituent Assembly had to sign the platform. By doing so, the party became politically paralyzed, because

the gist of the platforms was simply that the military would retain power for a transitional period of three to five years and that the Assembly elected on 25 April [1975] would have as its sole function the writing of a Constitution which would serve for the transition period. (Sweezy 1975, 11)

Thus, under the platform agreement, the MFA would in effect be the power center for three (or very likely five) years, starting in 1975. Ironically, the agreement, designed and implemented to maintain the military in control of the state apparatus, might actually have had the opposite effect, for it might have initiated the fall of the military. The elections for the Constituent Assembly, held on April 25, 1975, humiliated both the MFA and the Communist Party (see Table 7.1).

Shortly before the elections, some military leaders made public appeals for blank votes from those who had no party affiliation and wanted to vote for the military. It was assumed that a large number of blank votes would indicate "support for the MFA" (Pimlott 1978, 9). But, out of more than 90 percent of the total votes, only 7 percent were blank. According to the prevalent interpretation, the results showed that the majority of the Portuguese people did not support the MFA. And the lack of support was tantamount to questioning the legitimacy of the military rulers.

The "Hot Summer" of 1975

Following the Constituent Assembly elections, the Portuguese situation was critical. There were violent anti-MFA demonstrations, and attacks on the Communist Party offices in the conservative northern section of the country. There was also a decline in troop discipline. The polarization made the factions within the MFA more clearly defined: (1) radical faction I, the Gonçalvists, Prime

Minister Vasco Gonçalves with the collaboration of the Communist Party, who favored bureaucratic socialism from above; (2) radical faction II, Otelo S. Carvalho, who favored a revolutionary government based on popular power; (3) conservatives, Melo Antunes and Vasco Lourenço, who favored a social-democratic future for Portugal; (4) independent operationals, President Costa Gomes and independent officers, who favored a Western type of democratic regime; (5) the extreme left, composed of officers who identified with extreme left movements.

The extreme left military faction joined with extreme left civilians to organize the Frente Unida Revolucionária (FUR, United Revolutionary Front). Its main objective was to initiate dissatisfaction within the ranks of the military in order to form a new political movement of enlisted men, and to join the new movement with civilian mass movements. The plan worked, and FUR succeeded in organizing a movement of enlisted men called Soldados Unidos Vencerão (Soldiers United Will Win). The latter wanted a role in military decisions, and began challenging the military command hierarchy; lack of military discipline became a problem.

The Fall of the Fourth and Fifth Provisional Governments

The fourth provisional government collapsed when Mario Soares, leader of the Socialist Party, and the Popular Democrats resigned their government positions. Their main objection was the excessive influence of the Communist Party on Prime Minister Gonçalves. Almost immediately, in July 1975, a fifth provisional government was formed. In an attempt to prevent any further loss of control and to regain the power already lost, the ruling military, through the Council of the Revolution, based the fifth provisional government on a triumvirate made up of President Costa Gomes, Prime Minister Gonçalves, and Otelo Saraiva de Carvalho, the commander of COPCON.

But the fifth provisional government "was virtually stillborn." The Grupo dos Nove (Group of the Nine), led by Major Melo Antunes and Brigadier Vasco Lourenço, resigned from the MFA and made public their opposition to what they perceived to be a "bureaucratic dictatorship" of the military (Pimlott 1978). By then, the factional divisions within the MFA were irreversible and fatal. It became quite difficult for the MFA to rule the country. Limited social reforms, such as nationalization and land reform, had alienated the conservative MFA faction.

THE FALL OF THE MFA AND THE RISE OF A PLURALIST CONSTITUTIONAL REGIME

The Fall of the MFA

Prime Minister Augusto Vasco Gonçalves resigned at the end of August 1975. When, on September 19, 1975, the sixth provisional government was formed, the MFA and the military domination had ceased to exist. The sixth provisional government, under the moderate Admiral Pinheiro de Azevedo, brought members of the Group of the Nine, the Socialists, and the Popular Democrats back into the government. The right was in, the left was out. Four ministries were given to the Socialists, two to the Popular Democrats, one to SEDES, and one to the Communist Party. The Socialists and Popular Democrats viewed the sixth provisional government as a "victory for democracy."

After September 1975 Portugal began to move toward a pluralist democracy of the West European type. The control of the armed forces was returned to the chief of the general staff of the armed forces, and the former MFA members returned to the barracks. State power was to be transferred to the independent operational faction of the former MFA.

Foreign Intervention

As a dependent country in the capitalistic system of production and international division of labor, before, during, and after the revolution of 1974 Portugal was subject to direct and indirect foreign intervention. After April 25, 1974, foreign importers canceled orders of Portuguese goods as a protest against what they perceived to be a Communist revolution. Tourists stopped vacationing in Portugal, and immigrants stopped sending their remittances. The former strong balance of payments (strong thanks to remittances and tourist revenues) began to show a deficit. The deficit in the balance-of-trade account also increased. The growing need to borrow abroad, combined with the need for basic imports and for export markets, made Portugal a very dependent country.

Furthermore, by 1974 multinational corporations controlled one-third of Portugal's economy, with another third controlled by firms financially linked to the multinationals. Approximately nine hundred foreign corporations were operating in Portugal, "with West German corporations taking the first, and those of the United States second, place" (Green 1976, 80). Thus, what happened in Portugal was of much importance to Western capitalism.

Interested in protecting their investments and opposed to what they mistakenly considered to be a leftward turn of the revolution after March 1975, Western capitalists played an important role in the fall of the MFA. Dow Chemical terminated negotiations for the installation of an ethylene refinery, allegedly because the Portuguese government demanded a 50 percent state ownership. Both Exxon and Mobil Oil terminated negotiations for the construction of petrochemical plants. Faced with workers' demands for wage increases, Allied Magnets closed its plants. ITT cancelled investments in and shipments to Portugal. And the World Bank refused the Portuguese military government credits that had been negotiated and established before April 25, 1974 (Green 1976).

U.S. Secretary of State Henry Kissinger opposed the presence of Communists in the Portuguese government and wrongly believed that Portugal was moving toward socialism. On his orders, Portugal was expelled from NATO's nuclear planning. He also replaced the American ambassador to Portugal, Stuart Nash, with Frank Carlucci, who had served in Brazil from 1965 to 1968 and spoke fluent Portuguese. Carlucci was a specialist in secret warfare (Green 1976).

Intelligence agencies also intervened in Portugal's internal affairs. The CIA and the West German SPD financed the Portuguese Socialist Party, and the Soviet Union financed the Portuguese Communist Party.

The Associated Press reported on 25 September that the CIA had sent between $2 million and $10 million per month to the Portuguese Socialists since June. The West German Social Democrats had also contributed several million dollars to the Soares party. Support from the Soviet Union to the PCP was placed at $45 million since the April coup. (Maxwell 1986 [article], 130)

The End of the Revolution: November 25, 1975

The Portuguese revolution that began with the coup of April 25, 1974, ended on November 25, 1975. Never truly a revolution, the upheaval lasted only nineteen months. The process of democratization from above initiated by Caetano and his technocrats had taken a detour, but after November 25 it was back on the right track. The operational military officers (conservatives), with the approval of the Group of the Nine (moderate/conservatives), began military preparations to prevent a likely coup from the left. They gathered troops at the Cortegaça air base, in northern Portugal, and at the strategic Amadora commando base, just outside Lisbon.

On November 25, 1975, the former Gonçalvists, extreme left units, and the PCP attempted to regain power. Their putsch collapsed, however, because no other military units joined them and because the operationals, under the command of Colonel Ramalho Eanes and Major Vasco Lourenço, moved decisively to crush the left-wing units. The suppression of the left-wing uprising was so "coolly planned and executed" that it has been considered a "centrist coup" (Pimlott 1976, 393). Afterward, left-wing officers were purged and the

operationals placed themselves in key command positions, and the moderate faction of the former MFA, the Novistas, under the leadership of Melo Antunes, was now in complete control of the Portuguese situation. On that day the "radical" faction of the MFA ceased to exist, and "some 200 [radicals] were arrested including Otelo Saraiva de Carvalho and Dinís de Almeida." (Robinson 1979, 250)

After November 25, 1975, what had appeared to be a revolutionary process turned into a democratic-pluralistic transition. The Revolutionary Council was purged and reconstituted, COPCON was disbanded, the forces of social control (GNR and PSP) were kept, and "revolutionary" intentions were abandoned. On February 26, 1976, the military signed a revised pact with the major political parties. Under its terms, the newly constituted Council of the Revolution would be the guarantor of democracy for the next four years. In the new pact there was no reference to the MFA, to the armed forces as the vehicle of the revolution, or to any military commitment to socialism (Robinson 1979). On the contrary, the military "in a symbolically important move acceded to the demands of the conservative parties that it remove from the pact a preamble reaffirming its commitment to preserve the revolution's transformation of socioeconomic structures" (Hammond 1982, 94).

The masses of Portuguese workers reacted to the events of November 25 with much indifference, for by then the spontaneous movements from below had, for all practical purposes, disappeared. The workers had become aware that

in many ways the forces which came out on top on 25 November were the ones which appeared to offer the easiest way out, for to carry through the projects of FUR (United Revolutionary Front) or COPCON would have brought the wrath of Europe and America down on the workers' heads. (Mailer 1977, 341)

CONCLUSION

The MFA

The MFA was not, in the beginning, a radical group. The few left members, such as Vasco Gonçalves and Otelo de Carvalho, constituted a very small minority. Most MFA members were either moderates or quite conservative. And the MFA itself "had only minority support in the officer corps all along . . . it was riven throughout by major contradictions, and, above all, the politicization of the majority of officers was ambiguous and had distinct limits" (Poulantzas [1975] 1976, 141).

The MFA became temporarily radicalized for three reasons: (1) the rather premature attempts of Spínola and his followers to obtain total control of the state; (2) the dislike many petite bourgeois military officers had for the monopolistic groups, a dislike that had deepened while fighting the colonial wars; (3) the people's acceptance of the MFA, and the spontaneous mass movements from below, that turned the original Captains' Movement into a movement of liberation and opposition.

We must keep in mind that the MFA, while being anticolonialist and antimonopolist, was never anticapitalist. Hence, it was not, and could not have been, the revolutionary party organizer of the workers' class movement, nor even a reform group within a capitalist system. The two main forces of mass control during the reactionary coalition's regime, the GNR and the PSP, were never dismantled or restructured, even when the military radicals, the Gonçalvists, were in control. To the MFA, the GNR and the PSP were always potential instruments of control, a task both had executed exceedingly well in the past. This shows that the MFA was never a radical movement. Furthermore, the MFA itself created COPCON, whose initial task was to control spontaneous movements from below. Finally, the MFA placed severe limitations on the workers' right to strike.

Even during the most radical period of the "revolution," March–September 1975, the radical faction of the MFA was not really interested in the social transformation of Portuguese society or in the initiation of the transition to socialism. Instead, the Gonçalvists and the Portuguese Communist Party demonstrated their petite bourgeois distaste for the monopolistic groups through their willingness to nationalize large monopolistic firms. Hence, this policy was not born out of a plan to collectivize production or to engage in other forms of revolutionary social transformation, but was a consequence of class interests. Those interests also explain why both the radical and the conservative factions of the MFA showed a profound mistrust of any popular movement from below, even though such movements were never for collectivization.

There Was Never a Revolution from Below

Between April 1974 and September 1975, Portugal witnessed many spontaneous mass movements from below. There were demonstrations involving thousands of people, and there was a radicalization of the working class and even some experiments in popular power. But the upheaval from below was never properly connected to the MFA, and never sufficiently organized and strong enough to make possible the leap into socialism. The Portuguese working class, including the most politicized and radicalized (a minority of the entire working class), did not know anything about open class struggle. The reactionary coalition kept the majority of the people in almost total ignorance. It was indeed

an illusion . . . to see even the most radical occupations [of firms and dwellings] as representing some anti-capitalist collective consciousness when, to the contrary, they were often inspired by long-standing aspirations toward private ownership. (Lomax 1983, 121)

There Was Never a Transition to Real Socialism

As Poulantzas so aptly observed, "the beginning of a transition towards socialism did not take place in Portugal" and "socialism was never really on the agenda" ([1975] 1976, 135–136). The endogenous objective structures of the Portuguese society, combined with the latter's position in the international division of labor in 1974/1975, made the transition to socialism impossible. More specifically,

Given the characteristic dependence of Portugal on foreign capital, it is clear that not just a process of transition to socialism, but even an effective "anti-monopoly" policy, could not be carried through without radical anti-imperialist measures. (Poulantzas [1975] 1976, 63)

And even if it had been possible, despite the dependence, to initiate the transition to socialism sometime during the nineteen-month period of the revolution, the process would not have been carried through. For it would have been quite difficult to find a group sufficiently capable and willing to implement anti-imperialist measures.

The Portuguese Communist Party was able to take advantage of the possibilities presented to it by the April 25, 1974, coup, due to its superior organization, resources, and cadres. It soon had the sympathy of some members of the MFA, and actually became the MFA's most loyal political party. But the PCP was not interested in the development of democratization from below. It did absolutely nothing to organize a working class that had great need to secure its own permanent political power. The party's activities were instead directed toward the consolidation of "organizational" influences through "conspiratorial infiltration and installation of trustworthy people in sensitive and important positions" (Polulantzas [1975] 1976, 138).

The PCP was interested neither in socialism nor in the betterment of the working class; it was interested only in itself.

Condemning "unrealistic" and "irresponsible" strikes and "unauthorized" occupations and seizures of private property as playing into the hands of reaction, the Communist party was to show itself more interested in establishing for itself positions of power and influence within the existing social order, than in leading any revolutionary offensive against it. (Lomax 1983, 114)

The struggle of the working class and the transformation of Portuguese society also were not the concern of the Portuguese Socialist Party. Mario Soares, the leader of the PS, was a pseudo-socialist, a cryptoprofessional bourgeois politician par excellence. The true political colors of the PS were bourgeois social-democratic. Its proclivities were basically rightist, and its policy "was never more than that of a democratization process under the hegemony of the domestic bourgeoisie, and [as] the process accelerated it progressively showed itself a privileged representative of this class" (Poulantzas [1975] 1976, 149).

The Real Class Conflict

The real class conflict did not begin with the coup of April 25, 1974. It was not class against class, but faction against faction within the old hegemonic class; it was intraclass, not interclass. The systemic contradictions of the economy of the reactionary coalition became more acute and difficult to solve in the early 1960s with the outbreak of the colonial wars. These contradictions gave rise to interest conflicts between the "traditional" segment of the hegemonic class, "the coalition of rural landowners, small businessmen, rentiers, and entrepreneurs," and the "modern" subsegment, the "commercial and industrial [monopolistic] capitalists" (Logan 1985, 149; Arrighi 1985, 23).

The principal class conflict [in Portugal] has been between competing factions of capital tied to irreconcilable strategies of coping with their country's relationships with the world system. These two factions can be broadly defined as a traditional landed and mercantilist class and state bureaucracy linked to an autarchic (and colonialist) strategy, against an internationalist, developmentist class aspiring to integration with western industrialization. (Logan 1985, 149)

It was in the interest of the latter class faction that Marcello Caetano attempted a mild liberalization of the reactionary coalition's regime in the late 1960s and early 1970s. It was also to articulate and realize the interests of the modern segment that a group of young technocrats founded a new group of interest representation, the Society for the Study of Economic and Social Development (SEDES) in 1970. This group sought social change that would permit the incorporation of Portugal into the industrial and democratic world of modern Europe.

It has been postulated that the class faction conflict in Portugal during the 1970s was between a modern and Europe-oriented domestic bourgeoisie and the older agrarian and financial interests, and the *comprador* bourgeoisie that was tied to foreign capital. In this argument, the conflict arose because the domestic bourgeoisie wanted more progress and demanded structural changes (Poulantzas [1975] 1976, 135). It has also been argued that if there was a domestic bourgeoisie, "it would not have been found in the more progressive sectors of capital" but, instead, in "the small and medium sized firms that were protected by fascist legislation" (Lomax 1983, 124). Both arguments are incorrect.

First, there was no autonomous domestic bourgeoisie in Portugal. Second, since March 1945, when the Law of Development and Industrial Reconstruction was passed, the reactionary coalition's legislation ceased to protect the small and medium-sized firms, and gave rise to monopolistic capitalism, whose interests the law protected and enhanced.

Other capitalist countries, despite often ruthless anti-trust legislation, have failed to resist the trend towards larger concentration of industrial power. Portugal actually encouraged the process. Industries in which monopolies or oligopolies already existed . . . were protected from even the possibilities of fresh competition. Salazar used the banks consistently and deliberately to encourage a few private empires, protecting them both from small businessman and (until the 1960s) from the encroachment of foreign investment. (The Insight Team 1975, 57)

Monopolistic capitalism was the reason for the emergence and popularity of General Humberto Delgado in 1958, and the radicalization of a few MFA members. Since the early 1950s, monopolistic capitalism had been proletarianizing many small and medium-sized businessmen.

The revolution of 1974 actually began much earlier, when a split occurred between the traditional landowning class and the modernists. The former wanted the preservation of the status quo; the latter, systemic changes, specifically in the political and ideological spheres of Portuguese society. After April 25, 1974, the representatives of the modernists, the Spínolists, moved too aggressively and too fast to seize power. Their actions caused a backlash, and brought to the center of power the radical faction of the MFA, whose members had petit bourgeois origins and had seen the effects of monopolistic capitalism both on the Continent and in the colonies.

With the Gonçalvists in power, the revolution took a detour and acquired the appearance of being truly revolutionary. Many people believed that Portugal was moving toward socialism. In reality, however, the revolution never derailed. Beneath all that revolutionary appearance, it kept moving toward the attainment of bourgeois democratization from above. As Lomax aptly observed,

> the high point of leftist politicizing in Portugal thus proved to be the low point of the revolutionary movement. How else can one explain the complete rout of the left and the popular movement in the face of the right-wing coup of November 25 [1975]? (1983, 123)

Democratization from Above

In 1926, the military overthrew a parliamentary government and seized power on behalf of a reactionary coalition. Almost half a century later, the military overthrew a bureaucratic dictatorship, and after nineteen months of control it surrendered the state apparatus to the modernist bourgeoisie. In 1974, the military was acting as if on behalf of the modernizing segment of the hegemonic class. This segment had to seize state power in order to transform the economic, political, and social structures of an anachronistic bureaucratic–authoritarian regime into a capitalist democratic member of the European community of nations. And this had to be done because changes in the forces of production warranted new social relations. Before April 25, 1974,

> An increasing number of businessmen . . . asked: if the Premier [Caetano] tells us that we cannot restore freedoms until the African wars are finished, if we cannot go into partnership with the Common Market unless we democratize, why not find a way to do just this? The importance of Western Europe in Portugal's trade now clearly outweighs the African colonial trade; in 1973 only 15 per cent of Portugal's exports went to Africa. (Wheeler 1974, 1–2)

Portugal's transition to a bourgeois liberal democratic and pluralistic system was imposed from above.

On January 3, 1976, outside the Custoias prison, near the city of Pôrto, a unit of the Republican National Guard took positions facing the crowd of family members of the leftists taken prisoner on November 25, 1975, and opened fire. Four persons were killed, and seven were seriously wounded. On January 20, Otelo Saraiva de Carvalho, the leader of the popular movement, a truly radical but politically naive leftist member of the MFA, and a friend of the working people, went to prison. On January 22, General Kaúlza de Arriaga, an *ultra* and a loyal member of the former reactionary coalition, was released from prison.

In June 1976, the Portuguese people voted for president of the Republic. Ramalho Eanes, an army general, a right-wing conservative bourgeois, and the candidate of "law and order," received over 60 percent of the vote. It was indeed a victory for the bourgeoisie.

NOTE

1. Translated from the text in *O Commércio do Pôrto*, June 22, 1975; quoted in Sweezy (1975, 27–28).

8

Postscript

On November 25, 1975, the illusory revolutionary process of the previous eighteen months came to an end. That day in November marks the conclusion of the implementation of parliamentary democracy and free-market economy from above. Shortly thereafter, in the elections of 1976, the "operational" army officer Ramalho Eanes, the right-wing conservative bourgeois who had been rewarded with the rank of general for his countercoup, became the first president of the new constitutional republic. With the 1976 elections, a new era of bourgeois democratic rule, political instability, and economic crisis began for the Portuguese people.

Promulgated on April 25, 1976, the new Portuguese constitution had actually been written by the members of the Constituent Assembly in the latter part of 1975, before the countercoup in November. Hence, the language of the constitution reflected the conjuncture in which it was written more than the conjuncture in which it was enacted. It stipulated that to guarantee the smooth transition to socialism, Portuguese society was to be reorganized under a pluralistic system of free exchange of ideas and pluralistic political organizations. Socialism in Portugal was to come from above, via the bourgeois pluralist route.

But even the petit-bourgeois notion of socialism from above, incorporated in the constitution of 1976, was unacceptable to the major political parties and to international capitalism. Mario Soares, the Socialist Party leader and prime minister of the first constitutional government, considered the constitutional clauses stipulating a peaceful transition from above to socialism "excessive ideological ideas of more or less utopian character" (Soares 1979, 67; cited in Eisfeld 1986, 38). The Democratic Alliance (AD) considered the 1976 constitution "fundamental laws of Marxist, collectivist and militarizing orientation" (Alianca Democratica 1980; quoted in Eisfeld 1986, 38).

Consequently, immediately after the promulgation of the 1976 constitution, all major parties began disregarding the so-called leftist constitutional clauses and initiated steps toward constitutional revision to render the document more in line with a free-market economy and bourgeois interests.

Since 1975 there have been four major political parties in Portugal. The first is the Socialist Party (PS—actually a de facto social-democratic party), which historically has sided with business more than with labor. The conservative-liberal Partido Social Democrata (PSD) was founded in 1974 after the coup as Partido Democrata Popular (PPD) by the late Francisco Sá Carneiro, leading member of SEDES and of the liberal wing of the National Assembly after Caetano replaced Salazar. The PSD is the second major party in terms of voter support and has been in power since the 1987 elections. The third major party, the conservative Social Democratic Center (CDS), also was founded after the 1974 coup, and it opposed the 1976 constitution. The fourth major party is the Communist Party (PCP), the oldest in Portugal. The PCP has remained distant from the Portuguese workers, and in the last few years has suffered from its dogmatic positions, which have produced internal dissent from younger members.

In 1985 a fifth political party was formed, the Party of Democratic Renovation (PRD). The party began as an "Eanist" movement initially called "ex-CNARPE" (after the 1980 Comissão Nacional de Apoio à Recandidatura do Presidente Eanes). Even though President Eanes, who was at the end of his second and constitutionally last term in office, did not officially recognize the party, the PRD did extremely well in the October 1985 parliamentary elections. Two years later, however, in the general elections of 1987, the PRD's performance was an outstanding fiasco. Since then, and perhaps because of its instability, the PRD has had virtually no popular support.

Mario Soares has been the general secretary of the de facto social-democratic Socialist Party since he founded it in Geneva and renamed it in Germany. Soares has been described as "probably farthest to the right among Western European socialist party leaders" (Darnton 1983, 5; cited in Eisfeld 1986, 35). The conservative-liberal Social Democratic Party has been under the leadership of Anibal Cavaco Silva, the current prime minister. He is a former finance minister and a senior economist with the Bank of Portugal, holds a Ph.D. in public sector economics, and has lectured at two universities in Lisbon. Silva is well known for publicly favoring laissez-faire economics and politics. Both the PS and the PSD favor privatization of economic activities, reduction of the role of the state, and antilabor legislation. In late 1987 Silva submitted antilabor amendments to current labor law but, faced with much opposition, was forced to limit his proposals.

Between 1974 and 1987, there have been sixteen different governments in Portugal. Six administrations were provisional governments, and ten were constitutional governments formed after the promulgation of the 1976 constitution. From July 1976 to July 1978, there were two "socialist" administrations, the second in a coalition with the conservative CDS. Mario Soares was the prime minister. From August 1978 to December 1979, Portugal saw three presidential administrations led by presidential appointees. From January 1980 to June 1983, the administration of the government was led by the Democratic Alliance (AD), which included the PSD, the CDS, and the Monarchist Party (PPM). The prime minister of the alliance, which supported free-market economy and concomitant state reforms, was Francisco Sá Carneiro, who died in a helicopter accident in December 1980. He was succeeded by Francisco Pinto Balsemão, who later resigned, terminating the AD government. From June 1983 to November 1985, Portugal's government was controlled by a centrist coalition made up of the PS and the PSD. With Mario Soares once again in the prime minister's seat, this coalition was referred to as *bloco central* (central bloc) because it held a two-thirds majority in Parliament. In June 1985, the coalition could no longer find common ground and was dissolved. From November 1985 to the present, the administration of the government has been led by the conservative-liberal Social Democrats, a minority administration until July 1987 and a majority administration since then.

The Portuguese constitution of 1976 clearly demonstrates two fundamental facts about the current Portuguese situation. The first is the indisputable naiveté of the MFA officers and the representatives elected to the Constituent Assembly in 1975. Ignoring the effects of fifty years of reactionary bureaucratic-authoritarian rule, Portugal's position in the international division of labor, and the high levels of foreign investment in the country, they formulated a constitution that would guarantee a smooth transition to socialism and "conditions for the democratic exercise of power by the working classes." This was to occur without abolition of the former reactionary coalition's bureaucratic machine; without abolition of the National Guard (GNR), which for so long had been the coalition's loyal protector and proponent of its reactionary worldview; and without implementation of the mechanisms necessary to assure the people's access to power. Instead, Portugal was to become a classless socialist society via the pluralist bourgeois route, with the blessings of the soon-to-be-dispossessed owners of the means of production.

The second indisputable fact is the nature of the Left in Portugal between 1974 and November 1975. Contrary to what has been written on the subject, before, during, and certainly after the "hot summer," the Left in Portugal was illusory, not real. There were no leftists, only pseudo-leftists, crypto-rightists, and full-fledged rightists all along. And the rightists were real and numerous. This explains why, since November 1975, the cause of Portuguese political instability has been intraclass competition for the seizure of state power, not interclass conflict. Once again Portugal has witnessed ruling class homogeneity and heterogeneity concurrently. Poulantzas's perceptive conclusion that socialism was never on the agenda has been empirically confirmed. The 1976 constitution has already been considered rather ambiguous and subject to different interpretations. In the 1979/80 parliamentary elections a party coalition made up of social democrats, center social democrats, and monarchists ran on a platform demanding the removal of socialist clauses and principles from the constitution. In 1982, the required two-thirds majority in Parliament approved substantial constitutional revisions: barriers to free-market economy and private enterprise and references to a transition to socialism were removed.

With the elections of 1976, Portugal entered the new period of parliamentary democracy characterized by political instability and turnover of government administrations, discussed earlier. The political situation has stabilized since late 1985, but at the cost of a greater swing to the right. The Social Democrat Party has been in power, with Anibal Cavaco Silva as the prime minister. When the PSD received more votes (29.8%) than the Socialist Party, its major opponent for state power (20.8%), Silva formed the sixteenth national government since the coup of 1974.

The presidential elections of early 1986 terminated the mandate of General Ramalho Eanes. Mario Soares was elected in a narrow 51-to-49 percent victory over Diogo Freitas do Amaral, the former leader of the CDS. Campaigning on a platform of free-market reforms and less state power, the PSD won the 1987 parliamentary elections with over 50 percent of the vote. Furthermore, the victory gave the party an absolute majority of 148 seats in Parliament, the center of legislative authority, since Portugal has a unicameral legislature.

The electoral behavior of the Portuguese people since 1975 can be explained by the socioeconomic realities of the *three* Portugals: the North, the Center, and the South. These regions reflect old class divisions that predate the reactionary coalition's regime. Historically the PCP has attracted, and continues to attract, between 14 and 19 percent of the vote, mainly from the rural and industrial proletariat from the central region that constitutes the old Lisbon-Setubal industrial belt and from the small pool of agrarian labor in the South. Both the conservative-liberal PSD and the very conservative CDS obtain most of their electoral support from the small-to-medium landowners in the North, a region that historically has been conservative, strongly Catholic, and supportive of the reactionary coalition. The PS receives its electoral votes from more wealthy, urban (Lisbon and Porto), skilled workers and professionals.

In addition to political instability, Portugal also has experienced serious economic crisis since the coup of 1974. Today, Portugal remains the poorest country in Western Europe. According to OECD literature, in 1987 Portugal was the second poorest country, after Turkey. In the same year, the per-capita GDP was 51 percent of that of the United Kingdom "and over a third less than average wealth in Spain" (Hudson 1989, 2). Put in a different way, "on the basis of 1986 prices, the GNP per capita in 1983 was around $2,300" (Cravinho 1986, 112). By comparison, the per capita GNP$ of Greece and Ireland are 50 and 75 percent, respectively, higher than Portugal's (Cravinho 1986, 112). Other commonly used indicators also show the low developmental level and poor social conditions in Portugal. Thirty percent of the active labor force is still employed in the primary sector. Infant mortality is very high: 26 per 1,000 live births. In developed Western European nations, the number varies between 7 and 11; it is 10 in Spain and 11 in Greece (Cravinho 1986, 113).

Illiteracy, too, remains a problem in Portugal. The 1981 population census counted the number of illiterates in the population over age fourteen to be 1.5 million, or approximately 24 percent of the population. In addition, the number of functionally illiterate people, those who read but never graduated from elementary school, is 2.2 million people age fourteen and over. This means that of every five Portuguese people over the age of fourteen, three have not completed four years of primary education. This problem, inherited from long neglect by the reactionary coalition and given little consideration by the now-fourteen-year-old parliamentary democracy, is certainly an obstacle to meaningful popular sovereignty and to Portugal's further industrialization. The educational situation is even worse: first, out of a population of 6.3 million people age fourteen and over, the number of those with tertiary degrees, 155 thousand, is greater than the number of people holding secondary diplomas, 87 thousand. Second, only 29 thousand people hold degrees from professional schools. Finally, only 33 percent of the fifteen- to nineteen-year-olds are in school on a full-time basis. In the 1980s enrollment was 50 percent in Ireland and 45 percent in Greece (Cravinho 1986).

That the Portuguese economy has suffered a near-total state of structural crisis should not surprise anyone. While international conditions have, of course, affected the health of the economy, fifty years of introverted reactionary social formation caused much structural and psychological injury to Portugal and handicapped her greatly. And the political instability witnessed during the last fifteen years has not healed past injuries. It will be a difficult task to bring Portugal into the community of newly industrialized countries (NICs) in a way that is equitable and just to the working classes.

During the reactionary coalition's rule huge trade deficits characterized Portugal's political economy. But structural solutions to the deficit problem were not implemented, simply because the introverted model of economic organization was not designed to solve structural deficiencies and, more important, because the deficits were always offset by tourism income and huge amounts of workers' remittances. In 1973, the $914 million trade deficit was offset by $1.264 billion from tourism and remittances (Cravinho 1986). Since 1974, however, the Portuguese balance of payments has shown serious deficits which must be viewed as symptomatic of the structural problems inherent in the current Portuguese social formation. Portugal imports around 50 percent of its food needs. Between 1974 and 1977 the annual current account deficits amounted to $1.5 billion, $1 billion, $1.3 billion, and $1.14 billion. The last deficit figure represented 10 percent of the GDP (Cravinho 1986, 118). The current account was in deficit from 1974 to 1985.

Immediately after the coup of 1974, workers stopped remitting their savings, and tourism income dropped in light of Portugal's political instability and international economic conditions, worsened by the oil crisis of the mid-1970s. From 1973 to 1977, annual tourism income fell from $550 million to $360 million, and from 1973 to 1975, workers' remittances decreased from $1.081 billion to $821 million. Portugal had to offset the current account balances by using the foreign exchange holdings and by assistance obtained from the European Community (EC) and West Germany.

The seriousness of the balance of payments problems has required the involvement of the International Monetary Fund (IMF) in Portugal's fiscal policies and the imposition of austerity measures as part of two new loan agreements. As usual, the IMF has imposed substantial reductions in domestic demand and increases in exports via the devaluation of the Portuguese escudo. The first IMF intervention in 1978 succeeded in reducing the current account deficit to $50 million, or 0.3 percent of the GDP. The IMF success was facilitated in part by favorable external demand and massive entry of workers' remittances held abroad in previous years. But by late 1981 the success of 1978/79 was gone, and Portugal again faced serious financial problems. In 1982 the current account deficit reached $3.2 billion. In 1979, the deficit had represented 0.3 percent of the GDP; in 1980 it represented 4.4 percent; in 1981, 11.7 percent; and in 1982, 13.4 percent. Between 1979 and 1982, the external debt nearly doubled from $7.5 billion to $13.2 billion (Cravinho 1986, 119). Consequently, a new and even more austere stabilization program was imposed by the IMF in 1983. The current account deficit was reduced by half in 1983 to $1.7 billion, and in 1984 to $700 million. But the cost of this success was high—stagnation in 1983 and a 1.6 percent decrease in the 1984 GDP (Cravinho 1986, 121). Moreover, the labor share of the national income, which had increased after the 1974 coup, fell below 1970s levels. In 1986, workers' real wages were lower than they had been in 1973 (Maxwell 1986, 9).

The steps toward the imposition of representative democracy from above, as the only feasible political system for protecting the interests of the propertied classes preceded by several months the naive and illusory ideas of a transition to socialism. In May and June of 1975, during Portugal's illusory "hot summer," the European community first denied a loan and then "presented Portugal with what amounted to a 'virtual ultimatum' " to earlier (June 27, 1974) requests for EC economic support, and later (November 25–26, 1974) proposals for special trade terms. On July 17, 1975 France's president "vetoed a Community loan . . . for fear of subsidizing a socialist-communist alliance." Then the EC Council of Heads of State and Government forwarded their ultimatum (extortion?): "The EC, because of its political and historical tradition, can grant support only to a pluralist democracy" (Story 1976, 431; Szulc 1975, 9; CEC 1976, 8, quoted in Eisfeld 1986, 31).

In 1977, Mario Soares, as the prime minister of the first constitutional government, applied for Portugal's admission to the EC. While Soares stated that the membership application to EC was not "the decision of a government" but "the decision of a people . . . the meeting of a country with its destiny," 67 percent of the people in 1981 lacked a clear understanding of what the Common Market was (Soares 1978, 16; Diario de Noticias 25 December 1981, cited in Eisfeld 1986, 33). On January 1, 1986, Portugal joined the European Community. In the short period of twelve years, Portugal had experienced a difficult and total metamorphosis from a non-European, noncapitalist, and antidemocratic country to a member of the community of bourgeois pluralistic Western European democracies.

Membership in the EC, however, will present some additional problems to the new bourgeois hegemonic class. Competition in the domestic market will certainly increase. Portugal, a net importer of food, may face higher food prices in the very near future, and improvement in the overall condition of Portuguese workers in the Community may contribute to a substantial decrease in workers' remittances (Cravinho 1986, 156–57). On the other hand, entry into the EC may very well be the much-needed catalyst for the realization of inclusive structural transformations. In any case, there is no way back.

For five decades, Portugal was comatose. She recovered consciousness in April 1974, but in view of the length of the illness, recuperation has been difficult, with many complications: political instability caused by intraclass competition; economic crisis; opting for laissez-faire free-market economy and privatization; engaging in antilabor strategies; submitting the country's finances to foreign monetary regulatory agencies; inability to develop endogenous programs of socioeconomic modernization; and inability to develop a sense of national purpose to make Portugal a healthy nation once again.

What is to be done? The task is, of course, not an easy one. But Portugal must reassess the free-market, privatization, and planning options, implement programs for the diversification of its exports, increase current subsidies for research and development, use its EC membership to full advantage, and develop a deep commitment to the principles of social security and economic justice. And the new hegemonic bloc must realize that despite bourgeois ideological rhetoric, there can be no truly popular sovereignty in a country with the lowest labor wages and the highest illiteracy rate in Western Europe.

Bibliography

BOOKS

Almeida, Carlos, and Antonio Barreto. 1976. *Capitalismo e emigração em Portugal*. Lisbon: Prelo.

Almeida, Pinto de. 1961. *A Indústria portuguesa e o condicionalismo institucional*. Lisbon: Seara Nova.

Althusser, Louis. 1971. *Lenin and Philosophy and Other Essays*, trans. Ben Brewster. London: New Left Books.

Alves, Marcio. 1975. *Les Soldats socialistes du Portugal*. Paris: n.p.

Amin, Samir. 1973. *Neocolonialism in West Africa*. London: Penguin.

———. 1976. *Unequal Development*. New York: Monthly Review Press.

———. 1980. *Class and Nation*. New York: Monthly Review Press.

Andrade, Anselmo de. 1918. *Portugal económico, teorias e factos*. Coimbra: F. França Amado.

Arrighi, G., ed. 1985. *Semiperipheral Development: The Politics of Southern Europe in the Twentieth Century*. Beverly Hills, Calif.: Sage.

Baklanoff, Eric N. 1978. *The Economic Transformation of Spain and Portugal*. New York: Praeger.

Banco Português do Atlântico. N.d. *Investment Opportunities in Portugal*. Lisbon.

Beckinsale, Monica, and R. Beckinsale. 1975. *Southern Europe: A Systematic Geographical Study*. New York: Holmes & Meier.

Bender, G. F. 1978. *Angola under the Portuguese; The Myth and the Reality*. London: Heinemann.

Bhaskar, Roy. 1978. *A Realist Theory of Science*. Atlantic Highlands, N.J.: Humanities Press.

———. 1979. *The Possibility of Naturalism, a Philosophical Critique of the Contemporary Human Sciences*. Atlantic Highlands, N.J.: Humanities Press.

Bosgra, S. J., and Chr. van Krimpen. 1972. *Portugal and NATO*. Amsterdam: Angola Comité.

Bradford, Sarah. 1973. *Portugal*. New York: Thames & Hudson.
Bragança-Cunha, Vicente de. 1937. *Revolutionary Portugal, 1910–1936*. London: James Clarke.
Bruce, Neil. 1975. *Portugal: The Last Empire*. New York: Wiley.
Bruneau, Thomas C. 1984. *Politics of Nationhood—Post-Revolutionary Portugal*. New York: Praeger.
Bruneau, Thomas C., Victor M. P. da Rosa, and Alex Macleod, eds. 1984. *Portugal in Development: Emigration, Industrialzation, the European Community*. Ottawa: University of Ottawa Press.
Cabral, Manuel Villaverde. 1979. *Portugal na alvorada do século XX*. Lisbon: A Regra do Jogo.
Caetano, Marcello. 1938. *O Sistema corporativo*. Lisbon: Oficinas Gerais de O Jornal do Comércio e das Colônias.
―――. 1943. *Do Concelho Ultramarino ao Concelho do Império*. Lisbon: Agência Geral das Colônias.
―――. 1967. *Manual de ciências políticas e de direito constitucional*. Coimbra: Coimbra Editora.
―――. 1968. *Manual de direito administrativo*. Coimbra: Coimbra Editora.
―――. 1974. *O Depoimento*. Rio de Janeiro: Distribuidora Record.
Campinos, Jorge. 1975. *A ditadura militar, 1926–1933*. Lisbon: Publicações Dom Quixote.
―――. n.d. *Ideologia política do estado salazarista*. Lisbon: Portugalia Editora.
Campos, Esequiel de. 1923. *A Crise portuguesa. Subsidios para a política de reorganização nacional*. Porto: Porto Editora.
Cardoso, Fernando H., and Enzo Faletto. 1979. *Dependency and Development in Latin America*. Berkeley: University of California Press.
Carnoy, Martin. 1984. *The State and Political Theory*. Princeton, N.J.: Princeton University Press.
Castro, Armando. 1973. *A Economia portuguesa do século XX (1900–1925)*. Lisbon: Edições 70.
Chatelain, Jacky. 1976. *A Luta de classes em Portugal*. Lisbon: Editora Nova Crítica.
Chilcote, Ronald H. 1967. *Portuguese Africa*. Englewood Cliffs, N.J.: Prentice-Hall.
Collier, David, ed. 1979. *The New Authoritarianism in Latin America*. Princeton, N.J.: Princeton University Press.
Costa, Ramiro da. 1975. *O Desenvolvimento do capitalismo em Portugal*. Lisbon: Assirio & Alvim.
Crotty, R. 1986. *Ireland in Crisis, a Study in Capitalistic Colonial Undevelopment*. Dingle, Ireland: Brandon.
Cunhal, Alvaro. 1976. *Contribuições para o estudo da questão agrária*, 2 vols. Lisbon: Edições Avante.
Cutileiro, José. 1971. *A Portuguese Rural Society*. Oxford: Clarendon Press.
D'Assac, J. Plonchard. 1964. *Dicionário político de Salazar*. Lisbon: SNI.
Davidson, Basil. 1955. *The African Awakening*. London: Macmillan.
Dias, J. N. Ferreira. 1946. *Linha de rumo. Notas de economia portuguesa*. Lisbon: Livraria Clássica Editora.
Duarte, Amilcar G. 1962. *A Resistência em Portugal*. São Paulo: Editora Felman-Rego.
Duffy, James. 1961. *Portuguese Africa*. Cambridge, Mass.: Harvard University Press.

Emeth, Omar, et al. 1934. *El Portugal de hoy y su gobierno*. Santiago, Chile: Nascimiento Editora.

Engels, Frederick. [1878] 1969. *Anti-Duhring*. London: Lawrence & Wishart.

―――. [1884] 1972. *The Origin of the Family, Private Property, and the State*. New York: Pathfinder Press.

Faye, Jean-Pierre, ed. 1976. *Portugal: The Revolution in the Labyrinth*. Nottingham: Russell Press.

Fernandes, Hugo Blasco. 1976. *Portugal através de alguns números*. Lisbon: Prelo.

Ferreira, Eduardo de Sousa. 1974. *Aspectos do colonialismo Português*. Lisbon: Seara Nova.

Ferreira, Hugo Gil, and M. W. Marshall. 1984. *Portugal's Revolution: Ten Years On*. London: Cambridge University Press.

Fields, Rona M. 1976. *The Portuguese Revolution and the Armed Forces*. New York: Praeger.

Figueiredo, Antonio de. 1961. *Portugal and Its Empire: The Truth*. London: Victor Gollancz.

First, Ruth. 1973. *Portugal's Wars in Africa*. London: International Defense and Aid Fund.

Fonseca, Mario Mendez. 1963. *El fracaso del salazarismo*. Caracas: Moviment. Democrático de Liberación de Portugal y Sus Colonias.

Fonseca, Vasco C. da. 1975. *Eleições para a constituinte em processo revolucionário*. Lisbon: Editorial Estampa.

Frank, Andre G. 1978. *Dependent Accumulation and Underdevelopment*. New York: Monthly Review Press.

―――. 1980. *Crisis in the World Economy*. New York: Holmes & Meier.

Fryer, Peter, and Patricia McGowan Pinheiro. 1961. *Oldest Ally: A Portrait of Salazar's Portugal*. London: Dennis Dobson.

Gallagher, Tom. 1983. *Portugal, a Twentieth-Century Interpretation*. Manchester: Manchester University Press.

Galvão, Henrique. 1949. *Por Angola: Quatro anos de actividade parlamentar, 1945– 1949*. Lisbon.

―――. 1961. *The Santa Maria, My Crusade for Portugal*. London: Weidenfeld and Nicolson.

Giddens, Anthony. 1973. *The Class Structure of Advanced Societies*. London: Hutchinson.

Graham, Lawrence S. 1975. *Portugal: The Decline and Collapse of an Authoritarian Order*. Beverly Hills, Calif.: Sage.

Graham, Lawrence S., and Harry M. Makler, eds. 1979. *Contemporary Portugal, the Revolution and Its Antecedents*. Austin: University of Texas Press.

Graham, Lawrence S., and Douglas L. Wheeler, eds. 1983. *In Search of Modern Portugal, the Revolution and Its Consequences*. Madison: University of Wisconsin Press.

Gramsci, Antonio. 1971. *Selections from the Prison* Notebooks, ed. and trans. Q. Hoare and G. N. Smith. New York: International Publishers.

Green, Gil. 1976. *Portugal's Revolution*. New York: International Publishers.

Hamilton, Nora. 1982. *The Limits of State Autonomy: Post-Revolutionary Mexico*. Princeton, N.J.: Princeton University Press.

Hammond, R. J. 1962. *Portugal's African Problems: Some Economic Facts*. New York: Carnegie Endowment for International Peace.
————. 1966. *Portugal and Africa, 1815–1910: A Study in Uneconomic Imperialism*. Stanford, Calif.: Stanford University Press.
Harris, Marvin. 1958. *Portugal's African "Wards."* New York: American Committee on Africa.
Harsgor, Michael. 1976. *Portugal in Revolution*. Beverly Hills, Calif.: Sage.
Hudson, Mark. 1989. *Portugal to 1993, Investing in a European Future*. London and New York: The Economist Intelligence Unit.
Huntington, S. 1968. *Political Order in Changing Societies*. New Haven: Yale University Press.
Insight Team of the *Sunday Times*. 1975. *Insight on Portugal, the Year of the Captains*, ed. Simon Jenkins. London: Andre Deutsch.
Janowitz, M. 1960. *The Professional Soldier: A Social and Political Portrait*. Glencoe, Ill.: Free Press.
————. 1964. *The Military in the Political Development of the New Nations*. Chicago: University of Chicago Press.
Jessop, B. 1982. *The Capitalist State*. New York: New York University Press.
————. 1985. *Nicos Poulantzas*. New York: St. Martin's Press.
John XXIII, Pope. 1961. *Mater et Magistra*. In Anne Freemantle, ed., *The Social Teachings of the Church*. New York: New American Library, 1963.
Kay, Hugo. 1970. *Salazar and Modern Portugal*. New York: Hawthorn Books.
Kayman, M. 1987. *Revolution and Counter-Revolution in Portugal*. London: Merlin Press.
Keefe, Eugene K., et al. 1977. *Area Handbook for Portugal*. Washington, D.C.: U.S. Government Printing Office.
Kohler, B. 1982. *Political Forces in Spain, Greece, and Portugal*. London: Butterworth Scientific.
Korvetaris, G. A., and Betty A. Dobratz. 1973. *Social Origins and Political Orientations of Officer Corps in a World Perspective*. Denver: Denver University Press.
Lefebvre, Henri. 1969. *The Sociology of Marx*, Trans. Norbert Guterman. New York: Vintage Books.
Mailer, Phil. 1977. *Portugal, the Impossible Revolution*. New York: Free Life Editions.
Maraval, Jose M. 1978. *Dictatorship and Political Dissent: Workers and Students in Franco's Spain*. London: Tavistock.
Marques, A. H. de Oliveira. 1972. *History of Portugal*, vol. 2. New York: Columbia University Press.
Marques, J. A. Silva. 1977. *Relatórios da clandestinidade: O PCP Visto por dentro*. Lisbon: Edições Jornal Expresso.
Martins, Maria Belmira. 1975. *Sociedades e grupos em Portugal*. Lisbon: Editorial Estampa.
Marx, Karl. [1852] 1977. *The Eighteenth Brumaire of Louis Bonaparte*. New York: International Publishers.
Marx, Karl, and F. Engels. [1846] 1981. *The German Ideology*. New York: International Publishers.
Maxwell, K., ed. 1986. *Portugal in the 1980s, Dilemmas of Democratic Consolidation*. New York: Greenwood Press.

McAdams, John. 1952. "The Corporate State in Portugal." Ph.D. dissertation, Fordham University.

Medeiros, Fernando. 1978. *A sociedade e a economia portuguesas nas origems do salazarismo*. Lisbon: A Regra do Jogo.

Mercante, Paulo. 1975. *Portugal, ano zero*. Rio de Janeiro: Editora Artenova.

Miliband, Ralph. 1969. *The State in Capitalist Society*. London: Winfield and Nicolson.

———. 1977. *Marxism and Politics*. New York: Oxford University Press.

Minter, William. 1972. *Portuguese Africa and the West*. London: Pelican Books.

Mónica, Maria Filomena. 1978. *Educação e sociedade no Portugal de Salazar (a escola primaria salazarista 1926–1939)*. Lisbon: Editorial Presença.

Moore, Barrington. 1966. *Social Origins of Dictatorship and Democracy*. Boston: Beacon Press.

Morrison, Rodney J. 1981. *Portugal: Revolutionary Change in an Open Economy*. Boston: Auburn House.

Moura, Francisco Pereira de. 1969. *Por onde vai a economia portuguesa?* Lisbon: Dom Quixote.

Munck, Ronaldo. 1984. *Politics and Dependence in the Third World: The Case of Latin America*. London: Zed Books, Ltd.

Murteira, Mario. 1974. *Desenvolvimento e sub-desenvolvimento e o modelo português*. Lisbon: Editorial Presença/Gabinete de Investigações Sociais.

Neves, Orlando, et al. 1978. *O diário de uma revolução*. Lisbon: Mil Dias.

Newitt, M. 1981. *Portugal in Africa, the Last Hundred Years*. London: C. Hurst.

Nolte, Ernest. 1966. *Three Faces of Fascism*. New York: Holt, Rinehart and Winston.

Nowell, Charles E. 1973. *Portugal*. Englewood Cliffs, N.J.: Prentice-Hall.

Nunes, A. Sedas. 1969. *Sociologia e ideologia do desenvolvimento*. Lisbon: Morais Editora.

O'Donnell, Guillermo. 1973. *Modernization and Bureaucratic Authoritarianism: Studies in South American Politics*. Berkeley: Institute of International Studies, University of California at Berkeley.

Oppelo, Walter C., Jr. 1985. *Portugal's Political Development: A Comparative Approach*. Boulder, Colo.: Westview.

Organski, A. F. K. 1965. *The Stages of Political Development*. New York: Alfred A. Knopf.

Payne, Stanley G. 1973. *A History of Spain and Portugal*, vol. 2. Madison: University of Wisconsin Press.

Pereira, João Martins. 1976. *O socialismo, a transição e o caso português*. Amadora: Livraria Bertrand.

———. 1979. *Pensar Portugal hoje*. Lisbon: Publicações Dom Quixote.

Pereira, José Pacheco. 1976. *As Lutas operárias contra a carestia da vida em Portugal*. Porto: Publicações Nova Crítica.

Pereira, Miriam Halpern. 1971. *Livre cambio e desenvolvimento económico, Portugal na segunda metade do século XIX*. Lisbon: Edições Cosmos.

Peres, Damião. 1954. *História de Portugal*. Pôrto: Portucalense Editora.

Pintado, V. Xavier. 1964. *Structure and Growth of the Portuguese Economy*. Geneva: EFTA.

Porch, Douglas. 1977. *The Portuguese Armed Forces and the Revolution*. London: Croom Helm.

Poulantzas, Nicos. [1968] 1974a. *Political Power and Social Class*, trans. Timothy O'Hagan. London: New Left Books.

———. [1970] 1974b. *Fascism and Dictatorship*, trans. Judith White. London: New Left Books.

———. [1975] 1976. *The Crisis of Dictatorships*, trans. David Fernbach. London: New Left Books.

Rafael, Francisco, et al. 1976. *Portugal, capitalismo e Estado Novo*. Lisbon: Publicações Afrontamento.

Rego, Raul. 1974. *Diário político, os políticos e o poder econômico*. Lisbon: Arcadia.

Robinson, R. A. H. 1979. *Contemporaty Portugal, a History*. London: George Allen and Unwin.

Rodrigues, Avelino, et al. 1974. *O movimento dos capitães e o 25 de abril: 229 dias par derrubar o fascismo*. Lisbon: Moraes Editores.

Rostow, W. W. 1960. *The Stages of Economic Growth: A Non-Communist Manifesto*. Cambridge: Cambridge University Press.

Salazar, António O. 1939. *Discursos e notas políticas*, vol. 1. Coimbra: Coimbra Editora.

Saraiva, José Antonio. 1974. *Do Estado Novo a Segunda República*. Lisbon: Livraria Bertrand.

Schmitter, Philippe C. 1975. *Corporatism and Public Policy in Authoritarian Portugal*. Beverly Hills, Calif.: Sage.

Serrão, Joel. 1975. *Dicionário de história de Portugal*, vols. 2 and 5. Lisbon: Iniciativas Editoriais.

Sertorio, Manuel. 1970. *Humberto Delgado: 70 cartas inéditas (a luta contra o fascismo no exílio)*. Lisbon: n.p.

Sideri, S. 1970. *Trade and Power, Informal Colonialism in Anglo-Portuguese Relations*. Rotterdam: Rotterdam University Press.

Skocpol, Theda. 1979. *States and Social Revolutions: A Comparative Analysis of France, Russia and China*. New York: Cambridge University Press.

Skocpol, Theda, et al. 1985. *Bringing the State Back In*. New York: Cambridge University Press.

Soares, Fernando Luso. n.d. *PIDE/DGS, um estado dentro do estado*. Lisbon: Portugalia Editora.

Soares, Mario. 1975. *Portugal's Struggle for Liberty*, trans. Mary Gawsworth. London: Allen and Unwin.

———. 1979. *Confiar no PS—Apostar em Portugal*. Lisbon: Partido Socialista.

Sobel, Lester A., ed. 1976. *Portuguese Revolution 1974–76*. New York: Facts on File.

Spínola, António de. 1974. *Portugal e o futuro*. Lisbon: Arcadia.

Stepan, Alfred. 1978. *The State and Society: Peru in Comparative Perspective*. Princeton, N.J.: Princeton University Press.

Vilar, Rui, and A. Sousa Gomes. 1972. *SEDES—Dossier 70/72*. Lisbon: Morais Editora.

Wallerstein, Immanuel. 1974. *The Modern World System*. New York: Academic Press.

Watson, G. L. 1982. *Social Theory and Critical Understanding*. Lanham, M.: University Press of America.

Wheeler, Douglas. 1978. *Republican Portugal; A Political History, 1910–1926*. Madison: University of Wisconsin Press.

Wiarda, Howard. 1976. *Transcending Corporatism? The Portuguese Corporative System and the Revolution of 1974*. Columbia: University of South Carolina Press.

————. 1977. *Corporatism and Development: The Portuguese Experience*. Amherst: University of Massachusetts Press.

Wise, Audrey. 1975. *Eyewitness in Revolutionary Portugal*. London: Spokesman Books.

ARTICLES

Aliança Democrata. 1980. "Programa de revisão constitucional—linhas gerais." *Povo Livre*, September 17, pp. 5–6.

Altvater, E. 1973. "Notes on Some Problems of State Intervention." *Kapitalstate* 1: 100.

Alves, Vitor. 1975. Interview for *Expresso* (September 20).

Amaro, Rogério R. 1982. "O Salazarismo na lógica do capitalismo em Portugal." *Analise Social* 18: 995–1011.

Ameal, João. 1934. "Mostruário do império." In *O Mundo Português*, vol. 1. Lisbon.

Anderson, Perry. 1962. "Portugal and the End of Ultra-Colonialism." *New Left Review* no. 15 (May–June): 83–102; no. 16 (July–August): 88–123; no. 17 (November–December): 85–123.

Araquistan, Louis. 1928. "Dictatorship in Portugal." *Foreign Affairs* no. 7 (October): 41–53.

Atkinson, William. 1937. "The Political Structure of the Portuguese 'New State.' " *The Nineteenth Century* (September): 346–354.

Baklanoff, Eric. 1979. "The Political Economy of Portugal's Old Regime: Growth and Change Preceding the 1974 Revolution." *World Development* 7: 799–811.

Bandeira, António Rangel. 1976. "The Portuguese Armed Forces Movement: Historical Antecedents, Professional Demands, and Class Conflict." *Politics and Society* 6: 1–56.

Blackburn, Robin. 1974. "The Test in Portugal." *New Left Review* nos. 87–88 (September–December): 5–46.

Blume, Norman. 1975. "Portugal under Caetano." *Iberian Studies* 4, no. 2: 46–52.

————. 1977. "SEDES: An Example of Opposition in a Conservative Authoritarian State." *Government and Opposition* 12, no. 2: 351–366.

Bouscaren, Anthony T. 1981. "The Puzzles of Portuguese Politics." *Journal of Social, Political and Economic Studies* 6: 327–344.

Bruneau, Thomas C. 1974. "The Portuguese Coup: Causes and Probable Consequences." *World Today* 30 (July): 277–288.

————. 1975. "Portugal: The Search for a New Political Regime." World Today 30 (July): 478–487.

————. 1976. "Portugal: Problems and Prospects in the Creation of a New Regime." *Naval War College Review* 29 (Summer): 65–82.

————. 1979. "The Left and the Emergence of Portuguese Liberal Democracy." In Bernard E. Brown, ed., *Eurocommunism and Eurosocialism*. New York: Cyrco Press.

Cabral, Manuel Villaverde. 1977. "Situação do operário nas vésperas da implantação da República." *Analise Social* 13: 419–448.

————. 1978. "Agrarian Structures and Recent Rural Movements in Portugal." *Journal of Peasant Studies* 5, no. 4: 411–445.

Cardoso, Avelino. 1974. "Para onde vai o capitalismo português?" *Vida Mundial*, October 17, pp. 10–15.

Carrilho, Maria. 1982. "Origems sociais do corpo de officiais das forças armadas portuguesas ao longo do século XX." *Analise Social* 18: 1155–1164.

Commission of the European Communities. 1976. "Die Beziehungen zwischen der EG und Portugal." Brussels.

Cox, Andrew. 1981. "Corporatism as Reductionism: The Analytic Limits of the Corporatist Thesis." *Government and Opposition* 16: 78–95.

Cravinho, João. 1986. "The Portuguese Economy: Constraints and Opportunities." In K. Maxwell, ed., *Portugal in the 1980s.* . . . New York: Greenwood Press.

Darnton, John. 1983. "Soares—The Comeback of a Natural Politician." *International Herald Tribune*, April 27, p. 5.

Dubois, Jean-Pierre. 1974. "Portugal." *Agenor* nos. 45, 46: 11–18.

Ebinger, Charles K. 1976/1977. "External Intervention in Internal War: The Politics and Diplomacy of the Angolan Civil War." *Orbis* 20: 669–699.

Eisfeld, Rainer. 1986. "Portugal and Western Europe." In K. Maxwell, ed., *Portugal in the 1980s.* . . . New York: Greenwood Press.

Gallagher, Tom. 1979a. "Controlled Repression in Salazar's Portugal." *Journal of Contemporary History*, 14: 385–402.

———. 1979b. "Portugal's Bid for Democracy: The Role of the Socialist Party." *West European Studies* 2, no. 1: 198–217.

———. 1981a. "The Mystery Train: Portugal's Military Dictatorship 1926–1932." *European Studies Review* 11: 325–353.

———. 1981b. "The 1979 Portuguese General Election." *Luso-Brazilian Review* 18: 253–262.

———. 1983. "From Hegemony to Opposition." In L. S. Graham and D. L. Wheeler, eds., *In Search of Modern Portugal*. Madison: University of Wisconsin Press.

Ginner, S. 1982. "Political Economy, Legitimation and the State in Southern Europe." *British Journal of Sociology* 33: 172–199.

Gold, D. A., et al. 1975. "Recent Developments in Marxist Theory of the Capitalist State." *Monthly Review* 27, no. 5: 29–43; no. 6: 36–51.

Graham, L. S. 1979a. "The Military in Politics, the Politicization of the Portuguese Armed Forces." In L. S. Graham and H. M. Makler, eds., *Contemporary Portugal, the Revolution and Its Antecedents*. Austin: University of Texas Press.

———. 1979b. "Is the Portuguese Revolution Dead?" *Luso-Brazilian Review* 16, no. 2: 147–159.

Grayson, George W. 1975/1976. "Portugal and the Armed Forces." *Orbis* 19: 335–377.

Hammond, John L. 1982. "The Armed Forces Movement and the Portuguese Revolution: Two Steps Forward, One Step Back." *Journal of Political and Military Sociology* 10: 71–101.

Hanlon, Martin. 1974. "Beyond Colonialism: The United States, Portugal, and Portuguese Africa." *The Human Factor* 2–3: 91.

Harrison, Paul. 1974. "Portugal: A Social Revolution?" *New Society* 29, no. 615: 138–143.

Heydebrand, W. V. 1981. "Marxist Structuralism." In Peter M. Blau and Robert K. Merton, eds., *Continuities in Structural Inquiry*. Beverly Hills, Calif.: Sage.

Holland, Stuart. 1982. "Dependent Development: Portugal as Periphery." In Dudley Seers et al., eds., *Underdeveloped Europe: Studies in Core-Periphery Relations*. Atlantic Highlands, N.J.: Humanities Press.

Hume, Ian. 1973. "Migrant Workers in Europe." *Finance and Development* 10: 5.

Leeds, Elizabeth. 1984. "Salazar's 'Modelo Economico': The Consequences of Planned Constraint." In Thomas C. Bruneau et al., eds., *Portugal in Development*. Ottawa: University of Ottawa Press.

Linz, Juan. 1970. "An Authoritarian Regime: Spain." In Erik Allardt and Stein Rokkan, eds., *Mass Politics: Studies in Political Sociology*. New York: Free Press.

Logan, John R. 1983. "Worker Mobilization and Party Politics: Revolutionary Portugal in Perspective." In L.S. Graham and D.L. Wheeler, eds., *In Search of Modern Portugal*. Madison: University of Wisconsin Press.

———. 1985. "Democracy from Above: Limits to Change in Southern Europe." In G. Arrighi, ed., *Semiperipheral Development*. Beverly Hills, Calif.: Sage

Lomax, Bill. 1983. "Ideology and Illusion in the Portuguese Revolution: The Role of the Left." In L.S. Graham and D.L. Wheeler, eds., *In Search of Modern Portugal*. Madison: University of Wisconsin Press.

Lucena, Manuel. 1979. "The Evolution of the Portuguese Corporatism Under Salazar and Caetano." In L.S. Graham and H.K. Makler, eds., *Contemporary Portugal*. Austin: University of Texas Press.

Luckham, A. R. 1971. "A Comparative Typology of Civil-Military Relations." *Government and Opposition vol*. 6: 5–35.

Marques, António, and Mario Bairrada. 1982. "As Classes sociais na população ativa portuguesa, 1950–1970." *Analise Social* 17, nos. 72–74: 1279–1297.

Martins, Herminio. 1968. "Portugal." In S. J. Woolf, ed., *European Fascism*. London: Weidenfeld and Nicolson.

———. 1969. "Opposition in Portugal." *Government and Opposition* 4, no. 2: 250–263.

———. 1971. "Portugal." In Margaret S. Archer and Salvador Giner, eds., *Contemporary Europe, Class, Status and Power*. London: Weidenfeld and Nicolson.

Maxwell, Kenneth. 1974. "Portugal: A Neat Revolution." *New York Review of Books*, June 13, pp. 16–22.

———. 1975a. "The Hidden Revolution in Portugal." *New York Review of Books*, April 17, pp. 29–35.

———. 1975b. "Portugal under Pressure." *New York Review of Books*, May 29, pp. 20–30.

———. 1982. "Portugal and Africa: The Last Empire." In P. Giffor, and W. R. Louis, eds., *The Transfer of Power in Africa, Decolonization 1940–1960*. New Haven: Yale University Press.

———. 1983. "The Emergence of Democracy in Spain and Portugal." *Orbis* 27, no. 1: 151–84.

———. 1986. "Regime Overthrow and Prospects for Democratic Transition in Portugal." In G. O'Donnell et al., eds., *Transition from Authoritarian Rule, Prospects for Democracy*. Baltimore: Johns Hopkins University Press.

Miliband, Ralph. 1970. "The Capitalist State—Reply to Poulantzas." *New Left Review* 59: 53–60.

Miranda, J. David. 1969. "A população universitária e a população Portuguesa: Um confronto da sua composição social." *Analise Social* 7, nos. 25, 26: 158–165.

Mónica, Maria Filomena. 1982. "Industria e democracia: Os Operários metalúrgicos de Lisboa (1880–1934)." *Analise Social* 18: 1231–1277.

Murteira, M. 1975. "Sobre o conceito de independência econômica." *Analise Social* 44: 527–537.

Nun, Jose. 1967. "A Latin American Phenomenon: The Middle-Class Military Coup." In C. Veliz, ed., *The Politics of Conformity in Latin America*. London: Oxford University Press.

Nunes, A. Sedas, and J. David Miranda. 1969. "A Composição social da população portuguesa: Alguns aspectos e implicações." *Analise Social* 7, nos. 27, 28: 333–381.

O'Brien, Jay. 1974. "Portugal and Africa: A Dying Imperialism." *Monthly Review* 26, no. 1: 19–36.

O'Donnell, G. 1978. "Reflections on the Pattern of Change in the Bureaucratic-Authoritarian State." *Latin American Research Review* 13: 13–35.

———. 1979. "Tensions in Bureaucratic Authoritarian State and the Question of Democracy." In David Collier, ed., *The New Authoritarianism in Latin America*. Princeton, N.J.: Princeton University Press.

Oppelo, Walter C. 1978. "The Parliament in Portuguese Constitutional History." *Iberian Studies* 7, no. 1: 22–29.

Pereira, Raul da Silva. 1964. "Portugal em face dos niveis sociais europeus." *Analise Social* 2, nos. 7–8: 802–828.

Pimenta, A. 1935. "O Campo e a fábrica." *Diário da Manha* (September).

Pimlott, Ben. 1976. "Portugal's Soldiers in the Wings." *New Statesman* September 27, p. 353.

———. 1977a. "Parties and Voters in the Portuguese Revolution: The Elections of 1975 and 1976." *Parliamentary Affairs* 30, no. 1: 35–58.

———. 1977b. "Socialism in Portugal: Was It a Revolution?" *Government and Opposition* 12, no. 3: 332–351.

———. 1978. "Were the Soldiers Revolutionary? The Armed Forces Movement in Portugal 1973–1976." *Iberian Studies* 7, no. 1: 13–22.

Pollack, Benny, and Jim Taylor. 1983. "Review Article: The Transition to Democracy in Portugal and Spain." *British Journal of Political Science* 13: 209–242.

Poulantzas, Nicos. 1969. "The Problem of the Capitalist State." *New Left Review* 58: 67–78.

Raby, David. 1983. "Populism and the Portuguese Left: From Delgado to Otelo." In L.S. Graham and D.L. Wheeler, eds., *In Search of Modern Portugal*. Madison: University of Wisconsin Press.

Remmer, K. L. and G. W. Merkx. 1982. "Bureaucratic Authoritarianism Revisited." *Latin American Research Review* 17, no. 2: 3–40.

Rutledge, Ian. 1977. "Land Reform and the Portuguese Revolution." *Journal of Peasant Studies* 5, no. 1: 79–98.

Santos, Américo Ramos dos. 1977. "Desenvolvimento monopolista em Portugal (fase 1968–73): Estruturas fundamentais." *Analise social*, 13, no. 49: 69–95.

———. 1978. "Economia portuguesa: Dez anos, cinco modelos (1969–1978)." *Economia e socialismo*, 25–26 (April/May): 15–65.

Schmitter, Philippe C. 1974. "Still the Century of Corporatism?" *Review of Politics* no. 36: 85–131.

———. 1975. "Liberation by Golpe." *Armed Forces and Society* 2, no. 1: 5–33.

Silva, Manuela. 1982. "Crescimento economico e pobreza em Portugal." *Analise Social* 17: 1077–1086.

Smith, T. Lynn. 1955. "The Social Relationships of Man to the Land of Portugal." *Revue Internationale de Sociologie*, 2, no. 2: 37–64.

Soares, Mario. 1978. "Portugal and Europe." *European Yearbook*, no. 24: 16.

Sousa, Alfredo de. 1969. "O Desenvolvimento económico e social português: Reflexão crítica." *Analise Social* 7, nos. 27–28: 393–419.

Story, Jonathan. 1976. "Portugal's Revolution of Carnations: Patterns of Change and Continuity." *International Affairs*, vol. 52, n. 3 (July): 417–433.

Sweezy, Paul M. 1975. "Class Struggles in Portugal." *Monthly Review* 27, no. 4: 1–38.

Szulc, Tad. 1975. "Hope for Portugal." *New Republic* August 30, p. 9.

———. 1975–1976. "Lisbon and Washington: Behind Portugal's Revolution." *Foreign Policy* 21: 3–62.

United Nations. 1973. "Report of the Special Committee on the Independence of Colonial Countries and Peoples." A/9023/ADD3 and A/9023 pt. IV. New York (September–October).

Wheeler, Douglas L. 1972. "The Portuguese Revolution of 1910." *Journal of Modern History* 44, no. 2: 172–194.

———. 1974. "Days of Wine and Carnations: The Portuguese Revolution of 1974." *New Hampshire Council of World Affairs Bulletin*.

———. 1979. "The Military and the Portuguese Dictatorship, 1926–1974: 'The Honor of the Army.' " In L. S. Graham and H. M. Makler, eds., *Contemporary Portugal*. Austin: University of Texas Press.

———. 1983. "In the Service of Order: The Portuguese Political Police, and the British, German, and Spanish Intelligence, 1932–1945." *Journal of Contemporary History* 18, no. 1: 1–25.

Wiarda, Howard J. 1974a. "Portuguese Corporatism Revisited." *Iberian Studies* no. 3: 24–33.

———. 1974b. "Corporatism and Development in the Iberic-Latin World: Persistent Strains and New Variations." *Review of Politics* no. 36: 3–33.

———. 1975. "The Portuguese Revolution: Towards Explaining the Political Behavior of the Armed Forces Movement." *Iberian Studies* 4, no. 2: 53–61.

———. 1979. "The Corporatist Tradition and the Corporative System in Portugal: Structured, Evolving, Transcended, Persistent." In L.S. Graham and H.K. Makler, eds., *Contemporary Portugal*. Austin: University of Texas Press.

Zeitlin, M. 1981. "Class, State and Capitalist Development: The Civil Wars in Chile (1851 and 1859)." In Peter M. Blau and Robert K. Merton, eds., *Continuities in Structural Inquiry*. Beverly Hills, Calif.: Sage.

Index

ABOUT THE AUTHOR

DIAMANTINO P. MACHADO is visiting assistant professor of sociology at La Salle University. His research specializes in political sociology and the sociology of developing nations. He has also taught at Drexel University. He has participated in several sociological conferences, and his research has been published in *Iberian Studies*.

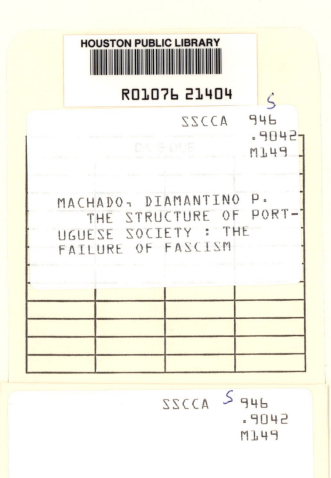